NEIGHBOURS AND NATIONALS IN AN AFRICAN CITY WARD

I0129609

Routledge Library Editions
Anthropology and Ethnography

AFRICA
In 26 Volumes

NEIGHBOURS AND NATIONALS IN AN AFRICAN CITY WARD

DAVID PARKIN

Routledge
Taylor & Francis Group
LONDON AND NEW YORK

First published in 1969
Published 2014 by Routledge
2 Park Square, Milton Park, Abingdon, Oxfordshire OX14 4RN
711 Third Avenue, New York, NY 10017
First issued in paperback 2014
Transferred to Digital Printing 2006

Routledge is an imprint of the Taylor & Francis Group, an informa business

British Library Cataloguing in Publication Data
A CIP catalogue record for this book is available from the British Library

Neighbours and Nationals in an African City Ward
ISBN 978-0-415-32998-9 (hbk)
ISBN 978-1-138-86191-6 (pbk)

Miniset: Africa

Series: Routledge Library Editions – Anthropology and Ethnography

NEIGHBOURS AND NATIONALS IN AN AFRICAN CITY WARD

David Parkin

Routledge
Taylor & Francis Group

LONDON AND NEW YORK

First published 1969
by Routledge & Kegan Paul Ltd
Broadway House, 68-74 Carter Lane
London, E.C.4

CONTENTS

LIST OF
SUPPLEMENTARY INFORMATION

INTRODUCTORY

In this book I analyse the way in which tribal ties are maintained in the development of a tribally mixed, middle-class community in Kampala East, Uganda. I show that while neighbours and friends may act towards each other as members of status groups, irrespective of tribe, they are drawn into alternative sets of relationships as members of their tribal or ethnic group. I go on to describe how these links consolidate into a type of solidarity when people feel they are under external political pressure. This solidarity may be expressed politically, or, as in this study, through recreation, 'ceremony', and ideology.

The study is focused on townsmen who migrated to Kampala from the neighbouring state of Kenya. These Kenyans became apprehensive at Uganda's independence in 1962 that they would lose their jobs because of their expatriate status. Many set about preparing for an anticipated mass dismissal from employment. This required the co-operation of loose groupings of people going under the name of 'kin' and of fellow-tribesmen. Rumours and apprehension proved groundless and there was no mass dismissal, a procedure which would in any case have been impracticable, due to the large numbers of Kenyans in the Kampala and Uganda labour force.

As future studies of urban Africa will probably show, political independence in most African countries will add a new dimension to the social processes operating in their towns. There may be many themes: the position of expatriate workers, as in this study; the effects of needy and possibly long-overdue legislation; the location of new industries as part of more planned and internationally assisted economic development; and the marketing and migratory influences on towns of realterations of national boundaries.

I have used the term 'townsmen' without definition. This does not mean that I ignore the value of the many brilliant qualitative and quantitative studies dealing with the problem of urbanization. My primary interest in this analysis is to consider social process rather than the structural elements at work in a town's population which indicate the points of strain and incorporation in an urban

ix

system of relations. My concern is thus with urbanism, the way of life in town. I am aware that Wirth's classic distinction[1] does not imply a study of one concern to the exclusion of the other. They do indeed complement one another, though undoubtedly the emphasis so far has quite rightly been on the problem of urbanization.

I am dealing, therefore, with a category of Kampala's population whom I regard as already highly involved in the town's system of relations. I believe that students of urbanism may begin by assuming the existence of an overall status system based on socio-economic criteria, even, nowadays, among such 'traditionalistic' towns as those of the Yoruba and Ibo in West Africa. The status system may be expressed in distinct residential localities, in ranked associations, and in varying spheres of recreation and leadership. One useful type of study is to focus on a local group of people and to analyse intensively a sphere of overlapping activities in which they are involved. From this study a picture emerges not only of the way in which statuses are ranked and expressed but also of how people move through them, the techniques they manipulate and their experience of conflicts. Small networks of relations are seen in detail from the inside and, in equal detail, the effects on them of political decisions of national consequence are observed.

My method of presentation is to provide many cases, some of which are illustrative, others of which extend over years or months and require individual analysis. Some personalities recur frequently in different cases. One of them recurs throughout the book. Professor Gluckman's exhortation to use each or both types of case not only ensures that the evidence of analysis is presented but, in the opinion of many at least, that something of the flavour of the social life described is conveyed. In addition to its theoretical aim, then, this book is intended to perform this function in an area of study where more details on day-to-day life are still needed.

The book may be regarded as falling into four parts. The first includes a standard description of Kampala, its suburbs, and its important East ward, particularly two housing estates in which this study is set. Kampala East is socially significant in mostly accommodating better-off townsmen, including Kenyans, who prefer not to be associated with the city's 'host' tribespeople, the Ganda. The second chapter includes a detailed description of a municipal council election occurring in the ward shortly before Uganda's independence. The description shows the relevant interplay of ethnic, regional and national interests. The ward is a microcosm of the state and the municipal election seems to point the way to the future participation of Kenyans in Uganda's affairs. The roles which leaders play at local, sectional and wider levels are exposed in the one situation.

The local context of activities for both leaders and ordinary townspeople constitutes the second part. In chapter three, the emphasis is on the subordination of tribal membership to socio-economic status attributes in a person's ordinary neighbourhood relationships. The multi-tribal neighbourhood is an arena of status competition for primary group relationships. It is more relevant for women than men.

Men express their status difference in recreational activities located outside the immediate neighbourhood in one or more of the ranked localities. This is a theme of chapter four. They, rather than their wives, make the decision to move from a less to more prestigeful locality or estate and so unconsciously subscribe to the status system of which they have become part. Personal status is very much reflected in the minor struggles for leadership and influence at these local levels. There is little material gain in being a leader here, but the prestige offered is much sought after by those so disposed. Politics thus begins at the level of locality, whether in a clan, tribal, or tenants' association. It is possible to climb a ladder of leadership and reach the more positively bene-ficial position of municipal councillor. The disfranchisement of Kenyans in July 1963 deprived them of positions at this superior level and seemed to confirm the fears they had expressed at the approach of Uganda's independence.

The two main Kenya tribespeople in Kampala, Luo and Luhya, had indirectly emphasized their cultural differences from other tribespeople even before independence. This cultural emphasis, which consisted of a marked kinship ideology and a type of ceremonial expression of ethnic ties through soccer clubs, other associations and public meetings, kept Luo and Luhya in a ready state of communication. The system of communication both sustained and expressed their respective ethnic economic ties in Kampala.

In the following three chapters constituting the third part,

xi

therefore, I describe cultural differences among tribespeople in Kampala East. My point is that though these differences have primary relevance in urban domestic relations, they provide a framework of established relationships among an ethnic group which may have solidary political significance if rights seem threatened.

In chapter eight, I focus all the above factors on a discussion of Luo associations and activity in Kampala East. I try to show that it was not expedient for Luo to organize themselves politically to oppose what they regarded as post-independence discrimination in Uganda. They had little alternative but to accept their expatriate status and to hope to continue in their jobs and businesses in Kampala. Dissident, more militant sections of Luo in Kampala were dissuaded from action which might appear hostile to the Uganda government. This publicly aired policy of acquiescence was made much more easy and effective through the established framework of communication and leadership referred to.

I have followed what seems to be an accepted and agreeable pattern in sociological monographs on African towns and deal with theoretical implications of the study in a brief concluding chapter. I suggest three things. One is that more attention might be paid to ethnic differences in systems of sanctions and restraints on the individual in urban status competition. Another is that many of the excellent theories and typologies for distinguishing urban and rural society might be applied *within* a town to the various sub-groups in the system of relations. The third is that certain social processes described in towns must, by definition, share similarities in their concomitance of variable factors with processes in non-urban situations.

The fieldwork for this study was carried out in the two housing estates mentioned from July 1962 to March 1964. Bounding much of Kampala city are 'suburbs' which are administered by Mengo municipality, capital of the former kingdom of Buganda. Kampala-Mengo is a single urban system comprising perhaps 120,000 persons. A study had already been made of two Mengo suburbs.[2] Apart from a substantial élite, many of the residents in Mengo are shifting migrants, not earning much, and not immediately involved in the workings of a city with secondary industry like Kampala. But the housing estates in Kampala East accommodate workers practically all of whom are members of the industrial labour force proper: clerks, artisans, machine operators, labourers, drivers, maintenance men, and supervisors. They serve public and private industry. Such men hold on to their jobs and are only migrants in the sense that they originally migrated from a rural area and were not born in Kampala. Though many will eventually return to their rural homes and certainly pay periodic annual or biennial visits there, they are likely to continue in urban employment for many years. The special feature of the Kampala housing estates in accommodating stable workers had been observed in the study referred to,[3] and this helped my choice of a social and geographical unit.

My method of investigation was that of participant observer. Epstein[4] quotes a passage from W. F. Whyte's famous analysis of Cornerville, an American slum district, and draws upon certain similarities in social conditions between it and some accounts of African urban life. Implicit is his appeal for studies in African towns of the type that Whyte himself undertook. My own fieldwork developed through stages into a type of network analysis with myself an integral part of the network. It is pointless to criticize this approach on the grounds that close involvement in a small group of people hinders objectivity in observation and analysis. The value gained far supersedes personal prejudice in relations, which should not in any case really affect trained investigation.

After deciding on the two housing estates, Nakawa and Naguru, as my areas of study, I set out to arrange residence there, with the intention of splitting my time evenly between the two. A high-ranking housing officer then pointed out that the long waiting list of two to three years would prevent my hoping to rent a house in the normal manner. My wife and I would have to receive privileged treatment and jump the queue. Apart from the social injustice of such an action, it is doubtful whether it would have been fair to expect the housing authorities to engineer matters with the respective estate managers on our behalf. It would have been obvious that we had been given special treatment if this had been done. The initial resentment caused might have provided more complications than could be dealt with. It was necessary to commute daily from the East African Institute of Social Research to the estates in Kampala East, five or six miles away.

So, for the first six months of fieldwork my wife and I participated in as many recreational activities as possible, making friends, being invited to their rural homes, without worrying too much about collecting data round a problem. We spoke at debates, went to dances, community shows, beer-parties, and bottle- and 'African' beer-bars, football matches, attended or helped run clubs and societies, and became *de facto* tenants, on several occasions being called on to speak at tenants' association meetings on behalf of the tenants and rather against the authorities.

Inevitably special friends emerged. One of these literally gave us complete and absolute open house. We regarded, and others came to regard, this house, which is situated in what is known locally as Upper Nakawa, as our central base, but we continued to commute for practical reasons of accommodation as well as problems of 'illegality'.

At this point the significance emerged of separate social networks for men and women. I was drawn much more into the all-male company of a small group of mostly Luo, while convention required that my wife and I occasionally go together to families in their houses. Home-based relationships are thus quite distinct from the more widely dispersed recreational relationships of husbands and their friends.

I inevitably became associated with one tribal and local grouping. I was seen to mix with Luo more than other tribespeople and with tenants of Upper Nakawa more than people of other localities, but over time I ramified my ties more substantially to other tribal and local groupings. In situations of conflict I was obliged to support 'my' side, or the side seemingly closest. Early on I had to favour a friend by acting as his checking agent when he was a candidate at the 1962 municipal council election and, beforehand, of helping him campaign. But far from providing undue problems of empathy, this involvement awarded insights into the election and related situations which would not otherwise have been provided.

I have used figures to give general pictures of Kampala-Mengo as a whole, the city of Kampala itself, and, particularly, the two housing estates in Kampala East. I have also used them to back up certain generalizations based on empirical impression.

The figures relating to the housing estates were not collected by means of a door-to-door survey. For a single sociologist to visit the 1,468 households of Nakawa and Naguru in this way would have been a formidable and highly time-consuming task. I was, of course, directly responsible for the collection of qualitative data, including the recording of observed and recounted events, diaries and life histories. But, with regard to the more obviously quantitative data, such as the collection of figures for a 100 per cent household sample, limited resources prevented me from enlisting the help of paid assistants and I had to use what documentary data was available. My wife and I investigated what are called personal record cards of each household head, which are kept by each estate manager. When an applicant accepts an offer of a house, he is asked to provide certain personal details which are then filled in on his card. With the estate managers' help and through as much personal checking as was possible, we tried to bring the details up to date and to compile tables from them. This crude system has its deficiencies but I believe that the figures were largely correct at the time of their collection and compilation, which extended over August, September and October 1962, at the same time as more intensive analysis. Other figures from small samples were acquired through intensive, open-ended, informal discussion, only after established relationships with informants had developed.

I had received a thorough training in Swahili at the same time as I received my instruction in anthropology at the School of Oriental and African Studies. This training extended over three years. My 'standard' Swahili had to be adapted to the Kampala East dialect but this provided very few difficulties. It became useful during the course of fieldwork to learn some DhoLuo to a very elementary standard, and to learn Luganda to an even more elementary standard. Swahili and English were, of course, the languages spoken most widely, but in some cases, the specific use of either DhoLuo or Luganda, not just with Luo or Ganda, made the initial establishing of a relationship much easier.

I do not use vernacular prefixes for names of tribespeople. I speak of 'Ganda' rather than 'Buganda' and 'Luo' rather than 'Joluo'. An exception is 'Jonam', singular 'Janam', which seem to be the only generally accepted forms for this people.

I have used fictitious personal names throughout but have retained genuine clan and place names. It is impossible to preserve complete anonymity among those familiar with the area during the time of study. I hope that the accounts recorded are accepted as accurate renderings.

It should be emphasized that the study does not apply to events after March 1964, when I left Kampala, though I do make an occasional general reference to constitutional developments relating to the kingdoms from 1966.

My acknowledgements are extensive. I firstly thank the East African Commonwealth Scholarship Scheme for an award tenable at Makerere University College, Kampala, Uganda, and extending over the two academic years during which I carried out my fieldwork. I also thank the East African Institute of Social Research for awarding me the status of Associate and providing me with a host of facilities. I am grateful to the School of Oriental and African Studies, University of London, for providing financial assistance in the writing up of a thesis, presented for a higher degree at the same university, on which some of this work is based.

I am indebted to very many persons. Professor A. W. Southall provided constant guidance and advice while I was in the field and after I had left it. He has taught me a great deal. Professor P. H. Gulliver has been an untiring source of encouragement in many ways during the writing up of successive drafts. Dr. A. C. Cohen has been unstinting in his help. His influence on this final draft is considerable, and to him I owe a fuller understanding of the sociology of ethnicity. Professor A. L. Epstein spent altogether very many hours with me and on my behalf discussing points of theory and detail. Dr. M. Southwold kindly scrutinized my material in the light of his own highly substantial knowledge of Ganda society, especially, and theory generally, and offered many valuable comments. Professor F. G. Bailey and the late Dr. D. J. Stenning were always ready to advise me during the early stages of my research.

I thank the very many people of Nakawa and Naguru who were always eager to help me. I especially thank Zablon Onguto, Thomas Omolo, Eridondo Kayumbu and Isaac Kimami.

Finally, I am grateful to my wife who has assisted me all along the line, through the various stages of fieldwork, in compiling the tables, and in providing many insights in the writing up of successive drafts, most of which she typed.

School of Oriental and African Studies, D.J.P.
University of London.
20th October 1967.

NOTES

[1] L. Wirth, 1938, 'Urbanism as a way of life', *American Journal of Sociology*, Vol. 44, pp. 1–24.

[2] A. W. Southall and P. C. Gutkind, 1957, *Townsmen in the Making*, East African Studies No. 9., Kampala.

[3] A. W. Southall and P. C. Gutkind, ibid. p. 49.

[4] A. L. Epstein, 1958, *Politics in an Urban African Community*, Manchester University Press, p. 225.

CHAPTER I

SOCIAL OUTLINE OF KAMPALA

Kampala's Development

Kampala lies just north of the Equator, to the north-west of Lake Victoria, about six miles from the Lake itself. It enjoys an altitude of some 4,000 feet above sea level and a pleasant, equable climate, a dominant feature of which is the frequent showers of heavy rain. The seasonal variations are slight. There are no real rainy seasons, and temperatures rarely rise above 30°C. during the day or fall below 16°C. at night. Kampala and its environs are amply provided with green and lush vegetation all the year round.

It is a commercial, administrative and communications centre, with a substantial minority of small-scale manufacturers. The growth of industry has been especially conspicuous since 1946, due mostly to high sales of cotton and coffee after the war and also to the accompanying development of engineering factories and enterprises producing a whole range of consumer goods.

Since Uganda's independence in October 1962, Kampala has been the nation's official capital. In effect, it has always been Uganda's commercial capital and, through the years, has gradually assumed from Entebbe the position of administrative capital.

At independence, too, Kampala became a city. The city may be regarded as one of the two main areas which together make up a single urban agglomeration. The other area is Mengo Municipality which accommodates the palace and parliament of the former kingdom, now region, of Buganda and is its capital. The whole agglomeration may be referred to as Kampala-Mengo,[1] which is rather more precise than the older term, Greater Kampala.

Mengo Municipality lies to the west and south of Kampala city. Though adjacent, Mengo and Kampala are administratively highly distinct. Service benefits in Mengo for a long time lagged behind those in Kampala. With the old capital of Buganda kingdom acting as a focus, and with a degree of economic

1

specialization made possible by a cash-crop economy and individual land tenure, settlements of what is now Mengo arose spontaneously in a very self-sufficient manner to accommodate a whole range of migrants from professional to unskilled, with a preponderance of the latter.[2] Except for a very high status élite, mostly Ganda, the pattern of life in Mengo is of people moving fairly frequently from one room to another, and into and out of different areas. These movements would appear to constitute an element in a general pattern of internal movement in Kampala-Mengo as a whole.

The élites of Mengo and Kampala are highly involved. But Mengo has its own distinct system of relations. Though Mengo provides much of Kampala's labour force, many of Mengo's residents are self-employed and contribute towards its partial economic and social self-sufficiency. Most of these residents are of the local tribespeople, Ganda, whose customs and institutions have come to be accepted and imitated by certain other tribespeople.[3]

Until recently Europeans and Asians were politically dominant in Kampala, while Ganda were dominant in Mengo. In the years immediately after the Second World War, housing estates to the east of Kampala municipality were built. They were established on Crown land and administered by the Uganda Government. In 1956 they were brought into Kampala itself. This extension of the Kampala municipal boundary most clearly marks the beginning of what is at present a rapidly increasing political and social integration of Africans into their nation's capital.

The second major historical landmark in this process of integration was the decision in March 1962, by the Minister of Local Government of the then internally self-governing Uganda Democratic Party, that a larger proportion of municipal councillors were in future to be elected by popular vote. Up to this time all town council members had been appointed by the Governor, or by the Minister of Local Government during Uganda's short period of internal self-government. Now there was to be the election of councillors on a political party basis. The Uganda political parties are the Uganda Peoples Congress (UPC), the present ruling party, and the Uganda Democratic Party (DP). The Ganda Kabaka Yekka Party (KY) established a coalition with the UPC during the 1962 national elections.

2

For the purpose of its council elections Kampala was divided into three wards, Kampala South, West and East. The two former are still mostly European and Asian high-status residential areas, though an increasing number of high-status Africans have taken up residence in them. Kampala East is the one dominantly African area. It is the area of the housing estates. In the Kampala municipal elections of 1962, the potential power and effectiveness of Kampala East's population as leaders and voters was obvious. African candidates and elected were in the majority for Kampala East, while Asians were still in the majority in the other two wards. In Kampala East, Kenya African migrants had provided much of the drive in this ward's political activity.

By the time of the Kampala city council elections of February 1964, all persons who were not Uganda citizens were disfranchised. This disfranchisement included not only European and Asian non-citizens but Kenya Africans as well. A further clause disqualified non-resident property-owners, including many Ganda. The city elections of February 1964, therefore, concerned a much smaller number of people than in 1962. All three wards were indeed represented by a greater proportion of Africans to non-Africans, though the political drive and activity of 1962 were lacking. The point remains, however, that the population of Kampala East, as it stands, is one which is aware of the current demand for the greater political and social Africanization of a town like Kampala in an independent African State like Uganda. In contrast, with the exception of an indeterminate number of mostly Ganda of high status, the people of Mengo are largely disinterested in the problem of how quickly Kampala city may come under the greater commercial and social, as well as political, control of its African residents.

Why should the African population of Kampala East, most of whom live in city council housing estates or areas, be differentiated in this way?

In 1956, Southall and Gutkind noted the popularity of the estates in the long waiting lists for houses on them. They noted also that the population in the estates was above the socio-economic average for the African population in Kampala-Mengo as a whole. Their hypothesis was 'that the estates will in the long run cater principally for the non-Ganda whose skill and income is above the average level and who appreciate a more secure and conventionally

3

respectable existence than is at present possible for those who rent rooms in suburbs such as Kisenyi or Mulago' (the two areas intensively described and analysed by the authors).[4] Eight years after the statement, at least, it is possible from the evidence of my data to say that this hypothesis has been borne out. It was these authors who first drew attention to the developing tripartite structure of Kampala-Mengo, in which, in addition to the older duality of Kampala and Mengo, the people on the housing estates were emerging as a distinctive category in special relationship to both Mengo and Kampala municipality of which they were part.

Kampala-Mengo

According to the 1959 census the total population of Kampala-Mengo was 107,058. According to the census of 1948 it was 62,264. Even allowing for the fact that Kampala-Mengo in 1959 included the extension into Crown land of Kampala East, the overall increase in population is reasonably pronounced. The increases in non-African population are from 14,324 in 1948 to 26,800 in 1959 for Asians, and from 1,497 to 3,539 for Europeans. The increase for Africans alone is from 46,443 to 76,719. It is interesting to note that Europeans, followed by Asians and then Africans, have shown the greatest proportional population increase during these years, and after, even though this was a period of Africanization immediately prior to independence. Indeed, as some following figures show, the same period has seen a considerable decline in African labour.

The increase in African population from 1948 to 1959 is largely due to labour migration. The officially enumerated Kampala labour force itself increased from 29,381 in 1952 to 38,023 in 1957, declining to 36,635 and 27,878 in 1958 and 1961.[5] While the population of Kampala-Mengo has not dropped and is probably even higher than the 1959 census figures, the number of wage-earning employees listed by the government department of labour had dropped considerably in the year before independence. Fewer jobs were then available, and the wide-scale unemployment had already given cause for alarm.

Yet, in the estates of Kampala East, the number of unemployed is relatively low. Few household heads are unemployed, and it is

4

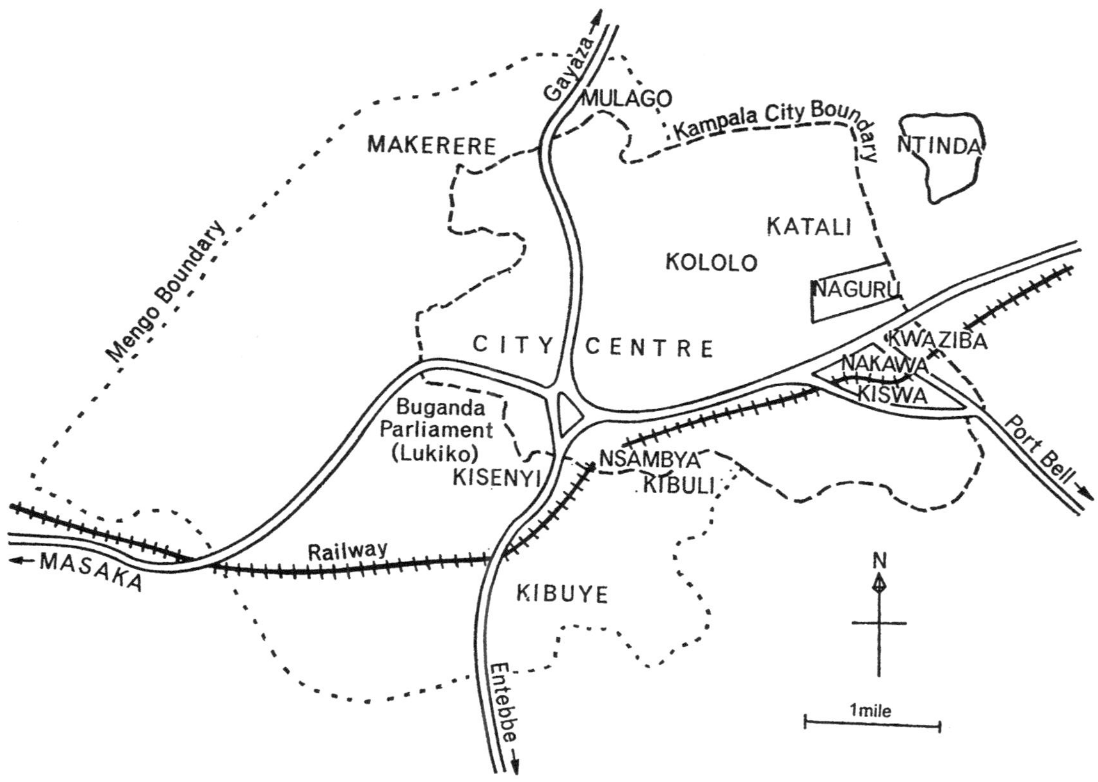

NTINDA

Kampala City Boundary

KATALI

KOLOLO

CITY CENTRE

KWAZIBA

NAKAVVA

KISWA

Port Bell

NAGURU

Gayaza

MULAGO

MAKERERE

Buganda
Parliament
(Lukiko)
KISENYI

NSAMBYA

KIBULI

KIBUYE

Entebbe

Railway

Mengo Boundary

MASAKA

N

1 mile

MAP I

KAMPALA — MENGO

relatives who are seeking work or have just lost jobs and who may be lodging with them who are likely to constitute the majority of unemployed in the ward.

The 1959 census also gives figures indicating the distribution of persons according to rather arbitrary age-groups in Kampala, Mengo, and Kampala-Mengo as a whole.

	% under 16	% 16–45	% over 45
Kampala	25·8	69·0	5·1
Mengo	31·8	57·9	10·3
Kampala-Mengo	29·9	61·5	8·6
Uganda (estimated)	43·5	43·7	12·8

As might be expected, migrants in Kampala-Mengo fall mostly in the 16–45 age group. There are more of this age group in Kampala, presumably due to the larger proportion of migrant employees. In Mengo the greater proportions of old persons, especially, and also of children are related both to the large numbers of Ganda who have owned land and property in the area for a long time and to the general tradition of residence by Ganda families at the king's capital.

Within the working age-group the proportions of males and females are:

	% Males	% Females
Kampala	69·9	30·1
Mengo	60·6	39·4
Kampala-Mengo	63·8	36·2
Uganda	48·9	51·1

The proportion of males to females is significantly higher in Kampala than in Mengo. Yet, as I shall illustrate, on the estates I studied in Kampala East, there is much less of this imbalance. But there are considerable variations in the adult sex ratio for individual tribespeople. I cannot reproduce the approximate proportions for the 16–45 age group but the general sex ratio according to tribe probably reflects the adult ratio. Thus, of the Ganda in Kampala-Mengo 50·5 per cent are females, a ratio of females to males of 101·9 per cent. The Ganda are the only tribespeople in Kampala-Mengo among whom females outnumber males. They are followed by the Soga and Nyoro, among

6

whom the ratios of females to males are 76 per cent and 64 per cent respectively. The ratios for the Acholi and Jonam are 53.5 per cent and 50 per cent, but no other tribespeople have as many as half the number of females to males.

The average length of residence in Kampala by migrants is not given in the census, but Elkan puts it at about only two years.[6] Mitchell puts it at eight years for Luanshya in Zambia.[7] As I shall show, the people of Kampala East are generally well above the city's average in length of urban residence and may be regarded, therefore, as including those with the most vested urban interests.

The figures gained from the census with regard to the tribal distribution of Kampala-Mengo's population (Table I) give a general picture of the categories represented, though some important tribes are not specified. Not all the tribes indicated by the census figures are numerically highly significant in the housing estates of Kampala East.

The Tribespeople of Kampala-Mengo

TABLE I. TRIBAL DISTRIBUTION OF AFRICANS IN KAMPALA-MENGO (1959)

Tribe	Total	% of African Population
Ganda	37,464	48·8
Toro	5,832	7·6
Luo	5,544	7·2
Ruanda	2,829	3·7
Kenya n.s. (mostly Luhya)	2,818	3·7
Ankole	2,492	3·2
Tanganyika n.s. (many Haya)	2,163	2·8
Acholi	2,080	2·7
Kiga	1,982	2·6
Nyoro	1,920	2·5
Sudan n.s. (mostly Nubi)	1,483	1·9
Teso	1,321	1·7
Samia	1,070	1·4
Soga	1,009	1·3
Lugbara	914	1·2
Congo	826	1·1
Other	4,982	6·5
TOTAL	76,729	99·9

7

Following the conventional linguistic classifications, Kampala's African population may be divided into Bantu, Nilotic, Sudanic, and Nilo-Hamitic groups, with the Muslim Nubi, originally from the Sudan, of indeterminate classification but not, as their name might suggest, from either Nubia or the Nuba mountains. The Bantu and Nilotic groups are by far the largest.

Overlapping these linguistic classifications are those based on national origin. Thus, some Bantu and Nilotes are from Kenya as well as Uganda. Some Bantu are from what was formerly Ruanda-Urundi and from Tanzania as well as from Uganda and Kenya. The distances from Kampala of the rural homes of the main tribespeople mentioned is given in Map 2, below. Where possible their sizes, rural *per capita* incomes, and proportions of the Kampala-Mengo African population are also included.

To some extent cultural, traditional, political, and social characteristics coincide with the linguistic classifications. Thus, all the Nilotes, Nilo-Hamitic and Sudanic groups are, or were

MAP 2 — TRIBAL AREAS

8

Tribespeople		Size (1959) ('ooo)	1959 per capita rural cash income (£'s)*	Proportions of African population in Kampala-Mengo (as %) (1959)
Ganda		1,049	19·3	48·8
Eastern Province	Soga	502	11·3	1·3
	Teso	525	10·6	1·7
Western Province	Ankole	519	3·8	3·2
	Kiga	460	2·9	2·6
	Toro	208	8·6	7·6
Northern Province	Acholi	285	4·8	2·7
	Lango	364	7·5	0·9
	Alur	123		0·6
	Jonam	27	4·3	0·5
	Lugbara	236		1·2
	Madi	80		0·8
	Nyoro	188	12·8	2·5
Rwanda (in Uganda only)		379	n.a.	3·7
Kenyans	Luo	c. 1,000	n.a.	7·2
	Luhya	c. 850	n.a.	c. 3·5

* *The Gross Domestic Product of Uganda 1954–59.* E. A. Statistical Department. Uganda Unit. 1961. Entebbe, Uganda. Table 31, p. 35.

traditionally, politically uncentralized, most of them falling into the very broad category of segmentary lineage societies. So, too, are some Bantu, like the Kiga (sometimes spelt Ciga and pronounced 'chiga'), Luhya and Samia. All these uncentralized tribespeople have local descent groups of some scale, which are important in many political and social contexts.

Other Bantu, like the Ganda, Soga, Nyoro, Toro, Ankole, and Ruanda, are politically centralized with kings or paramount chiefs, but to varying extents. Very little is known regarding migrants from the Congo beyond the fact that they include certain Bantu, Nilotic, Nilo-Hamitic, and Sudanic elements. The Bantu groups, in the order in which they are listed in Table I, are Ganda, Toro, Ruanda, Ankole, Luhya, Nyoro, Haya, Kiga, some Congo, Soga and Samia.

The Nilotes are Luo, Acholi, and subsumed in 'others', Lango, Alur, Jonam, and Padhola. I mention these latter tribes even though they are not listed in the census-based table, because they are significant in my analysis of Kampala East.

9

The Nilo-Hamites in Kampala are almost exclusively Teso, except for a few Kakwa and Kumam. There are very few Nandi and Karamojong.

The Sudanic-speaking groups are predominantly Lugbara, together with the closely related Madi.

Of the Bantu, the Luhya and a quarter of the closely related Samia are from Kenya. The Luhya really consist of autonomous but very close sub-tribes who have come to constitute a single 'tribe' only in recent times for political and administrative purposes. About three-quarters of the Samia in Kampala come from the Uganda side of the border with Kenya. The Bantu Haya are from Tanzania.

Of the Nilotes, the Luo are from Kenya. Together, the Luo and Luhya, plus the relatively small number of Kenya Samia, have exerted considerable influence in post-war years in the development of African urban institutions in Kampala. Kenyans generally may be said to have experienced a more disturbing impact of the related forces of colonialism, urbanization, and industrialization than Ugandans. This experience has to some extent been diffused into Kampala's institutions. As a group of singular influence they are only surpassed in some respects by the local Ganda. All other Nilotes are from Uganda. The most numerous of them are the Acholi and Lango. Some Alur are also from the Congo.

The Sudanic Lugbara and Madi, and the Nilo-Hamitic Teso, Kakwa and Kumam are mostly from Uganda, though some Sudanics and Kakwa are from the Congo.

Very generally there are certain associations of tribe and occupation in Kampala-Mengo. The Ganda as the local and most numerous people inevitably reflect a wide range, from the many self-employed occupations especially available in Mengo to the greatest number of clerical, managerial and professional positions. High- and low-status Ganda alike commonly commute to their places of work in the city from their individual plots in Mengo or another suburb. The many Toro from Western Province also show a wide range, with a smaller proportion of them in high status jobs. Many Toro are domestic servants. The Nyoro from Western and the Soga from Eastern Province include both those who are unskilled and a significant number, probably a minority, who hold clerical and managerial positions, while the Haya from Tanzania are almost entirely in self-employed and unskilled jobs.

The Ruanda, the Kiga and Ankole from Western Province, and the Lugbara from Northern Province, are reputedly preponderant in unskilled occupations. Excepting the Ankole, these peoples suffer very high population density at home. The Kenya Luo and Luhya, and the Northern Province Acholi and Lango are also employed in a wide range of occupations. As well as working in large numbers for the Kampala branch of the East African Railways and Harbours, many Luo and Luhya are clerks, artisans and labourers. Many Acholi, Lango and Alur, and also Teso from Eastern Province, work in various capacities for the civil and special police. A large proportion of Lango and Teso are clerks.

These very vague impressions of tribe by occupation for the town as a whole are to some extent borne out by the more precise data given later in this chapter for the two estates studied.

The Ganda are, of course, dominant in Kampala-Mengo, where they constitute 48·8 per cent of its African population. In Mengo itself the proportion of Ganda is 62·5 per cent. But in Kampala city alone their numbers are considerably reduced and constitute only 18·8 per cent of the population. This reduction of numbers also applies to the other centralized Interlacustrine Bantu. The proportion of non-Ganda is, of course, increased. The Ganda and Luo are in many ways the key tribes in Kampala, not so much numerically as influentially. In Mengo and in Kampala-Mengo as a whole Luo are far outnumbered by Ganda. But in Kampala the two tribes are almost equally represented, Luo constituting 14·3 per cent of the city's African population to the Ganda 18·8 per cent. It is in the two housing estates studied in Kampala East that this equivalence of Ganda and Luo is most closely approached, and here it is the Luo who until their disfranchisement in 1963 assumed dominance. Very loosely, then, Kampala East is something of a microcosm of the city in the presumably future joint participation in its affairs by local and migrant tribes. Though Kenyans are now disfranchised and, out of expedience, may eventually return to Kenya, their position in Kampala East is very likely to be filled by an increasing number of people from the Northern and Eastern Provinces of Uganda, especially Acholi, Alur, Lango, Teso and Lugbara who are distinguished much more as migrants than the more local people of the Bantu kingdoms.

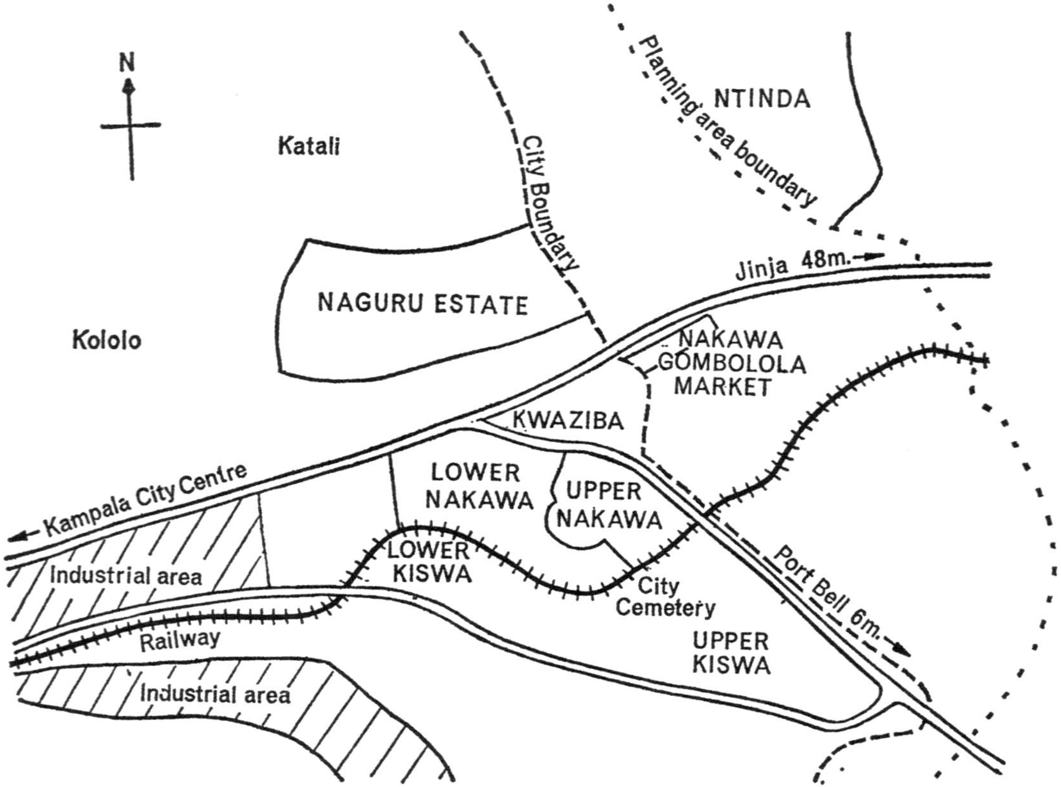

MAP 3
KAMPALA EAST

Labels visible on map:

N

Kololo

Katali

Planning area boundary

NTINDA

Jinja 48m.

City Boundary

NAGURU ESTATE

KWAZIBA

NAKAWA GOMBOLOLA MARKET

LOWER NAKAWA

UPPER NAKAWA

City Cemetery

Port Bell 6m.

UPPER KISWA

LOWER KISWA

Kampala City Centre

Industrial area

Railway

Industrial area

Kampala East

The history of the housing estates is only recent. Up until they were established shortly after the Second World War official policy did not specifically provide for the accommodation of African workers. Thus, a distinctive feature of Kampala and other Uganda towns was the tendency of its migrant workers to live outside the municipal boundaries in the suburbs. In Kampala and Jinja alone, where the need was greatest, employers were not obliged to house their employees. This was one reason why considerable spontaneous urban development, both residential and commercial, sprang up outside Kampala municipality and outside the town's control.

The two estates of Nakawa and Naguru were built in 1948 and 1949. In the *Uganda (Protectorate) Statement of Policy on African Urban Housing*, published in 1954,[8] official policy stated that '[Naguru] provided a better standard of housing for the higher income group of wage-earners, while [Nakawa] provided housing mainly for unskilled workers'. It was only later realized that '[this] sharp geographical distinction between low and high income groups is not desirable and that grades of property and population should be shaded into each other and not so abruptly divided as in the case of these two estates'.

Still later, two other forms of residence for Africans were established. One was the Home-Ownership Scheme estate at Ntinda. The intention here was to encourage Africans to buy or build their own permanent houses. The capital needed for a deposit on such a house was 20 per cent of the value of the house. This might mean an initial payment of Shs. 1000–1500/-.[9] Only a small number of people could afford this. The second of these later forms of residence was the Temporary Housing Development scheme. The idea was and is to encourage a man to build a temporary house, which would be inspected every five years by the Public Health and Housing authorities, and would be repaired if necessary. Such a scheme operates at Kiswa and Katali. In both these schemes, house-letting by absent landlords has developed. Rents at Ntinda may be Shs. 100–200/- a month for a house, and at Kiswa and Katali Shs. 30–40/- a month for a room.

Letting by absent landlords has also occurred in the areas

13

outside the city. A brief sample survey made during October 1962 in Wandegeya, Mulago, Kisenyi, Katwe, Kibuli, Nsambya and Kinyoro, revealed that over two-thirds of the rents were in the Shs. 20–40/– range.[10] Here the normal urban amenities and facilities are negligible, and though residents are not subject to petty restrictions, the lives they lead are generally insecure.

At Nakawa, rents range from Shs. 7/– for a bedspace to Shs. 17/– and 23/– for houses. Amenities such as street-lighting, a fair number of water taps, daily collection of garbage, and, in admittedly only a few Shs. 23/– houses, electricity, seem to offer most people better value for their money than residence in other areas. Even such forms of self-employment as laundering, tailoring, shoe-mending, fish, vegetable or charcoal selling, beer brewing and prostitution, though officially discouraged if they are carried on in private houses, are entered into by a few residents. At Naguru, amenities are greater and rents are, generally, considerably higher.

Nakawa and Naguru are roughly divided by the main Kampala to Jinja road (see Map 3, page 12). Naguru is slightly set back from this road. It occupies an area of about a third of a square mile and has 645 houses and a population of about 1,500 adults, nearly all of the 16–45 age group, and 600 children. Nakawa occupies an area of about an eighth of a square mile and has 823 houses and bedspaces. Though smaller in area it has a larger population, some 2,150 adults and 1,000 children and, as if to draw attention to this congestion, is not set back from the Kampala-Jinja road. Its boundaries adjoin this road and also a turning off it called the Port Bell Road. This road links Kampala with Port Bell, six miles away on Lake Victoria, from where the lake steamer ferries migrants to various ports around the lake, a chief one of which is Kisumu on its Kenya coast where many Luo board.

The triangular area formed by the junction of the Jinja and Port Bell roads and immediately facing Nakawa is called Kwaziba, which in Swahili means 'at the place of the Ziba'. The Ziba, or Haya as they are alternatively known, are a tribe in Tanzania to the south-west of Lake Victoria. Their women have a reputation in Kampala and elsewhere for prostitution. Ziba prostitutes and prostitutes of other tribes carry on their business in small mud and wattle huts at Kwaziba. Close to their huts and sometimes intersected by them are makeshift stalls at which trinkets and cheap finery are sold. 'African' beer[11] is brewed at Kwaziba. The liquor called *waragi* is distilled there, though illegally. 'African' beer, *waragi*, and prostitutes are cheap, the latter asking only 2/– for their services. Tribal drumming and dances abound in spontaneous fashion. Kwaziba is a thriving place of recreation and leisure, providing facilities which poorer urban migrants can afford.

At a little distance from Kwaziba, adjoining the Jinja road, but just outside the city boundary is Nakawa market. The stalls of this market are let on Nakawa *gombolola*[12] land by the Nakawa *gombolola* chief for fifty cents a day. All traditional tribal foodstuffs are sold at these stalls, tribespeople usually catering for their respective members. There are as many women sellers as men. Foodstuffs include banana plantain, dried fish, meat, and vegetables. Situated as it is, closer to Naguru than to Nakawa, yet bearing the latter's name, the market has come to be regarded as providing for residents of both estates.

To the south-east of Nakawa estate, and separated from it by the Kampala-Jinja railway line, is the temporary housing development area of Kiswa. Kiswa is divided into its upper and lower areas. People talk of Upper and Lower Kiswa. Upper Kiswa is the area in which plots of land are sold by the city council to persons wishing to build houses. The houses need not be of permanent structure, though, officially at least, they should be inspected by the city authorities every five years. Most of the houses, which may have four to six rooms each, are let. Each room is let to an individual or family for from 30/– to 40/– a month. A large proportion of residents are prostitutes, or just enterprising women of self-employed status, who charge considerably more for their services than the women of Kwaziba. Male residents of Kiswa, whether unmarried or with their families, include some unskilled or semi-skilled, though there is a highly mobile proportion of men of skilled artisan and clerical status. These latter frequently express their distaste of residence in Kiswa and attempt to move to Nakawa or Naguru.

Upper Kiswa has many so-called 'European' bottle-beer bars. This beer is, of course, far more expensive than 'African' beer. The bars are semi-permanent dwellings, seemingly modelled on the European-type small 'clubs'. They carry such names as 'Moonlight Bar' and 'Superjet'. The barmaids working in them live in Upper Kiswa and are also the prostitutes referred to. The prices of beer are fixed, and the proprietor employs a woman as a barmaid and no more. She carries on her own business of prostitution privately, outside working hours, and decides on the charges for her services herself. The fact is that, though residents in Upper Kiswa are mostly of relatively low socio-economic status, as a place of recreation offering the more expensive bottle-beer bars and women, Upper Kiswa attracts a clientele of higher than average socio-economic status who are themselves not residents.

Those persons owning the land plots, houses and bars are also of high socio-economic status. The number of landlords is 223, and includes 141 of the local tribe, Ganda, and 44 Luo.

Lower Kiswa as a place of recreation is quite distinct from Upper Kiswa and has much in common with Kwaziba. The same people tend to go to each. The rooms there are cheaper, and the houses less substantial, some of them of purely temporary materials like mud and wattle. Lower Kiswa accommodates the cheap 'African' beer stalls. These stalls are out in the open and consist of tables and benches arranged in on-facing squares. No stall has any particular name, though proprietors are individually known.

Nakawa estate itself has very few recreational facilities. There is one bottle-beer bar which, probably because of its isolation from other leisure activity, is never well patronized. There is a very small building called the community centre which is a fraction of the size of the community centre at Naguru. The estate has a small general store, a tailor's shop, and a small clinic, which is used exclusively for childcare by trained nurses who visit the estate a couple of days a week.

At the centre of each estate is the estate manager's office. The estate manager is a full-time public employee,[13] directly answerable to the city council housing committee. He has two assistant managers working under him in the office. His main tasks are to collect tenants' rents, which are brought to him at his office by the tenants themselves, to evict tenants who have fallen behind with their payments or who have violated the lives of other residents, and, ostensibly, to settle tenants' grievances. He is also responsible for the allocation of houses according to the waiting list which he has to draw up. For both Nakawa and Naguru, the waiting lists were always between seven and eight hundred persons. From the time he applies, an applicant has to wait from two to three years before he is offered a house. This system is handled fairly on the whole by the estate manager, even though it would seem inevitably to lend itself to graft and bribery, checked, perhaps, by the occasional visits sprung on managers by housing officers.

Each estate is divided into about thirty groups of from ten to over sixty houses. The latter groups are arranged in on-facing squares. A smaller group is usually either a single line of houses or two facing lines with a narrow road between them. The groups arranged in on-facing squares are more common at Nakawa then Naguru. Except for a single main road running through the estate, roads at Naguru are also narrow. Some Naguru tenants who own cars state that those who designed the layout of the estates 'never realized it would one day be possible for Africans to own cars'.

The cheaper houses at Nakawa and Naguru are usually four-terraced. Progressively more expensive houses are semi-detached. Nakawa has a number of what are called bedspaces, of which there are usually four to a room. Short-term migrants normally use these at a cost of Shs. 7/– a month. A few men with families, however, have taken over a whole room for 28/–.

Each estate is divided up into different rent zones. Like Kiswa, Nakawa has its Upper and Lower areas. These terms of reference were coined by the residents themselves, not by the housing authorities.

Naguru is also divided into different rent zones. A few residents talk of 'upper' and 'lower' Naguru, but the term is not commonplace as among the Nakawa residents. Presumably the fact that the majority of Naguru tenants are of relatively high status and can, as it were, look down on the majority of Nakawa tenants as socio-economic inferiors precludes much stress on a distinction of this sort within their own estate.

Naguru has a large community centre and a comfortable and well-supplied bar. There are usually a number of dances at the centre each week. At weekends the centre is often visited by persons living in the higher-status residential areas of the city and Ntinda. Talks, lectures and meetings are also carried out at the centre. A feature of both Nakawa and Naguru is the existence of a large mango tree at a little distance from the estate manager's office. At Naguru this tree is at the centre of a pleasant stretch of lawn. At Nakawa it stands somewhat awkwardly towards one corner of an on-facing square of sixty-eight cheaper four-terraced houses. The general meetings of some tribal associations and of the estates' tenants' associations are often held under the mango tree. People speak of 'the mango tree' as a point of reference to indicate, say, precisely where a dispute took place, or to direct someone to an address. Needless to say, the mango trees long preceded the estates.

Most houses at Nakawa have neither piped water nor electricity, though a few in Upper Nakawa have the latter. Water taps with laundry slabs serve about six or eight houses. Nowadays, individual pit latrines are provided for each house. Even more recently, a few water closets have been installed to replace the original communal latrines of the bedspaces, which had caused so much mutual disgust among tribespeople with different sanitary habits. There is a fireplace for burning charcoal in each kitchen, which in the Nakawa houses is more of a small cupboard-cum-outhouse. Some people prefer to cook on primus stoves by paraffin.

Nakawa houses have one room, in addition to the small kitchen. Most homes have a curtain drawn across the part of the room occupied by the husband and wife's single-sized bed, separating them from other members of the household sleeping (usually on clothes, blankets or cushions) in the room. The psychological difficulties of cohabitation experienced in these conditions by a man and wife with children are obvious. When there are more than two or three children of more than a few years of age, it is often necessary for one or more to sleep in the kitchen rather than in the room itself. 'Brothers' and lodgers also frequently sleep in the kitchen.

Though some Naguru homes experience these problems of congestion, more householders are more comfortably accommodated in their often considerably more expensive houses. A larger proportion of Naguru houses have piped water and electricity, as well as more than one room.

On both Nakawa and Naguru, back gardens are dug by either wives or husbands, and crops used in the preparation of traditional tribal foods are grown in them. A few Upper Nakawa householders grow flowers in front of their houses. A larger proportion have done so at Naguru. On both estates, front and back gardens are small and usually open, though some householders demarcate their gardens by growing hedges or banana trees.

Bus services from the estates to the city centre are infrequent.

People complain about this and about the fact that they have to walk to their jobs in the city centre or in the industrial area, which is nearer Kampala East but still half an hour's walk.

Against the background of individually different tribal tongues, the need for a common language emerges. For Kampala East, with its major population division between Interlacustrine Bantu and the rest, and with an overlapping division between 'educated' and 'uneducated', three major common languages emerge. These are Swahili, Luganda and English.

The fact that Swahili is spoken on a wide scale among sectors of Kampala's population causes both surprise and scepticism to those who have not investigated the phenomenon. The scope of the language is also questioned. Elkan goes so far as to claim that 'Swahili, as it is spoken in Uganda, is . . . a code rather than a language and its sole virtue is that it is easy to learn for all concerned'.[14] The first part of this statement was made with reference to a group of workers in a single workplace and obscures the possibility that in a local community the scope of Swahili may be greater, especially among specific sectors of the population. I would not dispute that the language is easy to learn.

Many Kenya migrants come to Kampala with a reasonably good command of a brand of Swahili. The Swahili may not satisfy the purists or be approved of by coastal people. But it is rich in vocabulary and expression. It is definitely not a form of 'kitchen Swahili'. The Kenyans constitute a key grouping in Kampala East and, in this ward at least, their brand of Swahili has been picked up in varying proportions by some non-Kenyans. Its use is far more widespread in Nakawa than in Naguru. The Nakawa tenants' association general meetings are held in Swahili, and the proceedings are translated into English. At Naguru, the association's meetings are held in English and translated into both Swahili and Luganda. Nakawa is very much more of a Swahili-speaking community than Naguru. Naguru is more of an English- and Luganda-speaking community. But Naguru, like the rest of Kampala East, does have a high proportion of Swahili speakers.

An immediate criterion distinguishing the general socio-economic statuses of the people of Nakawa and Naguru is the median monthly wage of the household heads of each estate.[15] For Nakawa the median wage is Shs. 164/- per month. For Naguru it is Shs. 319/-. For both estates taken together it is Shs.

243/50. According to the government department of labour assessment, the median wage for employees in Greater Kampala is Shs. 114/– (in 1961). In 1963 the legal minimum monthly wage payable in Kampala was increased from Shs. 75/40 to Shs. 120/–. My figures were collected before this increase and probably continue to have comparative value.

The differences in the range of occupations of each estate's household heads also illustrate the general socio-economic contrast between the two estates. Professional, clerical and skilled are 81 per cent of Naguru's household heads, whereas the figure drops to 48 per cent for Nakawa. At Nakawa there is a correspondingly larger number of unskilled, 52 per cent against 17 per cent at Naguru.

Taken together though, Southall and Gutkind predicted correctly 'that the estates will in the long run cater principally for the non-Ganda whose skill and income is above the average level . . . ' (see Tables II and III).

Ganda account for only 11 per cent of all household heads on both estates, which, considering the Ganda are the local tribe, is probably low in comparison with the percentage of local tribes on housing estates in other African towns. Ganda have a reputation for white-collar work, and significantly, they are much more numerous in the higher-status estate of Naguru than in Nakawa. In contrast, Southall and Gutkind's earlier findings indicated that the Ganda 'appear at the estates in large numbers only among the most unskilled and transient group'.[16] Thus, within a period of some eight years, low-status Ganda have left the estates, moving presumably to the suburbs, while certain high-status Ganda have entered them.

The Luo, Luhya and Acholi are numerous in both estates, followed by Ganda, Samia, Nubi, Teso and Lango. By grouping them together, the Interlacustrine Toro, Soga and Nyoro are also fairly numerous on both estates. But, like the Ganda, they are more numerous on the higher-status estate of Naguru. More of them have skilled and clerical than unskilled occupations. No other tribal grouping constitutes as much as 2 per cent of the households on each and both estates.

The Luo and Luhya show a wide span of occupations. This is partly a result of their large numbers, but is also probably derived from the generally longer and more extensive experience of urban

TABLE II. (a) NAGURU ESTATE
Household Heads according to Tribe and Income Category (as at October 1962)

	% of total House-hold Heads	MONTHLY INCOME RANGES Shillings:											1,000 and over	Un-known	Actual No. of House-hold Heads
Tribe		100	125	150	175	200	300	400	500	600	700	1,000			
Luo	22·64	2	7	7	17	9	44	31	13	8	—	1	2	5	146
Ganda	19·84	1	1	1	8	4	24	30	16	14	5	12	7	5	128
Luhya	10·54	1	7	2	7	2	18	10	6	7	3	4	—	1	68
Toro															23 ⎫
Soga	8·37	—	—	—	6	2	10	18	7	2	1	3	2	3	18 ⎬ 54
Nyoro															13 ⎭
Nubi	7·59	—	—	4	1	2	14	8	8	4	2	2	—	4	49
Acholi	5·43	—	3	1	3	2	9	11	3	—	1	—	1	1	35
Samia/Gwe	3·88	—	3	1	—	2	8	8	2	1	—	—	—	—	25
Teso	2·32	—	1	—	—	2	3	6	1	—	1	1	—	—	15
Lango	2·02	—	1	—	1	—	6	2	1	—	—	2	—	—	13
Lugbara	2·02	—	3	4	—	—	1	4	—	—	—	—	—	1	13
Others	15·35	—	3	4	4	6	22	22	14	7	5	6	2	4	99
TOTAL	100·00	4	29	24	47	31	159	150	71	43	18	31	14	24	645
Total %	100·00	0·62	4·50	3·72	7·29	4·81	24·65	23·25	11·01	6·67	2·79	4·81	2·17	3·72	100·01

21

TABLE II. (b) NAKAWA ESTATE

Household Heads according to Tribe and Income Category (including occupants of bedspaces)

Tribe	% of total Household Heads	MONTHLY INCOME RANGES Shillings:											Un-known	Actual No. of House-hold Heads
		100	125	150	175	200	300	400	500	600	700	700 and over		
Luo	21·99	1	29	33	20	25	50	15	1	2	—	1	6	183
Acholi	13·11	9	30	23	9	8	17	9	2	1	—	—	—	108
Luhya	9·60	4	18	14	14	9	14	4	—	—	—	—	2	79
Lugbara	7·90	9	18	15	6	1	13	2	—	—	—	—	1	65
Kiga	7·41	3	36	3	5	4	6	3	—	1	—	—	—	61
Samia/Gwe	4·98	2	8	5	5	11	6	2	—	—	—	—	2	41
Ganda	4·37	1	2	3	4	6	11	5	2	—	1	—	1	36
Lango	4·01	2	5	3	3	3	15	1	1	—	—	—	—	33
Toro														⎫ 13
Nyoro	3·90	1	7	4	4	1	9	4	2	—	—	—	—	⎬ 13 } 32
Soga														⎭ 6
Ruanda	3·77	3	6	6	5	5	4	1	—	—	—	—	1	31
Nubi	3·16	1	3	3	3	1	10	3	—	—	—	—	2	26
Madi	2·92	2	5	6	4	3	3	—	—	—	—	—	1	24
Jonam	2·92	1	3	6	4	1	6	3	—	—	—	—	—	24
Teso	2·92	—	2	1	3	2	8	6	1	1	—	—	—	24
Ankole	1·21	—	4	1	2	1	1	—	—	—	—	—	1	10
Others	5·59	2	10	5	4	5	14	3	1	1	1	—	—	46
TOTAL	99·76	41	186	131	95	86	187	61	10	6	2	1	17	823
Total in %		4·98	22·60	15·92	11·54	10·45	22·72	7·41	1·21	0·73	0·24	0·12	2·07	99·99

22

TABLE III. (a) NAGURU ESTATE

Household Heads according to Tribe and Occupation

Tribe	Occupation Categories						Total
	1	*2*	*3*	*4*	*5*	Unknown	
Luo	1	52	60	21	9	3	146
Ganda	21 (4f)	69 (5f)	18 (4f)	15 (2f)	2	3	128
Luhya	1	30	20	8	7	2	68
Toro						23	
Soga	2	41 (4f)	9	2	–	18	54
Nyoro						13	
Nubi	1	24	7	16	1	–	49
Acholi	1	17	11	2	4	–	35
Samia/Gwe	–	17	4	–	4	–	25
Teso	–	12 (1f)	2	–	1	–	15
Lango	–	6	5	2	–	–	13
Lugbara	–	4	3	3	3	–	13
Others	10	55	19	9	3	3	99
TOTAL	37	327	158	78	34	11	645
Total in %	5·74	50·70	24·50	12·09	5·27	1·70	100·00

f = female household head.

Occupation Categories

1 =*Professional, Technical
and Highly Skilled*
Lawyer
(Trainee) Accountant
Draughtsman
Surveyor
Teacher
Journalist
Clergy

3 =*Skilled not requiring
use of English*
Mechanic
Carpenter
Plumber
Electrician
Welder/Fitter/Joiner
Bricklayer
Tailor

2 =*Clerical & Skilled,
requiring use of English*
Assistant Manager
Clerk
Agricultural Administration
Civil Service Administration
Welfare Worker
Printer
Telephonist
Salesman
Storekeeper
Steward–Barman
Postal & Tele. Engineer
Gov't & Co. Engineer
Radio Broadcasting & Programme
  Planning
Bus Company Inspector
Meter Reader

23

4 =*Semi-Skilled*
Self-employed traders, shopkeepers,
   etc.
Driver
Machinist
Painter
Bus Conductor
Headman (of labouring gang)
Houseboy/girl/Cook

5 = *Unskilled*
Office-boy/messenger
Askari/Watchman
Porter

TABLE III. (b) NAKAWA ESTATE
Household Heads according to Tribe and Occupation

| Tribe | Occupation Categories | | | | Unknown | Total |
	1	2	3	4		
Luo	21	76	56	30	–	183
Acholi	16	26	20	46	–	108
Luhya	11	30	13	25	–	79
Lugbara	6	19	21	19	–	65
Kiga	10	3	2	46	–	61
Samia/Gwe	4	12	9	16	–	41
Ganda	12	12	10	2	–	36
Lango	13	13	2	5	–	33
Nyoro ⎱					13 ⎱	
Toro ⎰	7	13	6	6	– 13 ⎰	32
Soga					6	
Ruanda	2	7	5	16	1	31
Nubi	3	8	12	3	–	26
Madi	1	7	5	11	–	24
Jonam	4	10	7	3	–	24
Teso	11	9	2	2	–	24
Ankole	2	1	4	3	–	10
Others	15	8	4	18	1	46
TOTAL	138	254	178	251	2	823
Total in %	16·77	30·86	21·63	30·50	0·24	100·00

Occupation Categories

1 = *Clerical & Skilled,*
   requiring use of English
Clerk
Teacher
Draughtsman
Surveyor's assistant
Laboratory trainees
Librarian

Welfare Worker
Printer (Compositor)
Telephonist
Salesman
Storekeeper
Meter Reader
Barman

2 =*Skilled not requiring
use of English*
Mechanic
Carpenter
Book-binder
Plumber
Electrician
Tailor
Watch repairer/maker
Stores assistant
Welder/Fitter
Cable-jointer
Bricklayer
Shoemaker/repairer
Barber

3 =*Semi-skilled*
Self-employed (trader, shopkeeper)
Painter
Machinist
Tyre/Tube repairer
Bus Conductor
Driver
Houseboy/girl/Cook
Dobi (launderer)
Headman (of labouring gang)
Nursing Orderly

4 =*Unskilled*
Office-boy/messenger
Turnboy
Askari/Watchman
Porter
Kla. City Council cleaner/sweeper

work which Kenyans have had. It is the Kenyans who have provided the bulk of the artisans and, in the past especially, clerks. Additionally, many of them are unskilled workers. In common with other Nilotes, and with the Lugbara and Teso, the Kenyans are renowned for their large, muscular physiques, which particularly qualify them for heavy unskilled labour. Most of the Uganda Bantu are generally of small physique and slighter stature. Those of them who are unskilled tend to be employed in jobs in which the work is lighter. Differences in diet seem to account for these differences in physique during the course of many generations.[17]

The Kiga, Lugbara, Madi, and Ruanda are mostly unskilled workers. Most of them live at Nakawa. The Kiga migrate in large numbers from Kigezi, their home district, either to do unskilled work in Kampala or to work in rural Buganda for Ganda landlords. Kigezi suffers from high population density and land shortage. Lugbara and Madi districts also have high population density and land shortage and many Lugbara and Madi are forced to migrate to Kampala and Buganda. Few Lugbara and Madi are in well-paid jobs. So, in addition to their linguistic and cultural isolation, the Lugbara and Madi suffer a certain socio-economic isolation, in so far as few among them are represented in the higher occupational categories. Many Ruanda, almost all of them apparently of the lower Hutu 'caste', have come

25

to Nakawa not directly from Ruanda but from Buganda, where they have worked for many years. Some are the children of earlier migrants and were born in the Province.

Practically all tenants had to wait two or three years for a house, and they have usually worked some time in Kampala or Mengo before applying. The average length of residence on the estates is approximately four years[18] (see Table IV). Adding to this the two to three years' residence in Kampala-Mengo prior to moving to either of the estates, we have six to seven years as a very approximate average of total length of residence in Kampala-Mengo by people living on the estates, considerably higher than Elkan's suggestion of about two years for Kampala-Mengo generally.

The figures relating to length of residence were taken in October 1962. My fieldwork ended in March, 1964, shortly before when I collected the figures a second time. In this way I was able to test the stability of the estates' populations over the intervening period. General stability is, of course, a characteristic of the estates' populations. By March 1964 only 141 household heads, less than 10 per cent, had moved away from both Nakawa and Naguru. This figure does not include the number of household heads who moved from Nakawa to Naguru. It included some who moved to such higher residential areas as Ntinda or Kololo. Even without accounting for the number of household heads who moved to, say, Ntinda, Katali, or Kiswa, the figure indicates that relatively few of them, out of a combined total of 1,468 for Nakawa and Naguru, left Kampala East in the period of nearly seventeen months. Stated differently, the present rate of defection from both Nakawa and Naguru is only about one person in ten every seventeen months. Stated differently again, this indicates a current expected length of residence of fourteen years for each household head in both Nakawa and Naguru alone. The expected total length of residence for them in Kampala-Mengo is of course an indeterminate number of years longer.

I deal with the interrelation of these demographic features and marriage in a later chapter. For the general introductory picture it is sufficient to conclude that 1,157, or 79 per cent of the 1,468 household heads at Nakawa and Naguru are married. 1,009, or 87 per cent of these married persons have children (see Table VI, page 101). Most are tribespeople among whom the practice of a customary marriage arranged at home is still followed. Ignoring

TABLE IV. (a) NAGURU ESTATE
Length of Residence (to nearest year) as at October 1962

Tribe	Number of years 12	11	10	9	8	7	6	5	4	3	2	1	Less than 1 year	Un-known	Total No. Household Heads
Luo	1	2	4	4	2	6	9	8	28	27	26	20	5	4	146
Ganda	—	1	4	2	8	3	7	11	22	15	26	22	6	1	128
Luhya	1	—	—	1	1	2	5	2	14	13	10	16	1	2	68
Toro / Soga / Nyoro	—	—	1	—	1	1	3	1	13	9	10	14	1	1	23 / 18 / 13 } 54
Nubi	4	3	2	8	4	4	1	4	5	5	2	4	1	2	49
Acholi	—	—	—	—	1	—	1	4	5	5	6	13	—	—	35
Samia/Gwe	1	—	—	—	—	1	2	—	8	3	4	4	1	1	25
Teso	—	—	—	—	1	—	1	—	2	4	2	5	—	—	15
Lango	1	—	—	—	—	—	—	—	2	3	6	1	—	—	13
Lugbara	—	—	—	—	—	—	1	—	6	1	2	2	—	1	13
Others	—	1	3	3	1	3	6	5	16	17	13	22	6	3	99
TOTAL	8	7	14	18	19	20	36	35	121	102	107	123	21	14	645
Total in %	1·24	1·09	2·17	2·79	2·94	3·10	5·58	5·43	18·76	15·81	16·59	19·09	3·26	2·17	100·00

27

TABLE IV. (b) NAKAWA ESTATE
Length of Residence (to nearest year) as at October 1962

Tribe		Number of years												Less than 1 year	Unknown	Total No. Household Heads
	12	11	10	9	8	7	6	5	4	3	2	1			
Luo	1	1	5	2	6	5	16	12	31	32	27	27	16	2	183
Acholi	–	–	1	1	11	4	12	5	20	16	14	19	5	–	108
Luhya	–	–	–	2	1	2	5	5	19	19	11	12	1	2	79
Lugbara	–	1	1	–	2	1	19	5	6	13	4	7	6	–	65
Kiga	–	–	1	–	–	–	–	–	3	6	6	38	4	3	61
Samia/Gwe	–	1	3	1	1	1	–	1	13	5	4	6	4	1	41
Ganda	–	–	1	4	–	–	1	3	10	1	7	4	4	1	36
Lango	–	–	–	–	–	–	3	4	7	5	2	8	4	–	33
Toro ⎫ Nyoro ⎬ Soga ⎭	–	–	–	1	2	1	1	6	4	8	6	3	–	–	13 ⎫ 13 ⎬ 32 6 ⎭
Ruanda	–	1	–	–	1	–	1	5	11	3	2	3	2	2	31
Nubi	–	–	2	1	1	1	1	2	8	3	5	2	–	–	26
Madi	–	2	1	–	–	1	–	3	7	3	2	4	1	–	24
Jonam	–	–	–	–	–	1	1	3	5	5	2	6	1	–	24
Teso	–	–	–	–	–	–	2	2	5	4	5	5	1	–	24
Ankole	–	–	1	–	–	–	–	–	3	–	1	4	1	–	10
Others	–	–	–	2	1	3	4	2	8	8	7	6	1	4	46
TOTAL	1	6	16	14	26	20	66	58	160	131	105	154	51	15	823
Total in %	0·12	0·73	1·94	1·70	3·16	2·43	8·02	7·05	19·44	15·92	12·76	18·71	6·20	1·82	100·00

28

the considerable variations among individual tribespeople, this high ratio of wives to men contrasts with what is presumably a much lower ratio in Kampal-Mengo, where the ratio of both married and unmarried females to males is 66·5 per cent. The estates may be described generally as an urban area of stable workers, most of whom are married and have their wives with them for at least half the year, the other half usually spent by the wife at home in two spells of about three months at digging and planting, and harvesting times.

NOTES

[1] Suggested by A. W. Southall. The old Ganda capital of Mengo became a municipality in 1962 and was extended to include in its jurisdiction the sub-county previously known as the Kibuga, meaning capital in Luganda, of which Mengo was once a parish and then township. Since writing this book I have been told of the administrative merger of Kampala and Mengo.

[2] P. C. Gutkind, 1952, 'Accommodation and Conflict in an African peri-urban Area', *Anthropologia*, n.s., Vol. 4, No. 1.

[3] A. W. Southall and P. C. Gutkind, 1957, *Townsmen in the Making*, East African Studies No. 9, Kampala, have analysed in detail the relationship of the then Kibuga to Kampala.

See also P. C. Gutkind, 1963, *The Royal Capital of Buganda*, The Hague, Mouton & Co. This study deals with the extent to which a centralized political system either encourages or hinders 'modernization', including urban development, in this case in the Ganda kingdom's capital of Mengo.

[4] Southall and Gutkind, op. cit., p. 49.

[5] From the *Uganda (Protectorate) Annual Enumerations of Employees*, Government Printer, Entebbe.

[6] W. Elkan, 1960, *Migrants and Proletarians*, Oxford University Press for East African Institute of Social Research, p. 104.

[7] J. C. Mitchell, 1954, *African Urbanization in Luanshya and Ndola*, Rhodes-Livingstone Communication No. 6, Rhodes-Livingstone Institute, Lusaka.

[8] Government Printer, Entebbe.

[9] Twenty East African Shillings = £1 Sterling (100 cents = 1 East African Shilling).

[10] I am grateful to Mr. Serwadda of the Uganda Department of Labour for this information.

[11] This includes millet beer, which has nutrient qualities and is often regarded as much a food as a drink.

[12] Nakawa *gombolola* is a sub-county of Buganda and has to be distinguished physically, administratively and socially from Nakawa housing estate, though the latter does, of course, derive its name from the *gombolola* which once included the area which the estate now occupies. In 1963 it became Nakawa Township.

[13] Comparable, presumably, to the Location Superintendent referred to by Epstein, A. L. 1964, 'Urban Communities in Africa' in M. Gluckman and E. Devons (eds.), *Closed Systems and Open Minds*, Oliver and Boyd.

[14] W. Elkan, op. cit., p. 67.

[15] I regard as household head the member of a household family or domestic unit who is responsible, among other things, for the payment of the rent. Such responsibility normally lies with the father of a nuclear or compound family, or with the senior 'brother' of the household of siblings or friends. A small number of mostly Ganda and Toro women are household heads. They are unmarried or divorced, with or without children. A small number have 'temporary' husbands, but the house is rented in their name and they continue to regard themselves as household head.

[16] Southall and Gutkind, op. cit., p. 48.

[17] W. Elkan, op. cit., p. 86–7.

[18] In fact, it is greater than this, since many Naguru householders have previously lived at Nakawa. I have been unable to include in my table these extra periods of residence, which would have raised the average for both estates.

CHAPTER II

INDEPENDENCE AND POLITICAL CHANGES

The Setting

Politically the problem for most of the estates' population was one of identity. The Kenyans were numerous enough but had come to regard their political and employment rights in another nation as somewhat in jeopardy. Admittedly, during Pax Britannica this had hardly mattered since to move from Kenya to Uganda had never been difficult, except for Kikuyu during the Emergency from 1952 to 1959. But in the years approaching Uganda's independence of October, 1962, and with a decline in the number of jobs in the city, fears were being expressed that Ugandans might be given preference over Kenyans. It later transpired that these fears were partly warranted, but received heightened emphasis due to a general slackening in employment affecting everyone. But even while Uganda's independence was imminent, Kenyans in Kampala East were to be given a last chance to show their ability to organize politically. This was at the Kampala (then) municipal council elections of September 1962 which undoubtedly owed much of their vigour and success as exercises in municipal franchise to the industry of the Kenya residents, especially Luo. The elections occurred a few weeks before the formal declaration of independence. By the next elections in February, 1964, Kenyans were disfranchised, and many of the politically active had returned home or to alternative employment in Kenya towns. The elections were undoubtedly a failure, and the political and economic structure of Kampala-Mengo as a whole had already embarked on a shuddering process of social revolution.

If one could regard the Kenyans as one major national group, then one could almost regard the people from northern Uganda as another. Their position was ambiguous. Coming from societies which did not have kings and which were for the most part behind the educational, economic and, indeed, cultural development of the peoples of south Uganda, they felt as uneasy as the Kenyans about being 'foreigners'. In some ways people like the

31

Acholi, Lango, Alur and others felt closer to their fellow-Nilotics, the Kenya Luo, than to other Ugandans, especially the southern Bantu, though at best this was a tentative liaison. Northerners on the estates knew the value of independence. They, too, saw it as a possible means of displacing the many Kenyans in the offices and factories, and the trade unions. A question which remained was who would replace them. Would the Ganda continue their dominance over so many of the top positions or would the increasing number of educated men from the north step in? It was problems of this sort which people thought about and expressed in conversation as independence approached.

The position of the southerners must have seemed clearer-cut at about the time of independence than it did a few years afterwards when the Kabaka of Buganda was exiled and the kingdoms began to lose some of the constitutional privileges they had enjoyed for so long. At that time few would dispute the mastery of Ganda in Kampala-Mengo. Their political strength in the nation as a whole had seemed to be obvious when they threatened to secede from Uganda at the time of independence talks. Though often divided from Ganda on local issues, a notable one being the 'lost counties' dispute between Buganda and Bunyoro, people from the other kingdoms inevitably felt it relatively easy at the inter-personal level to graft themselves on to Ganda society while in Kampala. They lived where Ganda lived, and were thus, like Ganda, not numerous in the estates. They had similar languages and customs and, with the time and effort, could sometimes pass as Ganda, which they might frequently do in front of 'foreigners' from the north or from Kenya. They married Ganda, had Ganda mistresses and lovers, or established business partnerships, and so inevitably often appeared to the 'foreigners' as indistinguishable.

The municipal council elections of September 1962, which I now describe in detail, were finally to reveal how these groups stood, both in the nation and in an interesting microscopic manner in Kampala East also. The elections were to reveal also a new development in relations among the estates' tenants which was expressed in the much more poorly attended city council elections in the ward sixteen months later. Before then, in February 1963, by-elections were held for seats in the parliament of the Buganda kingdom in a number of constituencies around Kampala, including one adjacent to the estates. They were to confirm, if confirmation were needed, how Ganda were beginning to stand even more outside the activities of the city, and, in Kampala East, outside the life of the estates.

Council Election, Kampala East Ward, September 1962

For the first time municipal councillors were to be popularly elected, either under the banner of one of the two major political parties or as independent candidates. Previously councillors had been nominated by the Governor, or, since Uganda's internal self-government, by the Minister of Local Government of the then ruling Democratic Party. Adding to the atmosphere was the prospect of Uganda's independence a few weeks later in October.

Inevitably the fervour and excitement attending the campaigns, the rallies, and the polling were intense. There were many vested interests. The Asians,[1] who constituted a large and important part of Kampala's population, were apprehensive of what independence might bring them. Kenya Africans already claimed to have experienced discrimination in job-getting and were equally apprehensive of the future. Uganda Africans, especially the Nilotic northerners, saw their chances of acquiring the rapidly decreasing number of jobs blocked by the somewhat dominant position held by Kenyans, along with Ganda, in employment.

There were two other divisions cross-cutting the more general ones. The internally self-governing Democratic Party was alleged by many voters to be composed mostly of Catholics, though publicly the party denied this. The contending Uganda Peoples Congress had become powerful, seemingly composed of most Protestants, Muslims, Northern Nilotes, Kenya Luo and Asians. The power to decide the issue lay with the Ganda nationalist party, Kabaka Yekka, the only 'tribal' party in the country. The UPC forged an alliance with the KY and in the ensuing national and most local elections came to power convincingly.

The south and west wards of Kampala had majority numbers of non-African, mostly Asian, voters, and, realizing presumably that registered voters would have to be citizens by the time of the next elections, the party organizations directed a larger proportion of their time and energy to Kampala East, where middle-class Africans lived. It is doubtful if it had occurred to many of the organizers that the citizenship qualification, when it came, would bar Kenya Africans as well. The estates were inevitably the major target of electoral propaganda. Even so, only four of the ten candidates standing for Kampala East actually lived on the estates, though all except one lived in the ward. Three of the candidates were Asian, one a Sikh and the other two Muslims. They lived among and in a limited sense represented the minority but highly politically conscious Asian element in the ward.

Party-voting appeared to be the decisive factor in the results of the elections, since all four successful candidates were put forward by the KY/UPC alliance (see table). A possible reason for their success might be that this coalition party seemed to have the support of most of the secular and religious blocs, except Catholics, as I explained, though this is difficult to substantiate. Their propaganda was certainly more lavish than that of their rivals, the DP and the Independents, and many voters admitted to being swayed by their more advertised promises of better or cheaper housing often hours and even minutes before they entered the polling booths. But in fairness it must be recorded that a large majority of the estates' voters were people shrewd enough to realize that an independent national government without the Ganda party would be off to a shaky start, and many saw political stability and personal security in the success of the alliance. Both parties had considered very carefully the various people who had asked to be nominated as candidates. Their 'public images' and the leadership roles they were already

	Tribe or Ethnic Group	Nomination	Votes
1	Sikh	KY/UPC	1,112
2	Alur (Naguru)	KY/UPC	1,070
3	Asian Muslim	KY/UPC	997
4	Ganda	KY/UPC	990
5	Luo (Naguru)	DP	856
6	Asian Muslim	DP	818
7	Luo	Independent	732
8	Janam (Naguru)	DP	731
9	Samia	DP	629
10	Luo (Otieno of Nakawa)	Independent	194
			8,129

playing, on the estates or elsewhere, were all scrutinized before they were either selected or rejected. Indeed it can be claimed that the reasons for the selection and rejection of candidates by the political parties are of as great sociological significance as their actual performance at the election.

The three Asians, Nos. 1, 3 and 6, were established, politically active figures. They were businessmen and owners of property both in the ward and elsewhere.

The Ganda candidate, No. 4, lived some 20 miles from Kampala. He was a sub-county chief and was said to be of the royal clan. The KY/UPC officials explained that he had been selected in order to attract the votes of Ganda. He personally justified, as it were, the coalition of the KY with the UPC. He contrasted strikingly with the other candidates in standing aloof from the proceedings. He did attend meetings and rallies, dressed in his *kanzu* and jacket, the traditional Ganda dress for men, but a younger Ganda, dressed in a lounge suit and speaking impeccable English and Swahili as well as Luganda, addressed the meetings on his behalf. Ganda residents attending explained that they expected a Ganda chief to behave in this aloof manner. They were not at all affronted that he did not personally address the meeting, though others, notably the Kenyans and northern Ugandans, complained about this and also that a man, whatever his rank, who lived 20 miles distant could hardly be said to be in a position to represent the ward properly. But, as a figurehead for the Ganda, he was clearly successful and there is little doubt that most non-Catholic Ganda voted for him. This Ganda was the only candidate who did not normally live in Kampala East, or indeed Kampala, though he owned property there, and this was enough for him to be nominated under the 'colonial' voting registration regulations of the time. Neither he nor the three Asians lived in the ward and so had not associated with residents on the estates on an interpersonal basis before the election. They might conveniently be called 'outside' candidates.

The three Asians were already established members of the circulating élite which constitutes the core of any political party. The Ganda candidate was an established member of the Ganda rural hierarchy and appealed to the Ganda nationalist party. The relationships of these four to the electorate were categorical in that they represented the categories of political parties, which are meaningful to most of the electorate only at some great social distance, through the signs and symbols deriving from posters, public promises and radio broadcasts.

The other six, whom I call 'inside' candidates, all lived in Kampala East. They mingled with the people in bars, talked to them at tenants' association or other meetings, were neighbours to someone and had the mundane problems of neighbourhood like everybody else. While it is true that their incomes were above the average of their neighbours, the difference in most cases was not so high that they were out of touch with the ordinary financial difficulties of town life. They all had families and children, in some cases were prominent leaders in their Kampala tribal associations, or in other associations including trade unions, and so could rightly claim to know enough of the local scene to represent the people competently on the council.

Three of them were Kenyans, all Luo, and while in those days this was not officially a disqualification for nomination by a political party, the two Independent candidates had experienced a rebuff by the KY/UPC when they asked to be nominated. Both attributed this to discrimination against Kenyans, and Luo in particular, though in the case of No. 10, a more likely explanation is that the local party caucus did not regard him as coming up to the standards of a successful candidate. He lived at Nakawa rather than Naguru, and, as one party man put it, 'no one at Naguru would vote for a man living at Nakawa', while the reverse, he implied, could occur. He had, it is true, the highest wage of all Nakawa's residents and spoke reasonably good English, but these could hardly offset the lowered prestige of his place of residence.

That such things mean so much to people will emerge in the discussion. No. 10 did intend to remedy this position by moving to Naguru, but by the time a house became vacant over a year later he had lost the right to stand or vote at the next election. He was the only candidate living at Nakawa and in spite of widespread popularity as a leader on the estate fared dismally in the polls. Indeed, it was partly because of his close association with the estate that so few voted for him, including fellow residents. A neighbour voiced a typical comment, 'We know that he has tried his level best for us [Nakawa people] in the tenants' association, but we still have bad conditions on this estate, so how will he succeed as a councillor?' Yet this Luo, whom I call Otieno, had been asked by a number of fellow officers in the tenants' association in which he was active to stand and represent them. Being popular throughout the estate he had also been stopped by tenants passing by, who had made the same suggestion. But, when confronted by the choice of many obviously more powerful candidates and by the lavish propaganda of party campaigns, they had seemingly thought twice and withdrawn their support for him. Thus, there were at least two reasons for his failure. One was his rejection by the KY/UPC which obliged him either not to contest a seat or do so as an Independent, which he did but which cost him Shs. 2,000/– in deposit and expenses. The other was his strong identification with the less prestigeful estate of Nakawa. Popular but only in a restricted way, richest man on Nakawa but not rich enough as an Independent to exceed the relatively huge campaign budgets of the parties, aspiring but blocked, and Kenyan as well, Otieno is something of a marginal man. In his day-to-day relations he is very much like his neighbours, rising above most of them in income and local leadership, yet never really likely to move far out of their social milieu. Otieno's urban career is of interest in showing the interplay of status differences and aspirations typical of so many stable, better-off townsmen, and will be described in detail at a later stage.

The other Luo candidate who was obliged to stand as an Independent after rejection by KY/UPC was considerably wealthier than Otieno and, indeed, all the defeated candidates. He had two lucrative jobs, both of a professional nature. The lavishness of his rallies and numbers of cars and supporters he hired were considerable and almost compared with those of the two political parties. His failure thus cost him an enormous sum of money. All this was risked for a councillorship which offers no pay, not even expenses, and much work, though it does offer renown and useful social contacts, some of which may be of material benefit. This candidate lived in Kampala East, but in a higher status area even than Naguru. He owned the only bar at Nakawa, however, and was well known in the ward. Unlike Otieno he played no part in tenants' associations or the like, but, again unlike Otieno, was regarded as a prominent Kampala Luo leader, being secretary of the Luo Union and very obviously largely responsible for running its school and clinic and for organizing the provision of certain forms of aid. He was in many ways a tribal spokesman for Luo in Kampala. This probably counted against him when he asked to be nominated by the KY/UPC, who were naturally opposed to 'tribalism' and avoided supporting a candidate who seemed too closely associated with his own tribespeople, especially a people as numerous and active as the Luo, and expatriate as well. He did very well in the polls, attributable perhaps to his standing as a Luo leader, but did not manage to make the first four.

Many of his large retinue of supporters during the campaign were officers and members of the Luo Union, some helpers at the Luo school and clinic at Naguru and the Union's sports club, and others the usual regular hangers-on. As a figure of public significance to many Luo his progress was watched with anticipation. He had preached, perhaps ironically in view of his reputation as tribal leader, a proposed policy of 'non-tribalism', especially promising Luo and Kenyans generally that he would put an end to any fears that they had that they would be discriminated against in employment after independence. But he, too, failed. He had invested a great deal of time and effort, as well as money, in the arduous campaign and in the lengthy preparations preceding it. He had also used the time and efforts of officers and other Luo associated with the Union. The inevitable rival Luo who had opposed his candidature as councillor from the beginning now blamed him for the inefficiencies which had developed in the various societies affiliated to the Luo Union and in the Union itself. This condemnation was expressed on a much wider scale by the hundreds of Luo who attended the Union's annual election of officers a few weeks later. He was ousted as secretary amid some mild abuse and did not stand for any other office. Just over a year later he left Kampala and returned to Kenya. It was widely believed that he was rejected by the KY/UPC in the beginning because he was Kenyan. This probably was a reason, as also was his presumed leadership of a tribe who are fairly numerous in Kampala. It was only his wealth and some tribal support which, enabled him to go as far as he did as an Independent. But, finally, after his failure he experienced condemnation at the hands of those who were among the core of his supporters.

The DP seemed less concerned in having Kenyans as candidates, or perhaps had less choice, and the third Luo stood for them, coming fifth in the polls. He lived in one of the better, Shs. 150/-

houses in Naguru and had a reasonably well-paid job, though not of the level of the second Luo. But he did beat him in the polling, in spite of not being an acclaimed local leader, tribal or otherwise. Again, one could guess that the barrage of party propaganda, even of the less popular DP, had its decisive effect.

These three were Kenyans of the Luo tribe. Their failures were interpreted differently yet with common themes. Otieno was not a 'big man', at least not for councillorship. He was well liked by those of his lower-status estate, but this was not enough, especially since he was not even a tribal leader. The second Luo was financially well-off by any standards and was also a local 'big man' and Luo leader, but still seemed to need the extra booster of party support. The third Luo, though a Naguru resident and well-known, by his tribespeople at least, had no more than the usual casual relations with people around him. He did not attend the tenants' association meetings more than the average person and certainly did not attempt to become a leader in it. But he was supported by one of the parties and, in the absence of clearer evidence, this was responsible for his relatively good performance.

Many Luo saw these results as some sort of sinister plot to undermine Kenyans in Kampala. Some even suggested the ballots had not been counted properly, which was certainly untrue. Why, they asked, had two Luo been rejected by the KY/UPC in the first place, especially since so many Luo had pledged help and support to the UPC in earlier days? The other Kenya group, collectively called the Luhya, were every bit as uneasy as Luo about what would happen to their jobs after Uganda's independence, but none expressed the Luo rejections and failures as some sort of plot. In fact as individuals they were much less vociferous than Luo about political developments in Uganda. An impression which was partly confirmed by a row within the Luhya Association executive some months later, was that a fair proportion of Luhya, including the related Samia, supported DP. One of the DP candidates, allegedly from the Uganda side of the border, was a Samia, and an active trade union officer. Again, conversations in beer bars and at road corners suggested that Kenyans saw themselves as divided into two groups: those supporting UPC and summarily classed as Luo; and those behind DP, classed as Luhya. There may indeed have been some truth in this crude distinction for those few who were politically active. It was to some extent an extension into Kampala and Uganda political life of their home political division into the Kenya African National Union, solidly supported by Luo at the time, and the Kenya African Democratic Union, behind which at least a majority of Luhya stood. There were branches of these two parties in Kampala, which were especially active in the year or so before Kenya became independent, prior to the national elections to determine which of them should rule the country. As neighbouring peoples in their own country with not inconsiderable inter-marriage, sharing many customs though different languages, and as the only important Kenya tribal groups in Kampala, it was perhaps inevitable that their political division in Kenya should appear to be carried over into Uganda, both in their respective political party branches in Kampala and in their differing allegiances to UPC and DP. And in general terms this was probably the case, the exceptions often proving the point, as with the third Luo standing for DP and so, I was told by some Luhya, getting their support.

Though chagrined at what they thought were rebuffs of Luo by KY/UPC and the absence of an elected Luo councillor (one Luo had been appointed a councillor a year earlier under the old system), Luo expressed jubilation at the party's landslide victory, a victory which was of the same magnitude at urban elections all over the country. When the results were announced to the huge crowd gathered outside the town hall, the many Luo from the estates and elsewhere, so easily discernible as a physical type in any mixed crowd, left no doubt as to their allegiances, even if they continued to wonder with concern at their future in Uganda. The Luhya, much like any Bantu group to look at, could not be picked out, though individual Luhya expressed a guarded concern after the event. Thus Kenyans, while all anxious for their futures in Kampala, did not present a united front at the elections. It took what they regarded as an attack on them by the new government some months later to close their ranks, at least as far as associations and public expression were concerned, a development which I describe later.

Tribal and national affiliations apart, one of the ironies of the election results was that although of the ten candidates four actually lived on the two main estates and two in immediately adjacent areas, only one was among the four who were elected.

In other words, he was the only 'inside' candidate to become a councillor. Yet, though figures are not available, the bulk of the residents in the wards not only were Africans but came from the area of the estates. The Asians, a minority as residents, probably had a proportionally higher turn-out but in absolute terms did not outnumber the Africans. A few Asians and a fairly large number of Ganda were property-owners in the ward, an example being the Kiswa housing scheme next to Nakawa, where 141 of the 223 house, bar and plot owners were Ganda. The property and residence qualifications for franchise undoubtedly lowered the chances of more people from the estates becoming candidates and elected, but what was more important demonstrated how much under the control of 'outsiders' the estates were. This presupposes a sense of community for the estates which can be exaggerated but which did receive overt expression spasmodically when crisis situations developed affecting the tenants.

The one successful 'inside' candidate was personally more responsible than anyone for what community spirit existed on the estates. He was especially close to the electorate, being founding chairman of the Naguru tenants' association and for other societies on the estate, the owner of a bar at Kiswa where he often went to talk with people, and, perhaps less significantly, the president of his Alur tribal association, which like most tribal associations in Kampala, has its headquarters on the estates. Even at Nakawa he was looked up to as a 'big man'. His application for nomination by KY/UPC was readily accepted. Before the election tenants at Naguru spoke eagerly of his abilities, of the command he exercised in the tenants' association and of the success of his demands made to the housing authorities for better facilities. They said that once he himself became a councillor he would do even more for them. Residents of Nakawa, many of the politically conscious of whom themselves aspired to residence in the higher-status estate, echoed these sentiments. Nearly every tenant knew him by name. Many knew him personally either through his activities in associations or socially. Neighbours and other residents would come along to his house and ask advice about a neighbourhood problem, about how to settle disputing claims to hire the community hall for a dance or tribal or other association, or about the services provided by the children's clinic or a local school.

Because the Alur are so few in Kampala, it is probably no exaggeration to claim that every Alur in the town knew of him. Fellow officers and regular members of the tribal association which he had founded and other Alur constantly mixed with him. He had for a long time urged the greater recognition of the Alur people and language by the national government and by the Kampala local authorities. It seemed that nearly all Alur in Kampala voted for him. Party officials stated that his obvious local popularity and leadership qualities suited him for candidature. Some also expressed the view that his being a member of a small minority tribe helped because voters would then have no fear that he would be guided by large-scale tribal prejudice.

But those who bask in glory fall easiest from grace and within a few months he came under constant fire from Naguru residents. His devotion of time and energy to his new position as councillor brought accusations from them that he was neglecting his position as president of the tenants' association. Association officials and regular members harangued him for not doing enough for Naguru. His new duties prevented him from attending their meetings though he continued to be president. But it was noticed that he now mixed with a more prestigious circle of acquaintances at the city centre. He claimed that these were the necessary social obligations of councillorship. His accusers called it an excuse for neglecting them. After all, was it not they who had elected him? Whereas before the election his Naguru associates and fellow residents had exhorted his virtues of leadership, now, after the election, many subjected him to a barrage of condemnation. This situation did not last for more than a couple of months, and was really an indication of the strains felt by a group of people living together and with a general common interest in improving amenities, dependent on a leader and keen to see him represent them at higher levels yet anxious that he should not forget them. I interpret the outbursts against him as a type of ceremonial rebellion. The principal leader had to be reminded by those dependent on him of his duties, and this could only be achieved by accusing him of the neglect of these duties in tones of disrespect. But local Alur did not condemn him, even though, similarly, he had to relinquish all attendance at the tribal association meetings and to cut down on the number of personal visits he paid them. They felt privileged to have a member of their small minority tribe in a position of this eminence and expected he would be better able to remedy certain of their grievances.

The third Naguru resident who stood as a candidate was a Jonam, a very closely related independent branch of the Nilotic Alur who are also very few in Kampala. The Jonam was a Catholic and stood for DP, who had seen his bustling activity in the estate's associations as a sign of high standing there. In fact he was not as much a key figure in the Naguru élite as they thought, and really became well known after the election. A short while before being accepted by the DP he had spent many years at Nakawa where he had been an important member of the estate's local élite. Like so many status aspirants at Nakawa, he had moved to better housing at Naguru. This had displeased a number of his previous fellow residents, especially tenants' association officials, who accused him of withdrawing his much-needed support of this and other associations at a critical time when appeals had been made to the housing authorities for better facilities. Some of them were clearly jealous of his ability to move to Naguru. This jealousy became misplaced as an accusation of 'treachery', a favourite way of condemning people who withdraw their support of formal and informal associations on whatever grounds.

He was the driving force behind his tribal association and, after his failure at the council elections, was condemned by a number of Jonam for neglecting it during the lengthy preparations and campaigns. They claimed that the association's welfare activities had come to a temporary halt, that, without his organizational abilities, the customary flow of aid to distressed fellow-tribesmen had slowed, subscriptions and fines had not been paid, and internal quarrels had developed. Rightly or wrongly he was again accused of 'treachery', this time by people of his own tribe, who, being few in Kampala, could circulate gossip of this sort quickly among themselves. Many Jonam said that he had neglected the association for the sake of wanting to acquire prestige 'and a name' as a councillor, even though not all of them either expected to benefit from the association or attended its meetings. Perhaps if he had succeeded in becoming a councillor, his reception might have been more like that of the Alur, who was seen as something of a town tribal hero, a man from a small tribe who had made good.

43

Politics and the Community

This detailed account of candidates at the municipal elections reveals a number of factional elements in Kampala East. The Kenyans, always a politically active group, saw themselves on the threshold of a new relationship with their adopted town of employment. While dominant in the estates, they questioned for how long even their rights to work and live in the city would stand. The Ganda voters were themselves mostly resident outside the ward, being property-owners, using or hiring out shops, stalls and houses. Other African voters hardly constituted a clear grouping, consisting of people from the north and a few from other southern kingdoms. The Alur who was elected perhaps typified them, having little in common with either the Kenyans or Ganda and himself coming from a small northern tribe. The larger northern tribes, such as Acholi and Lango, and the Teso from the east, though numerous in the estates, had remarkably little to do with the political activity of the elections, providing no leaders in the ward and not evidently numerous at the polling booths. This is in spite of the obvious growing power and influence of certain individuals of these tribes in the UPC élite.

It was the Ministers of Labour and Information who first revealed publicly a glimpse of the newly independent government's attitude toward Kenya workers in Uganda only a month after Independence. They pointed out that there had been sixty strikes in Uganda between May and September of that year and claimed that most had been engineered by Kenya trade unionists. One of the ministers deplored what he regarded as excessive numbers of Kenya, Luo and Luhya workers in the country. A number of Kenya trade unionists were mentioned personally in the announcement. One, the secretary-general of the Uganda Breweries and Beverage Workers Union, a resident at Naguru, challenged each of the ministers to substantiate their statements that he was guilty of industrial sabotage in Uganda, that most of the sixty strikes had been led by Kenyans, and that Kenyans were in any case excessively numerous. He drew attention to the fact that of the twenty-two full-time officials of the Uganda Trades Union Congress, only four were Kenyans. He made no reference, however, to the large number of Kenya trade unionists working in an honorary capacity. Other prominent Kenya trade unionists protested, some drawing attention to the proposed East African Federation, which, it transpired, was not to emerge as early as had been suggested, but which at the time seemed inconsistent with this policy. The Minister of Labour later insisted that his remarks were aimed at individuals but not at Kenyans generally. But the news percolated down from the press to many Kenya workers who saw it as initial confirmation of the anxiety they had felt in the months preceding Independence. Some claimed to have seen or heard of government circulars distributed to employers and personnel officers requesting that Ugandans be given preference in employment.

Outbursts surrounding Kenyans later took more subtle forms, as when the president of the Uganda T.U.C. and of the Uganda Railway African Union claimed in October 1963 that Ugandan railway employees were not being promoted at a fair rate in Uganda. This same prominent trade unionist was clearly not simply anti-Kenyan since as MP for Kampala East he had some eight months earlier campaigned vigorously for recognition of Swahili as one of the official languages of Uganda, which, had it been accepted by Parliament, may conceivably have enabled some of the many Swahili-speaking Kenyans living in Kampala East to apply for citizenship. The sum result of these exchanges in press and parliament was to illuminate even more the problem of a large section of expatriate Kenyans in the Uganda mostly urban labour force. And problem it was in view of the rather drastic fall in the number of jobs in Uganda. The publication of the government's annual enumeration of employees in October underlined this scarcity. Wages had risen generally due to the March increase of the minimum level, but jobs were now fewer, and it was this which affected the labour market for Kenyans especially. The Uganda Government never officially stated that its policy was to deter Kenyans from working in Uganda, but this is how it appeared in practice. Official or unofficial, it was understandable. If national boundaries and citizenship were to have meaning then some sort of protection had to be given to the country's growing and increasingly more educated job-seekers.

In spite of Kenyans' fears and whatever the policy, the proportions of Kenyans in employment has in fact altered very little in the period from just before to a few years after independence. In Kampala they declined only from 17·9 per cent in 1961 to

15·4 per cent in 1965, and in Uganda as a whole from 8·1 per cent to 6·9 per cent. The decline will continue as more trained Ugandans are available but is so gradual as to belie completely the sudden mass exodus from their jobs which Kenyans feared might happen. In Kampala, indeed, the labour force increased in this period and there were slightly more Kenyans working in the town in 1965 than in 1961. The sociological significance here discussed is not in what really transpired but in how Kenyans mobilized themselves to deal with what had certainly seemed to be a threat against their economic position.

Ganda, as citizens, were hardly likely to lose their jobs. Yet both they and Kenyans were affected, though in different ways, by the new franchise qualifications which first came to the public's attention in July 1963. In the town of Jinja, forty-eight miles from Kampala, a Kenyan was surprised to have his application rejected for candidature at the forthcoming municipal council elections in September, because he was not a Uganda citizen. Protests by Kenyans in Jinja, Kampala and other towns followed, but a public announcement left the issue in no doubt. According to the Uganda Constitution, only Uganda citizens could vote in a by-election to choose a Member of Parliament, and only those eligible to vote at a by-election could vote at an urban council election. This disqualified most Asians, Europeans and Kenya Africans, but in practice many Ganda were also affected in Kampala city. The old qualifications had allowed the vote to owners and occupiers of rateable property in a ward. The new ones stipulated that not just citizens but only citizens who lived in the ward had the right to vote. Ganda were the only African tribal group in any appreciable numbers who owned property in the city, though, as explained, relatively few lived there, most preferring Mengo or other Buganda areas outside the city boundary. They, too, were surprised at not being allowed to register as voters.

Indignation rose among both Kenyans and Ganda, while, because the old electoral roll had to be scrapped and a new one drawn up, the proposed September date for the elections was postponed until further notice. It was strange, perhaps, that there had been a delay in scrapping the old electoral roll almost right up to the month when the elections were supposed to be held. Was this mere inefficiency in the town hall, an oversight, or was there a sudden change of policy eliminating the property and substituting the residence qualifications? If so, was the political motive to dispossess the Ganda of power in Kampala? Most Asians and Europeans were non-citizens and so were already disqualified, so removal of the property qualification was hardly likely to be aimed at them. In all likelihood there was no intention to unseat the Ganda, the move being an honest attempt to give control more to residents than property-owners. But Ganda interpreted the move as directed against them. With the dust still swirling after the July announcement the publicity secretary of KY stated in October that 5,000 Africans owning rateable property or paying rates for shops, offices and market stalls in the city would be disfranchised. Inadvertently drawing attention to the fact that they were mostly Ganda, he said that many KY supporters had complained to him that they were not allowed to register as voters for the elections, now scheduled for November. But the regulations stood and not surprisingly KY would not field candidates for the three city wards when the elections were finally held in February 1964. They left UPC and DP to compete alone.

This was a deepening of a rift which had started many months before between the KY and the UPC. There had been angry exchanges between the two not long after independence, chiefly over how much the UPC should be represented and allowed to have a distinct political identity in the Buganda kingdom. In February, 1963, the two parties did not form a coalition at the elections in nine Buganda constituencies for seats in the kingdom's Lukiko or parliament. In seven of the constituencies KY competed against DP only. In two of them KY actually stood against UPC as well as DP candidates. One of these three-cornered contests was in Naguru, adjacent to the estate of the same name but just outside the boundary of the Kampala city's east ward. Undoubtedly some Ganda who voted in this election had been among those represented in the previous September one as property-owners or users. With KY and UPC facing each other, DP emerged victorious by a small majority in this Buganda contest. The split between KY and UPC widened, and some of these same Ganda were to hear in a few months that they would not vote in the next elections in Kampala East. KY had ceased to be a political force in Kampala city. By April UPC had opened branches in two Ganda counties which, as rivals to KY, allegedly had to contend with opposition from local chiefs who supported KY and intimidated people who tried to join the new branches.[2]

The overall effect of disfranchisement in the city was inevitably to reduce the number of voters, but it is highly unlikely that anyone imagined how great this reduction would be. Whereas in 1962 8,129 mostly African votes were recorded in Kampala East for the municipal election, in that of 1964 only 1,947 were recorded. One of the reasons for delaying the election until February 1964 was to persuade more eligible voters to register. But lacking Kenyans, many Ganda, Asians and, surprisingly, Nubi, who could not prove that they belonged to Uganda rather than the Sudan, there were few people left with experience of political activity. There were certainly many more eligible voters than the meagre 3,000 who finally registered for the whole city, but interest and experience in politics is more important than numbers. Few Lugbara, Ankole or Kiga registered, nor many Acholi and Lango. DP, though its strength in the national parliament had waned, was able to capture the two council seats for Kampala East and did well in urban wards throughout the country. But the dismally small electorate gave the party's success a hollow ring. Defeated in Kampala East, one of the UPC candidates claimed that KY leaders, while not participating in the contest, had urged their previous supporters in the ward to vote for DP. This was later denied by KY but gives some indication of the ill-feeling which had grown between the two parties. Encouraged or not, the impression was that the few previous KY supporters resident there had indeed voted against UPC. A more decisive factor was that, with Kenyans disfranchised, the UPC lost the support of the biggest and most active tribe in the ward, Luo.

The very measures introduced at a national level by the UPC government to protect its citizens from domination in employment by foreigners and, by extension, from domination in urban politics by foreigners and non-resident property-owners had indirectly brought about their downfall in the important city ward of Kampala East. Admittedly the numbers were so small that the result was hardly representative of the residents. But it is important to see how a decision of national consequence can affect a single urban ward in this way. From being a key group in the estates and in the city labour force, the Kenyans suddenly found themselves unable to express themselves in Ugandan politics and apprehensive regarding their jobs.

I have outlined the developments in the period from September 1962, the first municipal council elections, to February 1964, the second (now city) council elections. Before this period a sense of community was being created in the estates. The estates were areas in which mostly migrants and relatively few Ganda lived. The sense of 'foreignness' was shared alike by Kenyans and Uganda tribes who did not come from the southern kingdoms. Very crudely this was a cultural division between Ganda and other kingdoms people, and the rest. But it was much more than this. In the context of Kampala as a whole it was expressed as being a division over declining employment opportunities. While the number of jobs in the Kampala African labour force declined from over 36,000 in 1957 to under 28,000 in 1961, the proportion of Kenyans in employment went up while that of Ganda went down. The number of Kenyans in the labour force increased from 10·0 per cent in 1956 to 17·9 per cent in 1961, accompanied by a fall of from 42·0 per cent to 31·5 per cent for Ganda. It is this 'invasion', as it is often called by Ganda, which probably gave support to the popular idea of rivalry between Ganda and Kenyans, especially Luo. Kenyans and non-Ganda, especially people not from the kingdoms, felt a certain affinity in a town, which, for all their numerical decline in the labour force, was still dominated by Ganda. It thus benefited Kenyans to direct their many leadership and organizational skills into trade unionism, with the result that, helped by international agencies, membership in newly created unions increased six-fold throughout Uganda from 1958 to 1961.[4] But, shortly after independence in 1962, the wheel came full circle and Kenyans were being attacked for their hold over jobs and trade unions, not just by Ganda, however, but by representatives of the national government.

This attack evoked protests but only minor ones. More than protests it eventually had something of the opposite effect. Various Kenyans, as individuals or through associations, went out of their way publicly to show that they acquiesced to the Uganda government's legislation and criticism. This consisted of either direct invitations to the government party for 'friendly' meetings or football matches, or an exaggerated direction of political interest to Kenya affairs, thus showing tacit acceptance of their expatriate status. This diversion of interests was, I believe, made much more peaceful than it might have been through the complicated chains of communication between Kenyan leaders in Kenya and Kampala. These chains had been kept alive and open through the existence of the extremely popular soccer league programmes among the Luo and Luhya, the two main Kenya peoples. It was really only interest in soccer which saved the Luo and Luhya tribal associations from being virtually defunct at one stage of their existence. The leaders in these associations were leaders in other spheres as well. Thus one of the Luo candidates at the municipal election of 1962 was also secretary of the Luo Union. Another Luo appointed councillor, not yet mentioned, was also prominent in the Union. These and other Luo operated through the Union and its affiliated associations to bring about the peaceful transformation I have referred to. The Luhya did similarly. A number of Luo leaders had minor business interests in Kampala and so had further reason to be in contact with members of their large ethnic clientele. I describe the process by which all this occurred in chapter seven.

This peaceful transformation of identities and interests enabled the housing estates to continue their important function of introducing people to the urban status system. In their development towards communities the estates are areas where tribe is not allowed to count for very much, if anything, in personal relations. It is to these aspects of life in Nakawa and Naguru to which I turn in the next chapter.

Communities grow from the interaction of the same people in neighbourhoods, friendships, gossip sets, and through marriage and business contacts. Their most important basis is that these people have common needs. Within the wider political framework which I have described, at least three factors emerged in the account of the first election which are of significance in understanding how a community works, and how an urban status system operates. One was the distinction between 'inside' and 'outside' candidates, which showed exactly how residents were represented to the local authorities. A second was what sociologists call the multiple performance of leadership roles, by which is implied the technique of acquiring a following, support or simply renown by spreading one's leadership in a number of different directions, both simultaneously and over time. Some candidates were leaders in tribal, tenants' and other associations at the same time. As applied to roles in general, and not just those of leadership, this is a standard technique in urban society for moving up in the social scale. A third factor, which is really part of the second, was the publicly recognized distinction between Naguru and Nakawa as high- and low-prestige-bearing estates. There are other areas in Kampala-Mengo which can be similarly ranked both in what people say and do, how they envy or even condemn those who move to a better area, yet move themselves given the chance. As house-hunters in Britain well know, area of residence is a definite attribute of status.

NOTES

[1] 'Asian' is the administrative and now local term referring to people originally from the Indian sub-continent.

[2] These were the two 'lost counties' of Buyaga and Bungangazzi which the neighbouring kingdom of Bunyoro claimed from Buganda. The Uganda Government favoured Bunyoro, whose people were a residential majority in the counties.

[3] I was myself checking agent for one of the candidates and was able to observe procedure at first hand.

[4] Cf. Roger Scott, 1966, p. 16, *The Development of Trade Unions in Uganda*, East African Publishing House for E.A.I.S.R., Nairobi.

CHAPTER III

NEIGHBOURHOOD, LOCALITY, AND
THE STATUS SYSTEM

Local Ties

'No one at Naguru would vote for a man living at Nakawa', said a party official after Otieno's failure at the elections. Another candidate, the Jonam, had previously lived at Nakawa but had moved to Naguru. Otieno followed suit some time later. Both did what many men regard as a logical move if they earn enough. Even within Nakawa there is the distinction between the cheaper 'Lower' area and the 'Upper' area. Many Nakawa and Naguru residents have moved from Kiswa, where there are also upper and lower areas. Otieno himself is an example of a man who moved from Kiswa to Lower Nakawa, Upper Nakawa and finally Naguru. And even further down the residential hierarchy many move to these estates in Kampala East from Mengo suburbs, such as Kibuli, where many Kenyans have stemmed from. Really top people may move from Naguru to the even more fashionable Ntinda, just outside Kampala East, or to the salubrious city centre.

Without going into details there is a hierarchy of some Kampala localities according to residential status. Strictly speaking there are two of them, one for Ganda and people who associate themselves with them, and another for non-Ganda migrants. The Ganda one is not well defined physically but operates outside the city for the most part. The non-Ganda is the one I refer to now, beginning in suburbs of the type mentioned and continuing within Kampala East.

A. L. Epstein applied the concept of locality to the Zambian town of Ndola, drawing a distinction between neighbourhood and locality while recognizing that the former is bound to shade into the latter.[1] As I shall try to show, the social units designated as neighbourhood and locality provide among the most effective contexts of change in urban relationships, especially when the physical establishment and administration of these units rests with external authorities, as with public housing estates.[2] Epstein shows how relationships of a mine compound differ from those of a municipal location. Residents in the former are employed by the same mining company. They thus interact both as residents and, potentially, as workmates. Residents in the municipal location are employed by diverse firms and do not, therefore, interact both as residents and workmates.[3] For similar reasons it may be that relationships in Nsambya, the Kampala railway workers' housing estate, differ significantly from those of the city council estates of Kampala East, whose residents are employed in a wide range of private and public enterprises.[4] Workplace conflicts and cleavages are perhaps carried into the neighbourhood and locality relationships of a single industry estate like Nsambya or a Zambian mine compound far more than they are into the relationships of an estate where there are no widespread common workplace conflicts and cleavages. Nakawa and Naguru fall into this category where there is generally little common observability of workplace and locality relationships.

For at least a year before the period of political changes described in the last chapter the residents on Nakawa and Naguru had become increasingly aware of their common interests on problems ranging from water and electricity supply, rent payments, house maintenance and decoration, recreational and social facilities for children and adults, protection against thieves, and the need for a regularized procedure for dispute settlement. Individually of course most people had been aware of such matters for years, but it took time for them to be dealt with collectively by the more public-spirited and prominent residents.

Records do not seem to reveal when tenants' associations or the like first appeared on the estates. The older residents, some of whom have lived there since the estates were built shortly after the Second World War, did not remember tenants' associations operating before the mid-fifties, while the present association officials, most of whom came during the mid- and late fifties, state that they were among the first to start them. This is too imprecise to be taken literally though it does suggest that, given the average length of residence on the estates as about seven years in 1962, community life either began or was revitalized by men who migrated or settled on the estates at that time.

The mid-fifties saw a rapid growth of African nationalism in

53

East Africa. The Kenya Emergency had been declared in 1952 and its effect quickly spread to Uganda and Tanganyika. Though in Kenya the colonial government only allowed political parties on a district basis to be formed in 1955 and not nationally until 1960, the nationalist slogan 'Uhuru', or Freedom, had become known and used throughout East Africa, certainly the urban centres, by 1958.[5] Residents who were on the estates then confirm this. They state also, as might be expected, that it was the Kenyans, especially Luo, who first advertised the slogan and 'spoke politics'. Uganda nationalism was, of course, already well-established, but the point of relevance for the estates is that nationalism throughout East Africa was seen as really one movement of all Africans against European dominance.

On the estates the tenants saw themselves as part of the same conflict. In their growing and increasingly effective demands for more facilities and improved conditions the tenants' associations had to make representation to the Uganda government African Housing Department, which was based in Entebbe, then the country's capital, but which had staff in each town. The senior staff in Kampala were nearly all Europeans, and it was inevitable that the problems of Nakawa and Naguru, unashamedly designated African Housing Estates, should be viewed in the light of the nationalist struggle. This lent an ideological framework to the relatively mundane demands of the associations, whose leaders developed as self-proclaimed mouthpieces of the tenants.

In tune with the ideology, the association officials condemned the evils of tribal prejudice and preached unity. In effect they were preaching what already existed among people obliged to live in tribally mixed neighbourhoods. As will be shown, tribal prejudices are soon eliminated in such neighbourhoods for most new tenants. At the personal level free and friendly association develops as the most practicable form of behaviour. At the wider level tenants are one under a remote and seemingly intransigent housing authority, and, for those most closely involved in urban life, a struggle for status may seem more important than tribal ties.

Status Divisions

While there is a progressive movement by status aspirants to more fashionable estates or part of an estate, where better and

54

more expensive houses are, there are many occasions when these same localities seem to compete with each other and to show a type of internal solidarity.

Early in 1962, Charles, a tenant of Upper Nakawa, received a suggestion from the Department of Social Development via the tenants' association that he and others start a debating society. The suggestion had already been made to Naguru and it was thought that competitions might be arranged between the two estates. Charles had some years previously been a chairman of Nakawa tenants' association, was known to be very proficient in English and seemed a suitable organizer.

About twenty fluent English speakers were contacted and the competitions started quickly and in earnest. Motions included [sic] 'Money is more useful than food', 'Educated ladies are better than illiterate ones', 'A teacher is better than a doctor', 'It is better to be in the town than in the village', 'Indians are more useful than Europeans', and others. While the proposers and seconders from each estate tended to be drawn from the same group of five or six men, the enthusiasm which English speakers showed for the debates exceeded all expectations, and membership numbers swelled. The debates were usually held at the Naguru community hall, since Nakawa had no building of sufficient size to accommodate the members.

Sometimes a group of forty supporters would march from Nakawa to Naguru as if the task ahead were a military operation, an analogy not without significance in view of such typical comments as, 'We are going to Naguru to do battle, and to show them that they are not superior to us'. The enthusiasm and societies lasted no more than a year. It was always Nakawa which threw out challenges to Naguru, as if to contest alleged superiority. Towards the end of the year a few principal speakers and supporters, including Charles, had themselves moved to Naguru and within another year over half the hard core of twenty or so members lived there.

During this period a YMCA branch was established at Nakawa, again including English speakers as its principal members. They were appealed to as 'big men' by the Ganda chairman, not himself from the estates, who said that they should take to heart the responsibility for the tenants' welfare. The first cyclostyled notice publicly inviting people to attend, also written by Charles, brought to their attention the 'shame' that Naguru already had a YMCA branch while Nakawa had none.

The sense of deprivation came out very clearly in a heated meeting between Nakawa tenants' association officials and the estate manager.

The meeting was arranged for a Friday evening in August 1962. The estate manager was to prepare the way for a later meeting with a European member of staff of the African Housing Department, which was to discuss the celebrations for Uganda Independence Day (October 9th). At this first meeting the estate manager wanted to know how many adults and children would be present so as to arrange for the delivery of free supplies of meat, beer and soda to tenants on the day. The tenants wanted scales and knives to be provided also so that the group leaders in the estate, elected annually with association officials, could distribute the food fairly. The manager had no authority to grant such requests and could only promise to make suggestions to the Department. To appease them he agreed to consider other matters not on the agenda.

At this concession the tone of the meeting became much more serious and demands were made for a primary school and social centre for the estate. The manager replied that these were unjustified since one school existed at Naguru and another at Kiswa, some classrooms of which were not full.

One of the more vociferous was Otieno, referred to in the last chapter, who declared, 'If children go to Naguru school they have to cross a main road. One child has already been killed. And to get to Kiswa you have to cross the railway line. Approaching trains never sound their whistles and this has also resulted in a death. This estate has enough children to fill our own school.'

The manager stayed his ground and the discussion moved on to the request for a social centre, or at least a larger one since there was already a very small building used for this purpose. The manager said, 'If you want to go to a dance, you can quite easily go to Naguru where they hold many dances.' Otieno: 'Most of the tenants here must go by foot to Naguru. When they return home late at night they are open to attack by thieves. Also we need a larger centre with separate rooms for our many thriving activities. Here we sometimes have to sit under a mango tree for our tenants' association meetings, so that, if it rains, the meeting has to be disbanded before we have finished our business.'

At about this point a boy with a number of others following behind came into the room with a book in his hand. He had come to a reading class, but on realizing the likely long duration of the meeting, went out again. Otieno pointed to this and became more excited. 'There, you see, they have come to a reading class, but because of us will have to leave it. It is the same with all our society and club meetings. You speak of us going to Naguru. We shouldn't have to do this. This is Nakawa.'

As Otieno's oratory rose the meeting was inundated with exclamations of agreement and approval. It was clear that they regarded Nakawa as a community entitled to its own amenities. Later, after expressing his sympathy and in a calmer atmosphere, the manager appealed to the twelve present, mostly committee members and a few group leaders, as the 'educated class', . . . 'to show our friends on the estate the advantages of cleanliness in the area and to prevent their children dirtying and writing on the latrine walls'. Here he was interrupted by Otieno, who saw it as further proof of a need for a school.

While the association leaders realized fully that the estate manager had no more than the unenviable task of trying to reconcile their and his superiors' expectations, they always considered it worthwhile expressing their grievances in this way. At the later meeting with the European, always a much less frequent affair, there was a marked emphasis on formality, almost courtesy, and grievances were aired much less effectively.

At a much later, quite unrelated general meeting of the tenants' association at Naguru, an angry outburst which received loud support was, 'Those people from Nakawa and Kiswa come to our dances and our beer-bar and cause much trouble. They get drunk more than our people and, because this is not their place, they damage the community hall, and are only after prostitutes. It is they who keep these prostitutes hanging round the beer-bar. Why don't you [to the housing representative] make them stay at Nakawa?' There was no truth in this claim which, like others of its sort, is an expression of a desire not to suffer a lowering of standards and loss of privileges at Naguru, while at Nakawa similar prejudiced statements are more usually expressions of the physical and social line of deprivation and of attempts to remedy it by claiming equal rights and prestige in residence on this estate.

Mock hostility may be directed at a person, as when one of the better speakers in the Nakawa debating society moved to Naguru half-way through the year and in no time at all was in the Naguru team. Some of the inevitable banter included accusations against him by Nakawa supporters of 'pride' and 'treachery'. And if these sentiments seem strongly expressed, consider this extract from a circular distributed by the chairman of the tenants' association to all Nakawa tenants for a general meeting in November 1962: '. . . All tenants are therefore requested to attend this Special MEETING [*sic*] without fail. Should you do so [i.e. fail to turn up] we shall call you a *traitor* to the Association and will keep your name in the Association's Record Book for future reference.' Admittedly few people are intimidated by what are in fact empty and almost jocular threats, but the technique brings personality and emotion into what could otherwise become a boring activity. Notices, like general meetings, are in Swahili as well as English, so that an attempt is made to attract all tenants.

Attendance at tenants' association meetings is not always a good index of public interest in an issue. In Lower Nakawa especially, there was a remarkedly widespread sense of inferiority. People there were as much concerned as others at the congestion in the houses and their bad condition at the time, but delegated the responsibility for transmitting their complaints to their group leaders, of whom there were about ten for about 600 households in Lower Nakawa.

People in Upper Nakawa, though a minority in the estate, were much more in evidence at association general meetings, rarely delegating responsibility to group leaders but preferring to speak for themselves. To some extent this can be explained by their generally higher status. They included the clerks and other white-collar workers and the more experienced and well-paid artisans. For some of them participation in the meetings led to membership of the committee, which could lead to higher positions in a number of associations. Most of the candidates in the municipal council elections of 1962 had started in this way, often complementing positions of importance in tribal associations with apparent leadership of an estate.

This voluntary exclusion of Lower Nakawa residents from their association's meetings is an expression of yet another line of deprivation, in many ways almost as great as that between Nakawa and Naguru. The deprivation is social but Upper Nakawa does stand on higher ground than Lower Nakawa. When there is heavy rain, it runs down from the Shs. 23/– houses to those below, leaving the latter often extremely muddy and the former able to dry very quickly in the sun. With rainfall all the year round in Kampala, Lower Nakawa residents complain about the mud, and even have to cope with the occasional snake brought along by the water, let alone having to tolerate the innumerable frogs which have made their homes in ruts and hollows created by the rains.

As explained, the cheaper houses and poorer workers are in Lower Nakawa. On Nakawa as a whole, 227 household heads earn no more than Shs. 125/– per month (as at October 1962) and may be classified as unskilled, including labourers, office messengers, sweepers and market stall assistants. They are 27·6 per cent of the 823 household heads at Nakawa, 212 living in Lower Nakawa and 15 only in Upper Nakawa. In addition to the very poor tenants in Lower Nakawa there are some 350 who fall into a spread of occupational categories from unskilled to clerical and skilled. It is from among the higher status of these that a steady movement to Upper Nakawa can be seen. Some go straight to Naguru if they can. Renting a better, Shs. 23/–, house in Upper Nakawa is prestigeful since it indicates occupational security and/or educational prowess. In addition to those who have come from Lower Nakawa, many of the 223 household heads in Upper Nakawa have moved there directly from Kiswa or a Kampala suburb.

The occupational breakdown of sixty-one who made the internal estate movement, from Lower to Upper Nakawa, is as follows:

(1) *Skilled or semi-skilled jobs requiring the use of English*

Clerk	12	Storekeeper	3	
Salesman	2	Telephone operator	2	
Assistant to draughtsman	3	Others	4	*Total 26*

(2) *Skilled or semi-skilled jobs not requiring the use of English*

Carpenter	3	Electrician	2	
Mechanic	9	Plumber	2	
Tailor	3	Bricklayer	2	
Driver	4	Others	6	
Headman (of labour gang)	2			*Total 33*

(3) *Unskilled jobs where no English is required*

Office messenger	2		*Total 2*

Two office messengers were the only unskilled to move, and even they claimed that, as they were English speakers, they expected to be taken on as junior clerks when an opportunity arose, which did transpire in the case of one of them. One reason why unskilled workers do not make this movement is the allocation of houses by the estate manager according to an applicant's economic status. But some, like the two office messengers, persuade the manager that a better house is within their means and that they are due for promotion, anyway, and so get over this regulation. Another reason, which tenants themselves often give, is a social deterrent. It is often observed that a poor unskilled worker living in an area like Upper Nakawa, where most of his neighbours earn more, are more educated, and have better jobs, tends to resent being an unprivileged minority and may be snubbed by his 'superiors' if he shows resentment or attempts to equate himself with them. This comes out more clearly in my description of neighbourhood.

Locality thus has much to do with status, or more specifically with enabling people to see where they stand, or should stand, on the social ladder. In general this is not different from most European urban societies, though the ethnic mixtures and retention of rural ties by migrants are greater in African towns, and it is this crucial difference at a time of rapid social change which makes localities and neighbourhoods so important in urban adaptation.

Relationships of locality can be distinguished from those of neighbourhood in so far as there is a difference of scale. Locality relationships are the domain of men. It is men who join associations, become leaders, send deputations to make claims to the housing authorities and take decisions about moving to another house or neighbourhood. It is they who are much more mobile physically in the town. They work in the city, travelling there on buses if they can afford it, going with friends to night clubs or the cinema in the evening after work, and, with exceptions, leading a social life segregated from that of their wives.

Women tend to be much more restricted physically. Many of them spend on average only half of the year in town, returning home twice a year for periods of three months for digging and planting, and for harvesting. Only wives of the very high status have jobs, while most women have domestic and child-rearing chores around the house and so are limited physically to the immediate neighbourhood except for trips to the nearest small market or shop for food.

Neighbourhood can be said to be much more significant for women than men, the latter's relationships being more widely dispersed through activities outside the immediate neighbourhood of their houses. This is not to say that neighbourhood is insignificant for men. Indeed, the converse is true, while the difference in importance to men and women remains marked. Both men and women are concerned about prestige and status and it is this mutual concern, differently expressed usually, which links the relationships a man and wife have with their respective associates. It is these considerations of prestige and status which are part of the social shading of neighbourhood into locality.

Non-tribal Norms

Localities may be distinguished not only physically and through the use of names, but also socio-economically, sometimes through an association and always in the way people evaluate the area. Neighbourhoods are less easy to define but to some extent are determined by the arrangement of houses. On Nakawa and most of Naguru, houses are juxtaposed and on-facing, either in squares or lines. In some parts of Naguru, juxtaposed but detached houses, with private gardens and hedges between them, make it less easy for neighbours to know each other, whereas at Nakawa and other parts of Naguru smaller houses grouped much more closely together not only facilitate but virtually enforce regular interaction between neighbours.

The difference is one of degree and there are common elements. The water tap is certainly a focus for neighbourhood gossip and activity, serving from ten to twenty houses and something of a 'neutral' area.[6] A mango or banana tree between two groups of houses may not seriously restrict the passage from one to the other, yet may be taken as a delimiter of frequent rather than occasional interaction. Obviously, though, neighbourhoods merge and overlap and, if they can be defined at all, revolve around a hard core of fairly frequently interacting tenants, male or female, though especially the latter.

The two most obvious features of this small neighbourhood are multi-tribal residence and status differentiation. Houses are given according to a waiting list as they become vacant and no one may choose his neighbours, who are from a variety of tribes. There are different grades of housing, each of which is rented accordingly and is territorially separate from any other. The policy of allocating houses according to economic status has the result that in any one neighbourhood of from ten to twenty houses, there will be a general parity of economic status among householders. This parity is never entire and there are usually a very small number of tenants who are below or above the average in income, education or skills, none of which are necessarily coincident. These status differences may be cross-cutting and, as an example, contrast a little-educated driver with an educated clerk, though both have similar incomes. They may be coincidental and sharply divide better-off, educated men with prestigeful occupations from poor, uneducated men with menial jobs. In either case, because of the otherwise parity of status such differences may be brought up in disputes or in gossip and mark off one or a few neighbours from the rest.

As I have already said, the neighbourhood unit is more significant as a field of interaction for women than for men. Women in the town often admit to long leisure hours during the day and may gather at a water tap or in front of a neighbour's house and gossip from early in the morning until shortly before the younger children come home from morning school. Much of the preparation for meals, the peeling of vegetables or plantain, or the brewing of tea, is done out of doors and provides additional contexts for the exchange of gossip.

Because of the very real threat of thieves, even during the daytime, women are wary of being out of sight of their houses, so that the tribal composition of a women's gossip set is definitely determined by the tribal composition of the neighbourhood unit. The tribal composition of the set, in turn, determines the language of conversation which may be Swahili, Luganda, or in the case of Nilotes, their respective dialects. Large numbers of wives and children, it may be noted here, speak fluent Swahili and Luganda in addition to their indigenous tongues. Few women speak English.

The following are paraphrases of some of these conversations heard by myself and a male informant from inside a nearby house.

1. A wife asked if any of the women could recommend a good African medicine to treat children's sicknesses. She said that most of the European medicines were far too expensive and, except for some fevers, did not seem effective. Another woman added that Nakawa was too wet and muddy so that there were many mosquitoes and that was why the children suffered.

2. A suggestion was made that one way of stretching one's husband's income was to buy only cheap food and to plant sweet potatoes and other vegetables in the garden for one's own use. Another woman suggested that if they stopped buying expensive items such as tea, or at least stopped having it daily, this would decrease expenditure. Yet another claimed that it was difficult not to use so much tea when one was continually having visitors.

The theme of expenditure on visitors cropped up elsewhere:

3. An 'experienced' woman (i.e. one of some urban seniority) stated that when you have lived long enough in the town you begin to select those visitors who are special enough to deserve the provision of tea and food. Another agreed and pointed to those 'foolish young wives' who treat all and sundry as special guests and never allow them to leave the house without having had tea or coffee. Others also wondered at the uneconomic behaviour of wives new to the town; at the way they were always off to the market. They pitied the husbands' wasted money, but said that such men are reluctant to scold their new wives.

4. There was enthusiastic agreement as to the virtues of wives trading, i.e. selling at vegetable and other stalls, and so supplementing their husbands' incomes. Some Acholi, Rwanda and Luhya observed that many Luo and some Luhya women do this sort of work and thought it was very good. Even the wives of some 'big men' worked in offices in town or as teachers, someone said.

5. A Lango 'temporary' wife (a very rare phenomenon) complained to the other women that she suspected that her Lango husband no longer had any intentions of making her his 'permanent' wife. She was therefore worried as to what would happen to her as she had been with him for two years and was not getting any younger. Most agreed that the man was acting wrongly, especially as they were of the same tribe, but one quietly remarked that she had not yet borne him any children and that he had to look after his own interests in this respect.

The theme of high urban expenditure is, of course, paramount in these conversations. Advice about how to budget or supplement one's husband's income stems from the set. Child-rearing occasionally presents problems which may be discussed by the women. The behaviour of husbands to their wives is open to criticism, but wives are not allowed to forget their own marital obligations. A distinction between 'experienced' and 'young' wives is held by the women and establishes a rough system of rights of arbitration according to urban seniority. In these senses a gossip set may be said to ascribe statuses and the appropriate norms of behaviour to its members.

In some neighbourhood units, however, these gossip sets harden into cliques with consequent policies of exclusion.

A certain set consisted of three Luo, two Lango, a Jonam and a Rwanda. The language used in conversation was Swahili. The occupations of the husbands of all the women of the group except one Luo were clerk, salesman, carpenter, storekeeper and qualified mechanic. The remaining Luo's husband was a houseboy/cook. The latter, though his job was far less prestigeful than those of his neighbours, had free food and some clothing as perquisites. With the money thus saved he was able to buy comfortable furniture and a transistor radio. His wife, in an attempt to overcome her husband's lowly occupational status, tended to brag about their material possessions and about her husband's 'wealth'. This evaluation of herself and her husband's social position was not accepted by the other members of the set, who pointed out that her husband was still only a houseboy/cook and uneducated, and that their own husbands had relatively skilled jobs, some of them requiring the use of English. The woman was gradually excluded from the gossip set. Following on her exclusion, attention was drawn by two other Luo women to the fact that she had ceased bearing at what seemed an early age. Referring to the connection between promiscuity, including adultery, and infertility, they said she must have been unfaithful to her husband. After a series of disputes into which even the woman's husband was dragged, she and the husband deemed it better to move to another neighbourhood, after explaining their position to the estate manager and being awarded a transfer.

What is particularly noticeable about this case is the fact that the woman who was excluded from the gossip set was a Luo, and that, though two other women in the set were also Luo, she received no help or defence from them whatsoever. Indeed, it was the two Luo women who intensified the friction by suggesting that the woman's early cessation of child-bearing was due to her marital infidelity and used this fact to eject her. This illustrates that what tribal solidarity between these women exists may diminish when the issue revolves around entry into an exclusive neighbourhood gossip set.

It may be noticed, too, that even when the women of the gossip set interact harmoniously by offering and receiving advice and by setting norms of behaviour, tribalism is not significant. Nor could multi-tribal residence be said to be responsible for conflict. In the case just described it was, again, status differentiation or at least open expression of it, which brought about the conflicting evaluations precipitating the ejection of the wife and husband from the neighbourhood unit. Another way of saying this is that in the intimate face-to-face relationships of a small group, ethnic heterogeneity *per se* is less likely to be the primary cause of conflicts within the group than the heterogeneity among its members of rights and privileges. This is especially the case in towns where such rights and privileges are far more open to achievement than in some rural tribal districts, and where individual competition is therefore more intense. The same applies to dyadic relationships of friendship and enmity.

Women usually have a larger number of close friends in the neighbourhood unit than men. Their friendships tend to be hedged by the jealousies typical of any small frequently interacting group, so that the friendships themselves may be broken and reconciled fairly often, and so may oscillate between different pairs of partners. Men, on the other hand, do not always interact as frequently with their neighbours, nor are they necessarily likely to have more than a few close friends in the unit. Their friends are as likely to be located outside the neighbourhood and may not know or come into contact with each other, so that jealousies between a man and his friends over their respective friendships are less obvious and less likely to cause friction.

A woman's neighbourhood friend is any person from whom she may borrow cooking utensils or crockery when she is entertaining visitors, or food if she has run short. Membership of the gossip set does not indicate mutual friendship in this sense, since a woman does not indiscriminately ask any member for a loan of this kind but rather refers to a particular member of the set with whom she is in an already established relationship of reciprocity. In one case this reciprocity consisted of a Kiga wife being taught how to make mats in a local style by her Ganda neighbour in exchange for the borrowing of cooking utensils. When the Kiga had become proficient in mat-making, her friendship with the Ganda wife continued and the reciprocity took other forms. In some cases friendships are established by neighbours for specific ends. In one case, a young Luo who was pregnant did not relish the idea of yet another child and asked her Luo neighbours the details of a traditional technique for procuring an abortion. Her Luo neighbours thought this 'immoral' and would not tell her. The woman therefore struck up a friendship with two Ganda women noted for their prowess in such matters, and, with their advice, successfully performed an abortion. In another instance, an Alur of Nakawa took a temporary wife and therefore felt obliged to find alternative accommodation for his younger brother who was lodging with him. He established a firm friendship with his next-door neighbour, a Luhya bachelor, and after some time, asked him to allow his brother to sleep at his house. When, some months later, he moved to Naguru, he invited his new neighbour, a Lugbara bachelor, round to his house for drinks. Again, after some time, he asked if his brother might sleep at the man's house. In both cases, of course, the friendships were based on reciprocity and could only be maintained as such.

If two male neighbours are employed by the same company or government department and leave work at about the same time each morning, they are more or less forced into a friendship with each other. There are also converse instances of friends at work becoming neighbours by one of them persuading a neighbour, sometimes with a gift, to exchange houses with his friend who may be living in another estate or a different part of the town. Clearly, the friendships in such instances have to be long-standing and in fact typify the friendships between fellow-tribesmen from common home-areas who may have been to school together.

A breach of the reciprocity in any relationship of friendship may convert it to one of enmity and, indeed, many outstanding enmities between neighbours, both men and women, were once friendships. Since most women's friendships are likely to be confined to the neighbourhood unit, it is they who tend to figure in most neighbourhood enmities and disputes.

1.   Two Luo neighbours had been friends for years. They came from the same home subtribe and had been to school together. The one had advised the other to come to Kampala and had helped him find a job in the same company in which he himself was employed. They were both semi-skilled workers and earned the same money. As unmarried men, they remained friends for years in town. Even when one of them married and succeeded in hiring a house at Nakawa, the other eventually managed to move almost next door

and also married. The former, however, was attempting to elevate his standard of living and had started saving in earnest, very much prompted, it seems, by his wife. The other man was less inclined to save, so that after some time there appeared a superficial but, to them, noticeable discrepancy in their standards of living and attainments. The more successful of the two friends suddenly became redundant in his work. Though of the same firm, his friend did not lose his job. The redundant man's wife accused the other couple of being jealous of their furniture, clothes and social aspirations, and of bringing about the husband's unemployment through sorcery. After redoubled accusations and counter-accusations and some fighting, one couple moved from the neighbourhood.

2. A group leader at Nakawa reported a series of disputes between a Rwanda and a Ganda woman. The Ganda woman had persisted in teasing her Rwanda friend about her husband's menial job and wage, though, in fact, her own husband only earned Shs. 50/- a month more. The Ganda wife boasted about her clothes and furniture. The Rwanda wife interpreted the persistent teasing as uncalled-for mockery and bitterly resented it. There followed a series of fights between them so that the estate manager, on the advice of the tenants' association, moved one wife and her husband to another group on the estate.

3. The wife of Jerenge, a semi-skilled Luo of Upper Nakawa, was extremely jealous of the furniture and household equipment of her next-door neighbours. She involved her husband in an argument with a man next door by accusing the latter of abusing her. During the arguments, the other neighbours supported the man who had been accused. Jerenge claimed that they were supporting him simply because they and the man were educated, while he himself was not. He pointed out that he had as much money as any of them, though in fact he had not. Eventually he and his wife moved to a less expensive house in Lower Nakawa where poorer and generally less educated people live.

These enmities were indirectly a result of the differences in material standards and aspirations between the disputing neighbours. More directly, they were brought about by one of the two parties feeling deprived in relation to the other, and to neighbours generally. Women were the first to feel this relative deprivation, but on the instigation of their wives, men, too, resented being a poor or uneducated minority and acted hostilely, sometimes breaking a former friendship. In every case, the disputes were ended not by reconciliation but by one of the couples moving from the neighbourhood. The movement, which is the breaking-point in the relationship, may be said to bring about a restoration of neighbourhood harmony, since, though this is not stated in the cases, neighbours would tend to cast the blame for the disturbances on the couple who had left the neighbourhood and would sympathize with the couple who had remained.

It is noteworthy that in the second case there was never any suggestion that the different tribal origins of the two women may have been responsible in some way for their conflict. It was generally recognized by neighbours and the tenants' association that the dispute was caused by open expression of prestige and status differences. This case is typical of most enmities between neighbours of different tribes in that the tribal membership of each disputant is regarded as either irrelevant or secondary as a cause of disputes to the expression of differing prestige awards. Sometimes, of course, a person may displace the cause of his hostility towards a neighbour by blaming the latter's different tribal origins. But this displacement is common only after a dispute is under way and, moreover, becomes inexpedient if voiced or proclaimed in a multi-tribal neighbourhood.

The only exceptions to this are some disputes, again dealt with through the Nakawa tenants' association, in which women from Nilotic tribes have accused unmarried women neighbours from the Bantu kingdoms of trying to seduce their husbands. Women from the kingdoms have a reputation among Nilotes for promiscuity and it is this which is often rationalized by Nilotic wives as a reason for husbands' neglect. The disputes relate to the varying marriage patterns among tribes, which are dealt with in chapter five. They are much less frequent than the disputes described above, and while being products of the neighbourhood, fall into a distinct category, though even these might be regarded as due to feelings of deprivation by the wives.

Children play or fight with other neighbours' children and inevitably draw their mothers and sometimes also their fathers into relationships with each other. Through their children new neighbours may become known and accepted. But neighbours of longer standing bearing mutual grudges may turn an otherwise trivial dispute between their children into an opportunity for airing their grievances. Prolific women may be the envy of those who are less productive. Envy and deprivation of this kind as well as that deriving from discrepancies in material possessions, occupation and education, are commonly behind expressions of hostility, whether through witchcraft or sorcery or through other means. Like friendships, neighbourhood enmities may also be purposive. One Lango confided that he had deliberately caused the eviction of his former neighbour because he wanted a fellow-tribesman who was already high on the housing waiting list to live next door to him. The bringing about of a neighbour's eviction, however, is more often a means of expressing hostility. It is easily practicable against a neighbour who is a so-called illegal tenant. An illegal tenant is one who rents a house which is in the name of someone else, perhaps a relative or friend, who has since left. An enemy who brings about eviction remains anonymous since all he has to do is inform the estate manager of the man's illegal tenancy, and the estate manager himself sends the notice of eviction. I have recorded fewer instances of sorcery and witchcraft between neighbours than this form of eviction by anonymous neighbour-hood enemies, which may therefore be a more common means of expressing intense hostility. It is probably more common than that of violence, which, by disclosing the identity of the enemy as well as the attacked, leaves the former open to retaliation by other members of the neighbourhood and by the attacked himself.

What these cases suggest is that not only is there the development of what we can call non-tribal norms based on socio-economic criteria, there is also the development of some consensus of them. This is not to suggest that people always agree. Indeed, as shown, they frequently do not. But the issues over which the disputes arose were not questioned, since they concerned a general struggle for status which affects most people on the estates to some extent. Moreover they evoked some sort of united reaction from a majority of neighbours, either of condemnation or appeasement. The minority's view was sacrificed for the harmony of the rest. This is an elaboration of the familiar scapegoat theme, whose importance in this context is in refuting overdone ideas of anomie or confusion over norms in urban migrant communities.

Four points emerge from this description of neighbourhood relationships. These are the statement of neighbourhood norms, the common causes of disputes, the place of the neighbourhood in urban status systems, and the part played by wives in helping define all these factors and in redefining their own relationships with their husbands. Both locality and neighbourhood are seen in the context of an urban status system, in which tribal criteria of behaviour are generally subordinate to socio-economic, a term which may be taken to refer to apparent or real differences of occupational, economic, educational and residential standing.

Neighbourhood, especially in a public housing estate of this type, is an arena of socialization, particularly but not exclusively for women. It introduces people to a new way of life based on behaviour and expectations which are normally different from those in their rural home area. Men are socialized much more at workplace, and through recreational activities and associations, the latter being identified very often with localities. To some extent a locality is a secondary group while a neighbourhood is a primary one. Since the latter are bound to overlap and are really the bricks of any locality, it makes sense to talk of the neighbourhood 'feeding' norms into the locality.

When men of the tenants' association are regularly brought in to arbitrate in disputes between neighbours of the kind described, and when they themselves may be personally involved in similar occurrences, they inevitably form what is a collective, general and consistant view of life in their part of the town. Other men get the same picture through their own, more widely dispersed gossip sets. Even if it is men who make the formal decision about where to live, it is their wives, and in some cases their sisters and daughters, who are largely responsible for the development of immediate neighbourhood relations.

Preserving this image, it is possible to talk of a single social dimension extending from the neighbourhood, a primary group, to the locality, a secondary group, to a collection of ranked localitites making up, say, Kampala East. With the neighbourhood emphasis on status and prestige, and with localities demarcating status groups, the whole dimension can be regarded as familiarizing the individual with the urban status system.

The competition for prestige among women implicates married men in a way that does not affect bachelors. In spite of a frequent reluctance to enter into wives' disputes, few husbands successfully ignore involvement, as was clear from the cases. Indeed, non-involvement will be regarded as indicating that 'the other neighbours' are correct in estimating his status lowly. He may become party to his wife's dispute merely in order to save face by refuting the charges made against him, through his wife, by other women. In this desire not to lose face the husband is very much dependent on the position occupied by his wife in the gossip set and in other relationships. In this limited sense a wife's behaviour has implications for her husband's status and gives her a modicum of extra influence in their relationship.

Locality, much more a social field for men, is where true political relations begin. Here the sensitivities of tribal and national membership are exposed. On the one hand there is the familiar struggle for power or influence among rival leaders, especially in the tenants' associations. On the other, all are concerned that this should not be expressed as tribal conflict or 'tribalism'. Cross-cutting the ideological concern with tribe is the very real division between Kenyans and Ugandans.

NOTES

[1] A. L. Epstein, 1961, 'The Network and Urban Social Organization, *The Rhodes-Livingstone Journal*, No. 29, M.U.P.

[2] Cf. P. Marris, 1961, *Family and Social Change in an African City*, Routledge, London.

[3] A. L. Epstein, 1964, op. cit.

[4] R. D. Grillo has undertaken research in this area during 1964 and 1965 as part of a study of East African railway workers.

[5] T. Mboya, 1963, p. 66, *Freedom and After*, Andre Deutsch, London.

[6] E. Mphahlele, 1962, *Down Second Avenue*, Seven Seas, Berlin, and A. L. Epstein, 1961, op. cit., in which we should note the universality of water taps as foci of social importance in many African towns.

CHAPTER IV

COMMUNAL UNITY AND POLITICS

Local Élites

I define as local élites those people at Nakawa and Naguru who monopolize positions in various associations established on and for each estate. These associations are distinct from those of individual tribes, which, going under the name of, for example, the Luo Union or Luhya Association, cater for the interests of a specific tribe or ethnic group. The estate or locality associations are open to all residents regardless of tribe, a claim which is not merely nominal but is of central concern to their organization.

Like the neighbourhoods and localities in which they operate, they are non-tribal, or at least expected to conduct their business on grounds other than tribal. If a tribal clique appears to be emerging, the norms of this ideology are invoked, a dispute occurs, the matter is thrown open to the public, even if only a few are represented, and the association is either disbanded or there is an appropriate re-shuffling of officers. This is what I was told had happened in a couple of cases, though detailed information was unavailable. From observation it remains very true, however, that people are very sensitive if tribal prejudice or divisions along tribal lines appear. I shall illustrate this below in the one clear instance in which there was an obvious restatement of non-tribal harmony following a previous 'tribal' dispute in the tenants' association.

The monopoly of leadership positions operates in four associations on each estate. They are the tenants' association, the debating society, the YMCA, and a political party sub-branch, which for both estates is that of the ruling party, the Uganda Peoples Congress (UPC). Attempts to form sub-branches of the opposition Democratic Party failed. With the exception of the tenants' associations whose origins are unclear, these were established either a little before or after independence, and were undoubtedly helped along by the spur of nationalism which made people much more aware of the value of leadership at the immediate local as well as national level.

From the authorities' point of view, the usual and acceptable chain of communication for residents' grievances is from individual tenants to tenants' association, from the association's executive committee to the estate manager, and from him to the city council housing committee, though the association at Naguru did once attempt to establish a more direct link with the city council. The intermediary but vulnerable position of the estate manager has already been touched on. In the higher-status estate of Naguru, and the nearby one of Ntinda, just outside the city but within its planning area, many men have better jobs and more education than the manager, a fact which can detract from the respect given him.

Offices in the tenants' association are unpaid, though involve considerable time for the more devoted in preparing circulars announcing meetings, the meetings themselves, and in drawing up agenda and recording recommendations. Committee members are given scope to display their powers of oratory and even to exercise a little authority and influence, as well as receiving prestige from their positions. They are 'big men' in the estates, not only because they are regarded as leaders, but also because they are likely to have been above the socio-economic average of the estate to have been elected in the first place. Prestige begets prestige. In what is essentially a 'modern' field of activity the tenants' association, with its written constitution, official communication with the city council housing committee, and quasi-bureaucratic administration, encourages people to think of leadership in it as the prerogative of the most educated tenants. Education, a superior occupation, and sartorial elegance are seen as going together and are associated with these 'big men'.

All the six officers of the Nakawa tenants' association's executive committee have seven or eight years of education. All but one are clerks and require the use of English in their jobs. Their respective monthly wages are approximately Shs. 750/-, 600/-, 500/-, 450/- and 200/-. Three of the six officers of the Naguru tenants' association have senior secondary or technical education, that is, over eight years, two have eight years, and one has six years, but has taught himself well beyond this standard. Four of the six are high-grade clerks, one is a full-time trade union official, and one a trained technician. Their monthly wages are Shs. 850/-, 800/-, 650/-, 610/-, 450/- and 350/-. The wages of officers in both associations are, with only one exception, above the median monthly income of Shs. 243–50/– for both estates. Even the one exception's wage is above that of the average of his lower status estate, Nakawa. For their respective estates, nearly all officers have above-average education and occupations which are highly prestige-ranked. Many are leaders in other associations, both tribal and non-tribal (see Table V).

It is significant that five of the six main officers in the Nakawa tenants' association figure among the twelve clerks, listed on page 59, who have moved from Lower to Upper Nakawa. These and other local association leaders also living in Upper Nakawa form the local élite and tend to regard only those resident in their part of the estate as eligible to enter their select circle. After meetings they may go their way together across from the community centre or mango tree to their houses. There they may continue their conversations, perhaps moving on to a beer-bar and splitting a bottle or two with a friend. A couple of active non-committee members who have not yet been awarded an official title walk in a different direction, literally down the slope, to their houses in Lower Nakawa. The physical seems to complement the social and they are really peripheral to the élite.

The debating society of each estate includes most of the same people, and committees of the less socially important YMCA and UPC sub-branches comprise at least some. The YMCA is not in fact exclusively male, Christian, or patronized by 'young' persons, but attracts people who feel they can help in the welfare of the community through discussion or organizing dances. Nevertheless, it is the tenants' association which is regarded as belonging much more to the non-speaker of English than the debating society or YMCA. The UPC sub-branches are mentioned since, again, it is the same people who run them, though neither is viable, being superseded in importance by wider scale organizations in the city centre.

Membership numbers are difficult to assess. Tenants' association general meetings are usually attended by between one and two hundred residents, nearly all male, though one at Nakawa is said to have drawn four hundred. The debating societies attract between forty and sixty if the motion is well publicized and the YMCA branches up to thirty at a discussion group, though as many as two hundred people, including women and children, to

TABLE V. (a) STATUS ATTRIBUTES OF MEMBERS OF THE NAGURU LOCAL ELITE

Association and Offices	Tribe	Income	Occupation	Years of Education	Years' Residence in Kampala	Age	Whether also leader in Full Tribal (F), Sub-tribe (S), or Clan (C) Associations
TENANTS' ASSOCIATION							
1 Chairman	Alur	850/-	Clerk	6	10	37	F
2 Vice-Chairman	Luhya	800/-	Trade Union Secretary	10	9	32	
3 Secretary	Acholi	650/-	Technician	12	6	31	
4 Assistant Secretary	Samia	450/-	Clerk	9	7	26	
5 Treasurer	Padhola	350/-	Clerk	8	10	35	F
6 Assistant Treasurer	Alur	610/-	Clerk	8	8	29	
DEBATING SOCIETY							
7 Chairman	see 1						
8 Vice-Chairman	see 3						
9 Secretary	Nyoro	480/-	Clerk	10	6	31	F
10 Assistant Secretary	Janam	780/-	Clerk	8	8	29	
11 Treasurer	Luo	470/-	Clerk	8	9	28	
12 Assistant Treasurer	Ganda	460/-	Clerk	8	9	32	
YMCA BRANCH							
13 Chairman	Toro	710/-	Office Superintendent	10	5	25	
14 Vice-Chairman	see 12						
15 Secretary	see 9						
16 Assistant Secretary	see 5						
17 Treasurer	see 12						
18 Assistant Treasurer	see 4						
UPC SUB-BRANCH							
19 Chairman	Soga	600/-	Clerk	9	6	25	
20 Vice-Chairman	Ganda	440/-	Copy-typist	8	7	29	
21 Secretary	see 2						
22 Treasurer	see 6						

75

TABLE V. (b) STATUS ATTRIBUTES OF MEMBERS OF THE NAKAWA LOCAL ÉLITE

Association and Offices	Tribe	Income	Occupation	Years of Education	Years' Residence in Kampala	Age	Whether also leader in Full Tribal (F), Sub-tribe (S), or Clan (C) Associations
TENANTS' ASSOCIATION							
1 Chairman	Janam	600/-	Clerk	7	9	31	F
2 Vice-Chairman	Luo	450/-	Clerk	7	7	27	F
3 Secretary	Samia	300/-	Clerk	8	8	30	
4 Assistant Secretary	Lugbara	500/-	Clerk	8	6	26	
5 Treasurer	Luo	750/-	Clerk	7	8	31	S
6 Assistant Treasurer	Luo	200/-	Storekeeper	7	10	28	S and C
7 Active non-com- }	Luhya	150/-	Painter	6	8	26	S and C
8 mittee members	Acholi	230/-	Clerk	7	11	36	F
DEBATING SOCIETY							
9 Chairman	see 5						
10 Vice-Chairman	Kiga	375/-	Clerk	8	8	31	F
11 Secretary	see 3						
12 Assistant Secretary	see 4						
13 Treasurer	Ganda	520/-	Salesman	10	11	34	
YMCA BRANCH							
14 Chairman	see 4						
15 Secretary	Alur	410/-	Clerk	9	6	27	
16 Assistant Secretary	see 3						
17 Treasurer	see 5						
18 Active non-com-	Lugbara	350/-	Telephone Operator	7	6	33	F (branch)
19 mittee members	Janam	290/-	Carpenter	9	7	27	F
UPC SUB-BRANCH							
20 Chairman	see 2						
21 Secretary	see 10						
22 Treasurer	Ganda	215/-	Storekeeper	7	10	31	

its dances or 'concerts'. The regular paid-up membership in any association is little more than the few officers themselves, though the tenants' associations are better served in this respect. But using this as a criterion for the 'size' of an association detracts from the social impact and image it may have on residents on an estate, who may attend a meeting or dance occasionally if not regularly.

Women hardly figure at all in the running of these associations, being more evident in the occasional colourful singing, praying and hand-clapping processions or other activities of the various Christian sects. The very few men who are constant members of church organizations appear to feel a definite conflict in participation in another associational sphere; often, trade unionists are spoken of as 'causing trouble', politicians as 'ungodly', and those concerned with recreation, the organizing of dances and football matches as in some way 'immoral'. The Catholic church, sited on Naguru Hill, just outside the estate, has an African and European 'middle-class' congregation who live as much at Ntinda or Kololo as at Naguru.

As can be seen from Table V the Nakawa local élite of 14 men fills 23 positions of leadership and includes three Luo, two Luhya/ Samia, two Lugbara, two Jonam, two Ganda, and one Alur, Acholi and Kiga. All except three leaders have more than one office. Of these three, two are Ganda and one an Alur. Six of the élite are leaders in various types of tribal association. Though the Kenyans, the three Luo and the Luhya, occupy half the positions in the more important tenants' associations, they do not in practice dominate proceedings. The Luo, No. 5, is Otieno, whose performance at the municipal council election in 1962 was described. He was also a leader in his subtribe association and had minor positions first in his trade union and later in a Kampala-wide KANU (Kenya African National Union) club.

The Naguru local élite numbers thirteen persons who occupy twenty-two positions in the four associations. Eight have moved to Naguru from Nakawa but have resided at Naguru for at least three years. The thirteen consist of two Alur, two Luhya/Samia, two Ganda, and one Jonam, Padhola, Luo, Acholi, Soga, Nyoro and Toro. As in the Nakawa élite, there is tribal variation which might almost be representative of the estate's population but which was not consciously intended.

Only three of the thirteen Naguru men are or have been full

77

tribal association leaders. None is or has been a leader of a lesser clan or subtribal association. Of these three, two were candidates at the 1962 municipal election, Nos. 10 and 1, the Jonam and Alur, the latter alone being successful.

This rather detailed breakdown of the two élites brings out the basic similarities in their composition with groups of ordinary tenants in neighbourhoods. Tribe is not significant in their membership while at least the superficial characteristics of high status are. In having moved from inferior localities they are not untypical of the ordinary tenant who is status-conscious and who does the same, or would like to if he could. They are important not only for the improvements in amenities they bring to an estate but also as a reference group in the way they act publicly, especially at meetings.

Rivalries and 'Tribalism'

I give the following case in detail to illustrate the linking of leaders and led, and the place of tribe in neighbourhood and community.

A crisis situation

One Sunday evening, the 4th of November, 1962, an Acholi young man of about nineteen climbed on to the roof of his 'father's' (in fact, his father's brother's) house in Upper Nakawa to retrieve some *malwa* (millet beer) straws which he had left to dry in the sun. He had come to Kampala to collect money for bridewealth and a celebration was planned for the next day. The boy could only get into a suitable position for jumping from the roof by supporting himself by the brick chimney. The chimney broke at its base and fell, bringing the boy with it and fatally crushing him. While the boy's 'father', a man of almost sixty who worked as an *askari* or security guard for a municipal department, yelled for help, neighbours, attracted by the noise of the falling chimney, rushed to the scene of the disaster, some running immediately to the telephone booth less than a hundred yards away to call an ambulance. The boy had died before the ambulance arrived.

Two associations turned to deal with the tragedy. One was the Acholi Association, which had not been very active since its inception in about 1960. Its job was to deal with personal crises of Acholi in town, to arrange dances and soccer trips to the homeland at Gulu. The association's leaders called a general meeting at Nakawa. Over a hundred Acholi came and a good collection was made which covered the cost of buying a coffin and sending the body home to Acholi. After this the Nakawa tenants' association directed its attention to the matter. A circular was issued on the 13th November calling a special general meeting at the mango tree on Sunday, the 18th. The circular gave news of the fatal accident and suggested that the association consider asking for the chimneys in the area to be repaired or replaced. It did not at this stage, it may be noted, refer to the possibilities of suing the housing authorities on behalf of the Acholi 'father'.

At a fairly large gathering of nearly two hundred tenants it was decided that money be collected and used to hire a lawyer for this purpose. It was the view of the association leaders who attended that the 'estate manager's ears are deaf to our complaints'. The duties of the hypothetical lawyer were then extended to cover what people claimed were grossly unhygienic conditions in the 'down groups', another expression for Lower Nakawa. It was agreed that 'later' someone would make a house-to-house collection. Other matters raised were the familiar ones of redecoration, electric wiring for each house, and a request for blocks of flats to be built in place of the worst houses.

The hard-working Samia secretary had been unable to attend the meeting, though it was he who drafted the circular, had it cyclostyled and personally distributed the copies. It bore the chairman's signature, a popular and very sociable Jonam. The chairman convened the meeting and controlled the time and order of speaking, but the vice-chairman, a Luo, put forward the association's suggestions, added others to them, and with great eloquence presented what seemed to those gathered as a fool-proof case, bound to succeed.

It was never discovered after the meeting why the Samia secretary had failed to attend, but he claimed his reason was a good one and that this was all he need say in apology. His abrupt reply was put down to the fact that the Luo vice-chairman had stolen the limelight with the tenants with his highly effective blood-and-thunder speech. In spite of the speech nothing had been done a week later to contact a lawyer and try to get compensation for the old Acholi, who told the Samia of this inactivity. The Samia was annoyed, saw the Luo's speech as 'words empty of action' and contacted the Luhya (No. 7 in Table V(b)) in an effort to collect subscriptions to build up a fund. In fact, the origin of the strains between the Samia and the Luo were a continuation of an earlier dispute.

The Samia and Luhya, both referred to as Luhya by others,[1] had six weeks earlier been involved in an almost violent dispute with the same Luo vice-chairman and the Luo treasurer, who is Otieno, already referred to. This was at a committee meeting about plans for Uganda's independence celebrations (following one with a European referred to in an earlier case). The apparent cause of the dispute was over the use of English or Swahili in committee meetings. About twenty-five men were present, including the committee and some group leaders, some of whom did not understand English properly. Normally these particular group leaders never attended a committee meeting but they were needed now in order to be informed of the arrangements for distributing meat and drinks.

These Swahili speakers protested at the absurdity of speaking in English. Otieno said that this was the language of committee meetings according to the association's constitution, but that the Luo vice-chairman would translate into Swahili for their benefit, a job frequently reserved for him at general meetings as well and earning him the nickname of Mr. Swahili. The Swahili speakers rebelled at this, saying that this would shame them by drawing attention to their inability to speak English. They insisted on Swahili being used, since all present, including myself, the 'visitor', knew it. Otieno replied that one or two Alur did not, but knew English.

By this time the Samia secretary, now firmly on the side of the Swahili speakers and sensitive to their claims, was trying to persuade the Luo vice-chairman, Mr. Swahili, to urge his 'companion', Otieno, to speak only in Swahili, to be followed by an English translation if necessary. They argued fiercely over this and accused each other of splitting hairs. Otieno in an attempt to restore order tried to pacify the Samia, addressing his pleas only to him. The Luhya, a deep-voiced man, who had meanwhile been growling his support also for the Swahili speakers, became suddenly angry when he thought Otieno was picking on the Samia and, switching from his excellent English to Swahili, furiously denounced what he called a tribalist attack by Luo on Luhya. He stormed out of the room, followed a little reluctantly but inevitably by the Samia, and also by the Swahili speakers, and the meeting came to a chaotic and undignified end.

A division between Swahili and English speakers, which was really yet another line of deprivation, had somehow developed into a Luo/Luhya split among four of the most active members of the committee. As in all such divisions the Jonam chairman remained calm and neutral.

It was this conflict between the four which re-emerged when the Samia sought the aid of his Luhya colleague to collect money for the old Acholi. The Samia did not convene another meeting for the purpose nor consult the two Luo, though he did inform the Jonam chairman. Through the third party of gossip, the two Luo heard of the Samia's annoyance and independent line of action. They both expressed surprise that so many tenants seemed to know of what they thought was a private dispute, even though it had been in the air for so long. They were very disturbed that people were interpreting it as a tribal conflict.

Luo and Luhya were at the time associated respectively with the opposing political parties in Kenya, KANU and KADU, and this reinforced people's beliefs that this was a conflict between Luo and Luhya in the committee. But, in fact, tribe had only a little to do with it. It was to be explained much more in terms of the internal rivalries typical of face-to-face élites. Otieno and the Samia had vied with each other, in an ostensibly friendly way, for the most influence and prestige in the committee. Both the Luhya and Luo vice-chairman, Mr. Swahili, had always managed to avoid taking sides on any issue between them, always referring a decision to the neutral Jonam chairman for his 'opinion' and then agreeing with it. The chairman did treat issues on their merits and so avoided an impression of favouritism, besides which his neutral position was clearly recognized as invaluable and therefor inviolable.

But the Luhya and Samia inevitably felt a sense of fraternity. They spoke the same language, shared similar customs, had a number of Luhya and Samia friends in common. It was perhaps significant that, like a number of his tribal group, the Luhya had succeeded in passing as a Uganda Samia[2] when he applied for a new job, after losing his previous one through what he claimed was 'redundancy caused by discrimination against Kenyans'. Similarly, Mr. Swahili and Otieno felt apprehension about their futures in Uganda. One or two Luo had tried to pass as Uganda Acholi but had been discovered very quickly, and this was not regarded as a serious solution of the problem for them.

The chain of events was as follows: In the original committee meeting, a status division between English and Swahili speakers, an equivalent of a division between clerks and manual workers, reached a critical stage and became an issue over which the two rivals, Otieno and the Samia, inevitably had conflicting views. With tempers raised, true alignments were revealed and the Luhya denounced the affair as 'tribalism'. In personal terms, the

Luhya and Samia were undoubtedly closer to each other than they were to either of the Luo, to whom the converse also applied. While neither pair were close friends, there was a mild cultural bond between those of the same tribal group. This bond would have been irrelevant had, say, the Luhya and one of the Luo been very close friends.

This was not the case and the Luhya, a bystander in the quarrelling and, as mentioned, normally peripheral to the élite, had to choose either to remain silent or to enter the issue decisively. His position would not have been helped by reticence. He was not a 'big man', so he had nothing to lose by speaking out, which he did. In speaking out he could enter the issue either in an attempt at reconciliation or by taking sides He did not attempt reconciliation. One can only speculate here that he dismissed this as unlikely to have any impact on the quarrellers. He therefore had to take sides. Again, more than merely voicing support for the Swahili speakers, he had to do something which made an impact if his participation in the affair was to have meaning. His role as member, even peripheral member, of the élite could gain capital if he was seen to be effective. He chose to take sides with the man who was closest to him culturally and also personally and appropriately condemned the Luo for tribal prejudice. Another factor underlying this choice may have been a preference to identify with the Ugandans in view of his own ambivalent position in the national division, but this is even more speculative.

Admittedly this can be no more than an interpretation of the way the Luhya used the choices available to him. He was not conscious of the choices, let alone why he made them. The only evidence are the case details presented and personal observation. The relevant point is that socio-economic status differences became an issue over which rival leaders disputed, and that when reconciliation failed the dispute was expressed in tribal terms. Since some of the Swahili speakers were themselves Luo, the status division was never expressed in tribal terms. The ordinary tenant got to hear of the dispute and its later development as between Luo and Luhya leaders of the estate, and it was this which worried the two Luo when the gossip reached their ears some time after the Acholi boy's accident.

It is not pleasant to have people believe that you quarrelled with a man because of his tribe, since this is known to be incompatible with community spirit, or against the norms. Few suggested the dispute was on KANU/KADU lines, which might have been another interpretation, and the two Luo had little alternative but to refute the accusation against them of tribalism and also to repair what was really a breach in the moral community. Meanwhile neither pair spoke to each other and no association meetings were held until a committee one in March with a European housing officer. The two Luo tactfully did not attend and left the Samia and Luhya to discuss the Acholi's case. They also did not attend a general meeting arranged by the Samia and Luhya a few days later when the Acholi's case was discussed with the Naguru committee, a development I describe a little later.

Individually the two Luo continued to point out to people that there had been a misunderstanding and that no grudges were borne. An opportunity to clear the air publicly came at the next general meeting of the tenants' association, which was really the last stage of this particular social drama.

On Sunday, May 19th, 1963, an annual general meeting was called to elect new officers. Beforehand circulars had been distributed, those in English to the Shs. 23/- houses of Upper Nakawa and those in Swahili to the cheaper houses in Lower Nakawa. Characteristically they urged all to attend and said that group leaders would take the names of people who failed to come and that their reasons for not attending would be scrutinized. Even so only about 120 tenants attended, though a number more looked in for a little while and passed on.

As usual the meeting was held under the mango tree, starting at eleven in the morning and not ten as advertised, due to a petition from a group complaining of delapidated housing, which had to be read by the chairman. From the start everything was in Swahili. The chairman gave his brief report on the past year. The vice-chairman, Mr. Swahili, acting as treasurer in place of Otieno who was unable to attend, gave his report, stating with some pleasure that Shs. 85/- had been collected in subscriptions over the past year and that Shs. 185/- was now in the First Permanent Building Society. It was here that he was able to repair the widely condemned disharmony between himself and Otieno and the Luhya and Samia.

The Luhya had in fact collected nearly all the Shs. 85/- over the year. Most had come from his own and a neighbouring group, especially in the latter few months, and all had been receipted and accounted for in a book which he bought with his own money. Mr.

Swahili dwelt on the Luhya's achievement for about fifteen minutes, praising him for his industry and urging others to be like him. Though credit of this sort was certainly due, its exaggerated form had the function of publicly asserting that nothing was any longer amiss between himself and the Luhya. As if to reassert community harmony even more, Mr. Swahili went on to point out that Naguru tenants' association had collected enough money to have their own headed notepaper and that, though he realized that they were better off, Nakawa ought also to do this.

Then came the election of officers. The Samia was at home on leave. He had needed to take his leave then because of domestic matters. The Jonam chairman had earlier given a very humble speech, saying that he had done his best for the association and was now prepared to hand over to someone else if the tenants wanted this. But he was proposed by the Luhya and was easily elected with seventy-one votes for his fourth successive year of office. Mr. Swahili came second with thirteen votes and once again became vice-chairman. A third nominee got only two votes.

Normally people who are not present cannot be nominated. This posed a problem since both the Samia secretary and Otieno were absent. They had been the two most active in the association and were regarded as local leaders. A precedent was set by general consent, therefore, that both should be nominated for the position of secretary. Another man, a Lugbara with an extremely good knowledge of English, was nominated as well and was elected with fifty-five votes. Years later he moved to Naguru and eventually became a city councillor, but this was his first office in a local association and a first step on what has proved to be a familiar ladder.

The Samia came second with twenty-four votes, thus becoming assistant secretary, while Otieno came third with sixteen. It is interesting that a number of tenants observed after the meeting that these two had been put on trial and that the community wanted to see justice. At the same time the majority had not wished to violate the 'law' that a nominee should represent himself personally and so the Lugbara had been elected as an impressive figure in his own right. By the same principle the office of treasurer, formerly Otieno's, was contested by tenants who were present but who had not figured in the cases described and who were not formerly significant in the élite.

Afterwards the group leaders were elected. The Luhya, in spite of the special praise awarded him and a certain renown for his part in the dispute, achieved no higher position than that of senior group leader, which he had held previously. He remained an active but untitled member of the committee or élite.

A notable feature of the election was that of the nine people nominated for the three positions mentioned only one, an Acholi, was proposed by a member of his own tribe even though numerically the chances were against this, since all but two were of dominant tribes. The same applied to the eighteen group and assistant group leaders elected, all unopposed. From observation this seemed to fit in with the emphasis on 'non-tribalism' at the meeting. The responses of tenants questioned afterwards confirmed this.

The meeting had thus been used to restate the values of non-tribalism and communal unity, which, by extension, included good neighbourliness. Even more indirectly it had been used to restate two other values.

A few of the tenants knew English but not Swahili and were shouted down when they attempted to speak from the floor on certain issues. They were only allowed to continue speaking when a translation was arranged. None were members of the committee. This opposition was another reflection of the general division between higher and lower status people and Upper and Lower Nakawa, as was the distribution of circulars in the two languages. The agreement to use a translater can be viewed as a statement of the value of communal unity over socio-economic differences. Secondly, since on the day before, May 18th, the pre-independence national elections had started in Kenya between KANU and KADU and the results were not yet out, Mr. Swahili's exaggerated courtesy towards and praise of the Luhya could additionally be seen as an appeal for unity among all Kenyans, a number of whom were gathered at the meeting. This again was confirmed by spontaneous conversation afterwards.

Mr. Swahili's own comment afterwards was revealing. 'It's true that I am a KANU man and that he [the Luhya] is KADU, but, you know, I have been here in Uganda for years . . . ' Much of the conversation among Kenyans for months had been over the problem of nationality and employment in Uganda, and I interpret this statement and others, and the implicit appeal for Kenyan unity as expressing their ambivalence. They are culturally and emotionally tied to their homes and view them as ultimate guarantees of social security, but at the same time they try to express some sort of allegiance to their place of employment, which they regard as a source of profit and self-advancement more than security.

85

New Political Influence

It will be remembered that Otieno and Mr. Swahili had tactfully left the Samia and the Luhya to continue trying to solve the problem of compensation for the bereaved Acholi. On March 10th, 1963, a general meeting was called by the chairman, but with the Samia and Luhya principally behind the arrangement. Two councillors for the ward were invited. These were the Ganda and Alur who had been elected the previous September. The Ganda, it may be recalled, lived twenty miles from Kampala, and the Alur at Naguru, the only resident of the estates to be elected. The invitation of the councillors to a general meeting marked a definite step forward in the association's means of representation to the housing authorities and signified a change in the power relationship of Kenyans to Ugandans in the Nakawa local élite.

In the committee meeting a few days earlier with the European housing officer, the Samia had asked to have the matter of compensation put forward for the bereaved Acholi referred to the housing authorities but said that the housing officer had refused to take responsibility. He then wrote a letter to the city council housing committee and asked the Naguru councillor to see that it was read and given fair consideration. Though by the time of the general meeting at Nakawa nothing positive had been done about the Acholi's case, the presence of the councillor gave more hope than before that tenants' complaints and requests regarding decorating, an electricity supply for those who wanted it, and a speed limit for Nakawa's roads would this time be considered. In other words, for the first time Nakawa was seeking aid from Naguru, which was now effectively represented on the council by one of its own residents. During the meeting a collection was made for the Acholi by the Luhya, who had already collected some money for this purpose. Eventually the Naguru councillor did reach some settlement with the city council over the Acholi's case and thus achieved something which probably could not have been done through the old system of indirect representation.

I have already described the meeting a couple of months later in May when Mr. Swahili reasserted locality harmony and indirectly proclaimed the ending of the dispute between the Luo and Luhya of the local élite. His actions and comments also revealed publicly the ambivalence Kenyans now felt more than ever. Kenya

PLATE 1(a)
Approaching Nakawa Estate from the City centre. The houses shown
are the cheaper, four-terraced ones of Lower Nakawa.

PLATE 1(b)

A Naguru semi-detached.

PLATE 2
Gathering at the water tap.

PLATE 3
Side-view of the back of a line of Upper Nakawa houses,
showing the kitchen and shower cubicle.

PLATE 4
A top "leader" of Nakawa. He has his name on his front door, one of the very few who do this.

PLATE 5
Lower Nakawa Bedspaces.

PLATE 6
Washday.
The wife of the
household head is
in the centre. His
mother and sister
(holding his child)
are right and left.
The mother was on
a few days' visit,
during which time
the household head
slept at a younger
brother's house
nearby.

PLATE 7
Refreshment.
Note the plantain
behind this Luo
child. This was one
of the few Luo
households who
regularly ate *matoke*,
the Ganda staple
diet.

national elections started a day before that meeting and emphasized the need for Kenyans to look for alternative employment in Kenya.

Excepting the Luhya, all the Kenyans so far mentioned, including the candidates at the 1962 council elections, had left for other jobs in Kenya by the end of 1964, often many months before. They typified an exodus of those with enough skills, luck and initiative. Others lost jobs and merely left for Kenya to search for employment, while the majority grimly hung on in Kampala. Stated thus the situation seems more dramatic than it was. It is the situation as Kenyans themselves saw it, though, as is shown by their only slight proportional decline in the labour force since independence, Kenyans were not singled out or discriminated against on any appreciable scale.

While Mr. Swahili summarized what was felt to be the position of Kenyans in Kampala very aptly, the political changes of independence had already made their choices for them. The entry of the Naguru councillor signified the future relationship of the estates to the city council. Putting it very roughly, Kenyans now no longer had power, Ganda had much less, and other Ugandans, especially from the north, were now the most numerous franchised category in the estates and were likely in future to provide the leaders and most voters.

Naguru is the better example of the new relationship to the city council. By virtue of having its own resident councillor and more articulate officers in the tenants' association, it was able to make immediate use of the new chain of communication with the city council.

An example was when the local Ganda *gombolola* chief ordered what was a periodic local government tax raid on all residents in Kampala East, including the housing estates. As usual the Ganda police, different from those of the Uganda central government, came early in the morning before six to demand entry into houses and an inspection of tax receipts. In some cases after one member of the household had opened the door, the tribal police pulled the bedclothes off those still sleeping, 'leaving some still naked'. Many people were arrested and taken to court. The time and manner in which the collection was made caused an uproar on the estates. Significantly Nakawa and Kiswa made protests to the housing committee but received no firm reply until Naguru tenants' association had complained. The latter had written to what was then the African housing department asking for central government intervention and succeeded in bringing about a more civilized form of collection.

Shortly after independence the central government African housing department was abolished and housing administration became the concern of committees on urban councils. This meant that the Naguru councillor was in an even better position to remedy residents' grievances. One particular issue illustrated the tenants' association's new confidence.

In about April 1963 the Naguru estate manager was 'summoned' by the association's committee to answer a charge against him by a Ganda girl of intent to seduce. The girl had been left in charge of her house by her elder brother. The manager was alleged to have tried to 'make friends' with her, but she refused his advances. She claimed that from then on he started to 'victimize' her by stating that she was an 'illegal' tenant. The girl went to the association who cautioned the manager, even though, technically, the girl was not the legal tenant, having lived there without her brother for some months, and even though her charge could not easily be proved. There was some reference by a few members of the committee to the manager's education, which, it was said, was far less than theirs and which perhaps warranted a new more highly educated manager anyway. Some suggested he should be replaced on the grounds of the charge against him by the girl. Most thought this too harsh, especially in view of his age, probably past fifty. No action was taken against him and the matter was not allowed to become public knowledge. It is relevant that the association's committee felt strong enough now not to have the matter referred to the city council housing committee. They could handle such matters more discreetly themselves.

Earlier in April the Naguru councillor had fought in the city council for greater official recognition of the Naguru tenants' association. He was, of course, still chairman of the association as well as being councillor, and with other officers had sent a letter to the city council which had asked for 'nothing short of full recognition [of the association] by the council to negotiate on behalf of all the tenants in Naguru on matters affecting conditions of tenancy, etc.'

At the time a number of general meetings held at the estate had brought to light many complaints, such as deteriorating housing, a need for redecoration, a request that latrines be adjoined to houses [*sic*], and that bus services be more regular. Many of these were dealt with. Later, approval was even made for a car enclosure to be built at Naguru, where roads were too narrow for parking, due, as one tenant put it, 'to the belief in the days when the estate was built that Africans here would never own cars'. On many British council estates also built immediately after the war, the same sort of remark might easily apply to what were originally lower-income earners.

There are other instances of this ability by the Naguru association to challenge the housing authorities much more directly and effectively than ever before. That this development should occur with a parallel declining power of the Kenyan residents was mildly ironic in view of their initiative in the early days, and a number remarked on this. In short, what had happened was the emergence of an incipient middle class, which had existed for many years as a socio-economic category above the African average in Kampala but which had much less constitutional influence before independence. Now it was able to produce its own politically effective leaders.

Though the leadership increasingly included fewer Kenyans, the latter were still very numerous on the estates. Yet no dislocation in community relations occurred. Kenyans still attended meetings to voice their domestic grievances like other tenants. Politically they withdrew from activities of Kampala East which did not concern their nation. But as neighbours they continued much the same as before. The relationships within and between localities, be they Upper or Lower Nakawa, Naguru or Kiswa, were part of the urban status system to and in which they had become committed and involved. They had little choice but to continue within this system. A call of 'back to the land' is least heeded by those so involved.

The three or four alternatives already mentioned seemed to face Kenyans then. They could act quickly and find employment in Kenya before losing their Kampala jobs. They could hang on in Kampala and take their chance. If they were in fact made redundant without having arranged employment in Kenya, they could either look for work in one of the Kenya towns or, say, on a sugar plantation, or they could return to the land temporarily or permanently. It would take a systematic follow-up study many years hence to find what in fact will have happened, but the little altered Kenyan proportions in the labour force suggest the fears were largely illusory.

My concern here is to explain how links were retained at home, and more especially in the various Kenya towns, to provide men with a multitude of 'safety-valve' relationships, to be utilized for jobs, accommodation or simply aid of some sort, if this were necessary. My thesis is that the tribal system, a phrase which I shall explain, was emphasized in ideology and ceremony among Kenyans in Kampala so that any man's network of relatives and friends from his tribe was both extensive and relatively effective.[3]

An important part of this ceremony[4] was expressed through the Luo and Luhya soccer league programmes, which had very high attendance rates and which gave rise to a pyramidal structure of organization involving a relatively large number of participants. Ideology was expressed through an emphasis on clan or descent ties in a number of situations, but especially those concerning the status of Luo or Luhya women, even though in reality socio-economic status differences were more significant for most relationships than descent ties.

None of this is to suggest that only the Luo and Luhya expressed a type of tribal solidarity in Kampala through ceremony and ideology. Other tribes certainly did, but none so strongly as these Kenya peoples. Nor were ties so expressed used anywhere near so effectively in exploring the job market in different towns, or in simply keeping in contact with a wide range of friends and kin.

I describe now the way in which the tribal system operated among tenants on the two estates. It functioned in the sphere of family and household relations and would occasionally be drawn beyond them. At the same time it was not allowed to become incompatible with the norms of locality and neighbourhood, or of community, which were both non-tribal and based on socio-economic status.

NOTES

[1] Samia is frequently regarded as a subtribe of Luhya. Luhya itself is a term referring to many subtribes. The Samia secretary was a Ugandan. The Luhya was a Kenyan, of the Marama subtribe.

[2] The Samia extend over both sides of the Kenya/Uganda border and were most easily able to 'switch' nationalities.

[3] A. L. Epstein, 1961, op. cit.

[4] By ceremony I refer to the etiquette, the proliferation of titles, the sometimes lengthy oratory, the jocular but regularized competitiveness, and in certain cases the special dress, singing and dancing, which characterize ethnic welfare and recreational associations, and which may occur in other contexts also. See J. C. Mitchell, 1956, *The Kalela Dance*.

CHAPTER V

THE TRIBAL SYSTEM AND FAMILY LIFE

Control over Women

As explained, most of the residents in the estates regard themselves as migrants of one sort or another. The Kenya Luo and Luhya are obviously so. People from the north and east of Uganda, such as Acholi, Lango, Alur, Lugbara, Padhola, Teso and others, had also for many years seen themselves as 'foreigners' in Kampala-Mengo. The Ganda were the host tribe. Neighbouring people from Bantu kingdoms such as Toro, Bunyoro and Busoga merge with the Ganda to constitute an ethnic group basically similar in their institutions and in striking contrast to the 'foreigners'.

One such institution is marriage, which in the Bantu kingdoms is usually regarded as a contract between bride and groom, who pays a bridewealth which may or may not be valuable but which is not normally recoverable under any circumstances. Sometimes wedding expenses, also payable by the groom, are much higher than the formal bridewealth. The man who actually begets children, the genitor, is entitled to them. A husband technically has the right only to children he has himself produced. Local courts uphold these rights of physical fatherhood, or, as they have been called, genitorial rights in a woman.

Local descent groups are not as important in marriage or the control and inheritance of land as among the other peoples referred to. A son may be favoured by his father as principal heir with no necessary reference to his or his mother's seniority. Daughters may inherit, increasingly so these days, while it is common practice for women to own property in their own right and to transmit or dispose of it as they please. The concept of corporate, land-owning lineages and clans has relatively little relevance for property and land rights, which are frequently recognized as accruing to an individual. *De facto* freehold land tenure is widespread, especially among Ganda.

I shall call these the 'host' people in Kampala, not because they specifically invited others to come to the town, though rural cash-cropping in Buganda has certainly encouraged immigrant labour for many years,[1] but because it was originally their, or at least Ganda, customs and institutions which inevitably dominated what was their traditional capital. People from outlying areas frequently found difficulty in adjusting to the different ways of the people of the kingdoms, while having to recognize that the Ganda were politically, economically and socially supreme, in conjunction with rather than except for the British.

The 'foreigners' I shall call 'migrants', not by reference to the physical distance they may have travelled in order to reach Kampala but because they have stepped, or originally did step, into a highly contrasting society. The Host people figuratively owned Kampala, while the Migrants moved into it. This crude distinction is clearly cultural but with historical, political and economic overtones.

The Migrants, among whom may also be included the Bantu Kiga and Ankole Iru, differ in all the cultural features mentioned for the Hosts. Marriages are still very much the concern of strongly patrilineal or agnatic extended families, even though bride and groom are allowed to choose each other. Bridewealth tends to be of high value, consisting of cattle, livestock, money, or a combination of these, and part at least usually deriving from the bridewealth received for a sister's marriage. Most importantly a complete or nearly complete transmission of bridewealth gives the husband rights as social father over all children born to his wife. Technically this means that even if he did not beget some of her children he is entitled to be regarded as their legal father. Alternatively he cannot be regarded as legal father of children he has begotten unless he pays over the bridewealth to their mother's family. Again, local courts uphold these genetricial rights in a woman. Bridewealth can be recovered by the groom's family if the wife breaks her marriage contract by leaving her husband and even, in some cases, by being barren.[2]

Because a sister's stable marriage is an important means ensuring brothers of a contribution to their own bridewealth, they are often very vigilant over a sister's activities before marriage and in the early period of her married life. She may not be 'promiscuous' since this is associated with infertility. She is allowed to reject a suitor but is discouraged from marrying a man who is thought unable to pay bridewealth to her family. As a result relatively few women are 'prostitutes', or live with men to whom they are not customarily married. By contrast, Host women are allowed greater freedom in choice of husbands and lovers, and most 'prostitutes', often an inappropriate English misnomer, and free marriages are of these people.

Among Migrants sons inherit property and land from their fathers according to the principle of what has been called the house-property complex.[3] In polygynous families sons inherit in the order of their mother's seniority, and in the order of seniority among their own full brothers. Cattle and land are given for marriage and in inheritance in strict accordance with this principle. The elders of a cluster of local descent groups are still important in settling land and marriage problems and operate alongside government courts. Women cannot inherit and it is rare to find them owning property of any value.

As a general relative comparison, brothers among Migrants are united by common interests in family land and in the social and economic status of their sisters much more than brothers among Host peoples. An excusable tautology is that these differences are also obvious in town. Their marriages are in direct contrast, and their concepts of the obligations of 'brotherhood' are different. Underlying these domestic differences is a general cultural one. Migrants, coming from societies which lacked a traditional hierarchy of political authority, express amazement at the highly centralized political systems of the Hosts, among whom chiefships of various grades often rest on access to or ownership of land and in which a non-egalitarian premise pervades the society at all levels from king to commoner.[4]

In spite of their division into Kenyans and Ugandans, Migrants understand each other's customs, which operate at the domestic level among family and kin even if they are irrelevant in the struggle for scarce jobs and the resultant political affiliations. They deplore the independent status of Host women, who often make their way to Kampala on their own, get a job if they can, find a lover, and have children and live permanently with a man, all without any special permission of their brothers or parents. In fact, in view of a woman's frequently low bridewealth value, her earning capacities in town are often of more benefit to her parents and siblings at home than they would be if she were formally married, when a much smaller proportion of her income would be due to her own kin. There is a striking difference in cultural values as was evidenced in a typical, spontaneous conversation in English between two workmates, both living in Upper Nakawa.

Migrant: We Luo don't marry girls whom we find in town unless their parents or strict brothers have looked after them. We fear disease [i.e. by implication barrenness as well] and do not like a girl who may have 'roamed' in the town with many men and who will run away when you try to keep her as your wife. I refer mostly to these Bantu women [i.e. of the Host peoples], but even some Luo girls could get like this if their parents and brothers did not control them.

Host, a Nyoro: I find it preferable to marry a girl whom I have found in the town because she is used to life there and will not run away when you marry her, whereas a girl who is brought from home will find her eyes opened up and will want to enjoy all she sees in town and will leave you.

In reality while the Nyoro's is a typical comment on the freedom enjoyed by Host women, it is partly a rationalization of a situation over which men have little control. Some frankly express envy of the greater control Migrants have over their women, and in earlier days attempts were made to remedy the situation. In 1955–6 Ganda feeling was sufficiently aroused that an unsuccessful attempt was made to drive out single women from Mengo. This was partly a result of growing resentment towards Europeans and Asians and was seen as a way of withholding African women from them as well as a possible return to traditional male control. The attempt failed because the emancipation of women was too entrenched, since in addition to the cultural factors mentioned many Host women have more education than others, which gives them the ability to organize should their rights seem threatened, as well as giving an increasing number 'respectable' economic independence through employment in offices or the professions. In the early 1950s Toro in the Kenya port of Mombasa hired coaches on a train to send unattached Toro women home but the local authorities regarded this compulsion as illegal and banned it.

By contrast, Migrants have constantly maintained a check of varying effectiveness on their womenfolk in all East African towns. Brothers do this, sometimes with the aid of relatives recruited for the purpose, or of tribal, subtribal or clan associations.

Clearly with more education for women and with a larger number of girls who are born and bred in town, this will change, Nairobi being the best example of this, even for Luo. But the difference in Kampala between Host and Migrant peoples remains marked. There are very few 'prostitutes' and unattached Migrant women in Kampala.

The two categories are in full view of each other, however, and cannot escape comparisons, as in these two cases of near neighbours.

James, the Nyoro in the conversation referred to above, met a Nyoro woman in Kampala, lived with her for two years and re-garded her as his wife. She bore him a child. Her parents asked James for what he thought was the exorbitant bridewealth of Shs. 600/-. He refused to pay this and the girl, more out of loyalty than submission to her parents, left him. The child is now with James's parents and is regarded as his according to customary law.

James now has another wife who has three children. Now that he is better off he has managed to pay money for bridewealth, though so far only about Shs. 300/-. Recently he arranged a marriage for a Nyoro neighbour at Nakawa by 'introducing' the man to his wife's younger sister. The couple lived together at Nakawa for some time, the wife became pregnant and they then went home for a Christian wedding ceremony. The man has not yet paid bride-wealth but intends to, though he is under no more than a mild pressure from his wife to do so, 'to help her parents'.

In a parallel case, a Migrant had to achieve the status of social as well as physical father in order to have custody of his child.

A Lango of Upper Nakawa came to know very well an unmarried Lango girl lodging with her brother in Lower Nakawa. The woman started living with the man, who agreed with her brother and parents to pay bridewealth for her in the customary manner. He made a special visit to her parents at home. The wife was by this time some months pregnant. After about eighteen months the husband was unable to meet some continual and heavy bridewealth demands. At the behest of her parents, brothers and some clansmen in Nakawa, the woman and child returned home. The Lango accepted without protest the fact that he had lost custody of his wife and child until such time as he could recontinue his bridewealth obligations. This he was able to do after six months. His wife and child then returned to him at Nakawa.

96

Marriage

Given the fact that Host women have more independent status, it is not surprising that most tribally mixed marriages and other types of cohabitation involve them. Migrant women are usually married to men of their own or a closely related tribe and rarely enter into a conjugal union in which the husband has not agreed to customary marriage, with the full transfer of bridewealth.

There are many variables underlying urban marriage patterns, only a few of which can be dealt with here. So far the cases and comments have touched on some. There are two types of mixed tribal 'marriage', using this last term to refer to any conjugal union, whether 'legal' or not, in which husband and wife have lived together for a reasonable time. One is of a couple who come from different but similar tribes, such as Ganda/Toro, Nyoro/Toro, or Toro/Soga unions, or, for Migrants, Lango/Padhola, Acholi/Lango, Alur/Acholi (a theoretical possibility though none recorded), and Luo/Luhya. The incidence of each combination varies considerably. Among Migrants there is little intermarriage even between tribes which share the same language and customs. Among Host people there is much more.

The second type of mixed marriage is between spouses from quite dissimilar tribes.[5] Examples are a Luo/Ganda or Acholi/Toro conjugal union. These are extremely rare. When they occur they are not usually legal marriages either in the customary sense of having paid bridewealth to the girl's parents or by virtue of a church or civil ceremony. They are more often unions in which a Host woman has agreed to live with a Migrant man, though even these are not common.

This brings us to a second variable, which is the distinction which residents themselves make between 'permanent' wives and husbands and those who are 'temporary'. Again, people make another, and in practice overlapping, distinction between marriages arranged in the home rural area and those established in town.

A 'permanent' union includes not only what would conventionally be regarded as legal marriage, according to either customary, religious or civil law. It includes also cohabitation in which the man and woman have lived together long enough for neighbours and kin to award it the title 'permanent'. The birth of children is usually an essential of this title, before which the union is called 'temporary'. If both spouses are of Migrant tribes pressure is brought to bear by kin on both sides to legitimize the union through payment of bridewealth. If the man is Migrant and the woman Host, the man's kin and friends usually dissuade him from taking the union too seriously. They say, 'She is wasting your blood, because soon she may run away', and express apprehension as to the future of any children he may have.

There are only two recorded cases of Host men living with Migrant women, an indication of the restricted status of the latter rather than disinclination by the former. In the many more cases of Host men and women living together, there is very little pressure from either kin or friends to legitimize cohabitation.

Other variables, such as the socio-economic and educational statuses of spouses, must be ignored in this account. The general point I wish to illustrate is that Migrant women do not marry or live with men of the Host tribes.

This point emerges when we consider 166 couples at Nakawa and Naguru who were known to me on anything from casual to close terms.[6] One hundred and forty constituted conjugal unions of some socially acknowledged permanence. Nearly all had children. Of these unions 133 were intra-tribal, most of them rural-established customary marriages, and most of Migrants, particularly Luo. Twenty-seven unions were inter-tribal. Although 204 of all spouses were Migrants, only eighteen of them were partners to an inter-tribal union. I list these inter-tribal unions below, underlining Host spouses. All wives have borne at least one child to their husbands.

LIST A: 'PERMANENT' INTER-TRIBAL UNIONS

	Migrant to Migrant			Migrant to Host	
	Man	Wife		Man	Wife
2	Luo	Luhya	3	Luo	Ganda
1	Acholi	Lango	1	Lango	Nyoro
1	Lango	Padhola	1	Luhya	Toro
1	Lugbara	Luhya	1	Kiga	Toro
			1	Lugbara	Rwanda
			1	Teso	Soga

(With the exception of the 2 Luo/Luhya unions,
all these are urban-established.)

Twenty-six unions were regarded by neighbours, kin and the partners themselves as 'temporary'. Twelve of them were intra-tribal. The remaining fourteen inter-tribal unions included five which were between partners of Host tribes and nine in which one spouse was of a Migrant tribe. I list these latter.

LIST B: 'TEMPORARY' INTER-TRIBAL UNIONS

		Migrant to Host			Host to Migrant	
		Man	Wife		Man	Wife
	I	Luo	Ganda	I	Nyoro	Luhya
	I	Luo	Toro	I	Rwanda	Kiga
	I	Acholi	Ganda			
	I	Lango	Ganda			
	I	Kiga	Ganda			
	I	Kiga	Toro			
	I	Alur	Nyoro			

(All unions are urban-established.)

The two exceptions to the rule that Migrant women do not marry or live with Host men occur in List B: a Nyoro is living with a Luhya girl, and a Rwanda with a Kiga girl. The Luhya and Kiga are Bantu, which alone might be expected to facilitate their integration with Host Bantu, both in marriage and in other spheres of activity. But this linguistic factor of integration operates only to a limited extent. The fact that these are the only instances in my sample of Host men living with Migrant women, let alone marrying them, suggests that the social and cultural factors I have described generally override mere linguistic similarity.

In List A five Migrant women have married men not of their own but of other Migrant tribes. But social and cultural factors are not ignored. Thus, two Luhya women are married to Luo men. These are rural-established, customary mixed marriages which quite frequently occur at the boundaries of Luo and Luhya country in Kenya. The Lugbara who married a Luhya girl was born and brought up in Buganda, to which his father had migrated many years before. Though he spoke Lugbara and maintained ties with his 'home' area in Lugbaraland, he was familiar with Bantu languages and customs. Integration was further eased by the fact that Luhya and Lugbara share the notion common to Migrants that bridewealth is recoverable and guarantees the husband's rights as social father over the children born to his wife. The Acholi/Lango and Lango/Padhola unions are intra-Nilotic and provided few difficulties in their conduct either for the spouses or for their respective agnates. Though initially urban-established, the marriages followed the customary transaction of recoverable livestock and money by the husband and his local descent group in return for rights over the woman's reproductive powers.

Migrants generally disapprove of any sort of conjugal union with Host women. But, as is evident from lists A and B, these do occur, though as a very small proportion of the customary intra-tribal marriages of these people. All eight 'permanent', urban-established unions in list A in which Migrant men live with Host women have been subject to varying proportions of disapproval voiced by the husband's kin and fellow-tribesmen. Together with the disapproval, social, cultural, and linguistic difficulties inhibit mixed marriages of this type.

In only a few cases do the barriers look like being overcome. In list A one Luo's Ganda 'wife' has borne him seven children and has visited her husband's rural home fairly frequently. She speaks DhoLuo and wants her children to speak DhoLuo as their first language, though, in fact, they normally converse with each other and with friends in Luganda. Yet, except for two unions I shall mention, this seems to have the greatest chance of surviving the husband's cessation of urban employment. The two which may survive for a much longer period are the Lugbara/Rwanda and Teso/Soga unions. In the former both husband and wife speak Luganda and have their families in Buganda, where they intend to settle eventually. The Teso man and his Soga wife are both of high educational and occupational status and do not envisage settling in either of their rural homes.

Something of this detailed picture also emerges for the two estates as a whole (see Table VI, opposite). At Nakawa household heads of Host tribes are only 13 per cent of the total, while Migrants are 83 per cent, the remainder being Muslim Nubi. At Naguru the proportion of Host household heads rises to 31 per cent, still much lower than the Migrants' 58 per cent. Approximately a quarter of the Host household heads at Nakawa are unmarried, which is only slightly higher than the proportion for

TABLE VI. MARITAL STATUS

Tribe	Unmarried	Married no Children	Married with Children	Total No. Household Heads
NAGURU ESTATE				
Luo	19	11	116 (2*)	146
Ganda	50 (15f, 6+c)	13	65	128
Luhya	10	7	51	68
Toro ⎫				23 ⎫
Soga ⎬	17 (4f)	7	30	18 ⎬ 54
Nyoro ⎭				13 ⎭
Nubi	7	2	40 (2*)	49
Acholi	8	4	23	35
Samia/Gwe	6	2	17	25
Teso	5 (1f)	—	10	15
Lango	2	3	8	13
Lugbara	1	3	9	13
Others	29	9	61	99
TOTAL	154	61	430	645
Total %	23·87	9·46	66·67	99·90
NAKAWA ESTATE				
Luo	22	16	145 (4*)	183
Acholi	15 (1f)	10	83 (2*)	108
Luhya	6	10	63	79
Lugbara	9	8	48	65
Kiga	45	4	12	61
Samia/Gwe	5	3	33	41
Ganda	7 (3f+c)	6	23 (1f)	36
Lango	4	4	25	33
Nyoro ⎫				13 ⎫
Tori ⎬	6	5	21	13 ⎬ 32
Soga ⎭				6 ⎭
Ruanda	7	4	20	31
Nubi	3	1	22 (1*)	26
Madi	2	3	19	24
Jonam	5	1	18	24
Teso	5	3	16	24
Ankole	4	2	4	10
Others	12	7	27	46
TOTAL	157	87	579	823
Total %	19·71	10·57	70·35	100·63

Key: * = with 2 or more wives.
       f = female household head.
   +c = with children.

Migrants. The highest tribal proportion of unmarried here are Kiga, three-quarters, whose average length of residence is very low (Table IV p. 28), indicating that, like many of their tribe in Kampala, they are short-term migrants who have come for the express purpose of acquiring enough cash for bride-wealth. Other tribes of any significant number approximate the average for the estate of a fifth of their population being unmarried.

Naguru has a proportionally larger number of unmarried household heads than Nakawa. This is at first sight surprising, in view of the larger houses and better amenities existing at Naguru. The explanation is that many high-status Ganda in particular, and other Host peoples, including women, have not yet contracted what they regard as legal, customary, or 'permanent' marriages. They are able to afford the more expensive Naguru houses by dint of their generally higher occupational statuses (see Tables II and III, pp. 21–24). Many Migrants whose need for larger housing is much greater may simply be unable to afford the higher rents at Naguru. So, lacking other applicants, it is those high-status but unmarried Ganda and other Hosts who obtain some of the Naguru houses.

In practice there is no favouritism or graft at work in this allocation of houses at Naguru. But the sight of relatively empty larger Naguru houses embitters many Nakawa tenants with large families and serves even more to set apart Nakawa and Naguru residents. In an even more general sense it signifies the difference in status at Naguru between Migrants, who exhibit the full range of skills and incomes, and Host peoples, who predominate in the upper categories. That this difference there should coincide with a difference in proportions of those married impresses upon many Migrants' minds the idea that Host people, even when they are well off, are not really concerned to marry and have children, but are content to have a series of lover relationships. In fact, unmarried Host residents may have their children living with parents in the country.

Distinct from Nakawa, where Host and Migrant proportions of unmarried are not very different, at Naguru about two-thirds of Host people are unmarried whereas the proportion is only slightly less than a quarter for Migrants. Additionally, of the unmarried Host household heads, over a quarter are women, some of them with children. At Naguru, in other words, the ideas Migrants have of the contrasting status of women among Host people seem to them to be given visible proof.

Briefly, Host/Migrant differences are much less sharply drawn at Nakawa than Naguru. To some extent this sharp distinction at Naguru is mitigated by the relative lack of participation by Host people in tenants' association or other communal activities. Thus, though I spoke ealier of a local élite at Naguru, there is in fact a large category of even higher-status tenants from Host tribes who are little in evidence. Other tenants often say, 'There are no Ganda at Naguru. They all live in Mengo.' In fact, Ganda are the second largest tribe there, even though they are proportionally far fewer than their number in Kampala-Mengo. They are typical of any upper middle class in having their social and other networks located much more widely than their immediate area of residence.

Yet, the fact remains that people continue to move from Nakawa to Naguru as a complement to status achievement, and that most of those who do so are from Migrant tribes. An interesting question then posed is what happens to Migrants who reach a sufficiently high rung in the social ladder to act as socio-economic equals with these high-status Host people.

The question ushers in a further crucial query as to what are the sanctions encouraging and discouraging change. This is where the long-due explanation of the tribal system is relevant. As shown above, there is a major institutional distinction which can be made between Migrants and Host people. The reasons underlying it stem from the very nature of their rural social structures. The obvious tautology is thus that people differ in their marriage systems and in their ideas on the status of women in town because they do so in their home districts. A reasonable assumption would be that as people become more involved in urban life and also achieve adequate economic and social security they depart more from the norms and sanctions operating at home. Most would agree from observation that this assumption is correct, but, with one notable exception,[7] the rate at which this may occur as between groups, and the manner, have not been studied.

Migrants share a highly complicated system of negative sanctions deriving from the tribal system, which are rarely any other than those of disapproval. For pragmatists it may be hard to concede that disapproval is a powerful weapon, and I shall need to illustrate my point with detailed and lengthy case-studies. The

Kenyans among the Migrants are especially likely to emphasize such sanctions through appeal to an ideology of tribal solidarity, often when the facts of a case contradict any real, political solidarity. And this, of course, relates to my thesis, that Kenyans were unable to organize themselves as a political force in Uganda and so expressed a mock solidarity in ideology and ceremonies instead. Because of differences in the tribal system Host people do not exert the same sanctions of disapproval over issues relating to marriage and the status of women.

NOTES

[1] A. I. Richards (ed.), 1955, *Economic Development and Tribal Change*, Cambridge, Heffer, for E.A.I.S.R.

[2] A. W. Southall distinguishes the 'Nilotic' and 'Interlacustrine' marriage types in A. W. Southall, 1960, 'On Chastity in Africa', *Uganda Journal*, Vol. 24. P. C. Gutkind suggests that adaptation in urban family life may be expected to vary among ethnic groups. 1962(b) 'African Urban Family Life', *Cahiers d'Etudes Africaines*, Vol. III, No. 10, p. 206.

[3] M. Gluckman, in A. R. Radcliffe-Brown and D. Forde, 1950, *African Systems of Kinship and Marriage*, O.U.P. for I.A.I.

[4] I include details and literary references on Host and Migrant peoples in Appendix I.

[5] J. C. Mitchell, 1957, op. cit., has distinguished these two types of marriage as inter-tribal and inter-ethnic.

[6] I have given more details on these unions in D. J. Parkin, 1966, 'Types of Urban African Marriage in Kampala', *Africa*, Vol. XXXVI, No. 3.

[7] P. Mayer, 1961, *Townsmen or Tribesmen*, Cape Town, O.U.P.

CHAPTER VI
SANCTIONS AND IDEOLOGY

Sanctions among Migrants

There is a Luo proverb which states that friends will help you more than brothers. This refers to the ambivalence in relations among brothers of a homestead: on the one hand they are expected to act in defence of common interests, on the other they are in competition for the resources represented by these interests. By contrast, friendships can be made and broken relatively easily without disrupting corporate property interests. As long as brothers each have a self-interest in preserving some degree of unity, they act as each other's keepers, condemning behaviour which might seem to disrupt this unity. Friendships rarely have an irreplaceable economic basis. They are established much more for leisure pursuits, unbiased advice, and as an escape from the unremitting demands of kin.

This contrast between friends and brothers is overdrawn but perhaps illustrates what I believe is a characteristic of societies in which the extended family is the primary unit of production and consumption, and allocation of land and property. It thus applies to the Migrant peoples, though with some variation. The Acholi and Lango claim that they have ample land and can 'just go and take it' if they want it. They contrast themselves with the Luo and Luhya whom they regard as land-starved, and often cite this as a reason for their coming to Kampala. There are many cases among the Kenyans, especially Luo, of sons in town being called upon by their father to send money to help him in a land case. His land is theirs, and they are all concerned. Perhaps the lesser scarcity of land among Acholi and Lango is the reason why such demands are rarely made among them.

The Kiga and most of the Lugbara in Kampala also suffer from land shortage. Most Kiga and some Lugbara stay for fairly short periods in Kampala and take their earnings back home with them intact, 'buying' or improving claims on land as they are able. A substantial number of Lugbara claim that they are 'landless' and that they shall work for as many years in Kampala as they can

105

in order to acquire land and improve their economic position generally.

Whatever their different land situations, all these Migrants have common notions of the function and value of bridewealth: that it gives a husband the right to be the social father of his wife's children, and that this right is worth paying dearly for. Sisters represent a receipt of bridewealth at their marriages, and the sons of an extended family have this common interest even if they are not bound to each other by land. Townsmen of the Migrant tribes continue to prefer to marry girls whom they have met at home, and undergo a customary ceremony. Links between town and country, between brothers and sisters, and between children and parents, are maintained through these institutional ties, as well as through the universal ties of affection.

Host people have marriage which is much more a matter between bride and groom alone, a type of freehold land tenure among Ganda and in some areas of the other kingdoms, preferential inheritance, a different notion of the function of bridewealth, and much more flexibility in regulations regarding the economic position of the extended family, whose incidence is anyway much less. Brothers and sisters, and even children and parents, are much less bound by common interests to behave in a specific way to each other. The less instrumental aspect of their family relationships should emerge in the discussion.

This said, it must be admitted that these contrasts are ideal types. Among Migrants the ideal type is, say, 'Luo (or Acholi, or Lango) law and customs', a phrase which men may use when pointing out the propriety or impropriety of a certain course of action in town. A man may be dissuaded from living with a Ganda woman because this is against the 'custom', which is that he should arrange a marriage at home with a girl of his own tribe. It is true that the ideal type is based on certain very real common economic interests, yet at the same time in many urban relationships the ideal is appealed to much more often than the economic facts would require. This is the ideology I referred to earlier. The tribal moralists are its proponents, operating in formal and informal situations, through associations and through ordinary networks of relatives and friends. But, in spite of them, urban life continues to provide the contexts for changing relationships which can only be accepted in the long run.

Life histories are sometimes offered by neighbours of a man of their own tribe as an illustration of how town life can corrupt. Though they refer to people who are still resident on the estates, they take on a mythical quality and express sanctions of disapproval as well as a realization that the forces of urban life are irrepressible.

Two life histories recounted as examples of urban life

I have condensed the following to avoid the verbatim repetition but have retained certain words and phrases used in the original English, denoting them by quotation marks.

1. Odhiambo, a Luo, has been in Kampala since 1950, and has lived for many years at Naguru. He was industrious and earned quite good money even though he had very little education. He never had 'a proper job' but sold vegetables at a stall he hired in Nakawa market, and did additional work in the evenings and weekends at the bar on Naguru estate owned by a prominent Luo. It is said that he did not get on well with other Luo. Nor did he have a job 'which could establish his name'. He had many lovers in the bar where he worked. These were Ganda and Toro girls who would either help in the bar or simply patronize the place waiting to be bought drinks by men who came there. Odhiambo had lovers in other bars too, and was known to spend all his money on them. He considered himself an expert in seducing these women and would latch on to a man who was a stranger in Kampala and take pleasure in introducing him to them. These were always short friendships, except with men who were 'rogues' like him. Other Luo came to realize his disrepute and, due to their intervention and warnings, his attempt to marry a Luo girl who had come to Kampala to lodge with her brother in Naguru failed. His poor reputation reached home and his attempts to marry there failed also.

He did not alter his ways, however, and continued to live a high life, always managing to dress well and sometimes moving in the company of men who had cars. 'They could even go to Top Life and White Nile night clubs, and yet he was only a vegetable-seller and barman.'

Though disapproved of by people of his own tribe he never appeared worried or offended and they marvelled at his self-assurance. Luo housewives in his neighbourhood would ask him when he was likely to marry. He gave one of two replies, either that he already had a Ganda wife or that he would go home and marry a

Luo girl shortly. These were stock responses for such a long time that the women in the end merely asked as a joke. Like the men, they believed he would never marry, at least not a Luo girl. 'Odhiambo had no man from a distant location to get him a girl who had never heard of his behaviour.' All the people he knew were in his own home location or area. He would go home looking for a wife and pretend that he was a clerk but they knew who he was. 'There was no one to recommend him.'

The last time Odhiambo went home for this purpose was in July 1963. He searched widely but met with the same response, until he came to know a girl of fifteen who had just had to leave school in Standard Five through lack of school fees. Odhiambo had only Shs. 60/– in his pocket but made her believe that he was a 'businessman in Kampala, owning a shop', but that he had no wife to help him mind it. He said that there were many expensive items in the shop which had to be left unattended when he went to the Asian dealer for his supplies. He explained that 'he wanted a humble girl who was honest and trustworthy and could read and write', willing to marry him and help in the business. He asked if he might see her another day, wondering all along whether she really knew of him. But she accepted and they met again. He implored her not to mention their relationship to others. They eventually agreed that she should follow him in a few days to Kampala. He gave her the fare for the steamer and arranged to meet her at Port Bell, the Kampala side of the lake.

They reached his house in Naguru and settled in. Odhiambo then made the daily pretence of tending his shop, but in reality would go to his usual market stall after collecting fish and vegetables from the larger city markets. After some days he could no longer resist her requests to see and work in the shop. One day he came back early looking very worried and broke the news that his shop had been broken into by thieves and ransacked, and that he was now 'bank-rupt'. He took her to a shop of permanent construction which had been abandoned some time before by an owner who had in fact gone bankrupt. The door was open, the shelves bare, and the girl believed his story. He explained that now there was no alternative for him but to trade at a stall in Nakawa market in dried fish and vegetables. Their short relationship had been a good one and the girl felt sorry for him and, at his request, agreed to help him at the stall.

He pretended he had now arranged his 'new business' at the stall and a few days later took her there. They are now living and trading together happily. 'Odhiambo at last left going about with prostitutes and became a good man and stuck to his business.'

The Luo women at Naguru who had earlier ridiculed his un-married status were surprised at the developments and change of personality. He had told them on his arrival from home that a young, pretty, educated girl would come to Naguru as his wife and would trade with him. They were amazed that this actually happened. The girl's relatives located her in Kampala after some weeks and came to retrieve her. Odhiambo welcomed them, expressed his good intentions and promised to go home and discuss bridewealth. He paid their fares home and gave them a little money besides and eventually fulfilled his promise.

To some extent this has the ingredients of a fairy tale with a moral. The basic facts recounted proved to be correct. The man did have a bad reputation and those Luo who knew him were un-willing to 'recommend' him to their own or friends' sisters. Women were, as usual, significant influences on his behaviour. What they thought seemingly did matter. A theme which often recurs in urban life histories is the period of adjustment, in this case a long one, during which some young men new to town wallow in the gaiety which is offered if they can afford it. Another implicit theme is the naïvety of wives new to the town. This cropped up in the description of women's neighbourhood gossip sets in chapter three.

The morals are fairly clear, that a man has to win the respect of his fellow-tribesmen before he can form friendships which will lead to introductions to possible wives, and that an honourable settlement over bridewealth should be reached even when a wife has been 'pulled' from her home to town. There is reference, too, to the virtues of husband and wife working at market stalls together. There are a number of Luo and Luhya who do this. Usually the women are left to work at the stall on their own if their husbands have alternative employment, though the husband manages the income and retains the right to retire his wife if he wishes. By contrast Ganda women often run the stalls as their own businesses, independently of their husbands if they have them.

Sanctions of disapproval, powerful though they may be, are not always enough.

2. Samson, a Luhya of Wanga subtribe, lives at Naguru and has been in Kampala since 1949. He used to work for Uganda Transport Company and, by travelling a great deal, earned a fair wage in addition to tips. He was dismissed by the company and, in only

getting an inferior job as a driver's mate, experienced a drastic reduction of income. He was always refused to marry so that his fellow-tribesmen colleagues have given up trying to persuade him, saying, 'Samson will never marry now'. Furthermore, he is regarded as a heavy drinker and it is common knowledge that he has always spent nearly as much as he earns on 'roaming' with women and prostitutes. He has constantly refused to join his subtribe association in town and, anyway, does not heed their requests for better behaviour. Samson rarely goes to his rural home but when he does, it is said he never dares visit his close relatives since they have heard of his misdemeanours in the town 'and he would feel shame before their anger'. There is speculation as to how he will eventually fare when he is too old for work.

His two sisters, moreover, are both in Kampala East and are reputed to be prostitutes. One of them is particularly notorious in this respect and 'even associated with a European'. Samson, as elder brother, is regarded as responsible for checking their behaviour, but it is considered that he himself needs correction.

Samson recently had a younger brother lodging with him, attending a Senior Secondary School in the city and studying for his Cambridge School Certificate. Samson and other siblings paid his school fees. But the boy failed his examinations. He was also accused of impregnating the daughter of a Samia at Nakawa but, after failing his examinations, left for Nairobi to get a job, never accepted responsibility, and, anyway, claimed his education put him at too superior a level to consider the girl as a wife. Though the girl herself was admitted to be rather coquettish, the boy was condemned not so much for refusing to accept responsibility for the girl's condition as for somehow using his achieved education for extending the social distance between himself, the girl's father and sympathetic kinsmen and colleagues of the latter. He could, at least, they say, have offered compensation to the girl's father. By not doing so he had acted 'proudly'. Contacting him, which would have to be done initially through his unpopular and unreliable brother, Samson, was pointless unless the boy himself desired to negotiate.

The whole chain of events and the family and girl involved in them are regarded as a slur on the reputation of Luhya, and Wanga subtribesmen in particular, in Kampala East, but people can no more than attempt to control the events through sanctions of disapproval.

Samson and his siblings do not fulfil ideal role-expectations. Samson was guilty on four counts: remaining unmarried; not joining his subtribe association; not controlling his sisters; and allowing his brother to 'roam' instead of encouraging him to study for an examination. The brother was guilty of using his higher status to escape from obligations consequent upon his making a Samia's daughter pregnant. Samson's sisters were condemned for their shamelessness, though not as much as were their brothers, since, being women, their activities were held to be so much the responsibility of brothers. One may speculate that, had the educated brother offered compensation to the girl's father, he might have been excused the more normal requisite of marrying her on the grounds of his claim that she was too inferior for him, and so would have been allowed to defect from an expected course of action.

There are instances from other Migrant peoples of men 'wasting' their money and time, failing to get married, or living 'only' with a woman from a Host tribe. There are instances, too, of brothers failing in their obligations to each other, or of sons not sending money home to 'help' the parents. But, like deviants anywhere, offenders of this sort get improportionately large attention and are still a minority. Most men from Migrant tribes do arrange marriages at home, as the earlier figures suggest. Few of their sisters are unattached in Kampala, and the parents are not usually ignored. What these instances and cases demonstrate is something of the new pattern which is emerging. Ethnic associations have never had more than a fairly small, fluctuating membership, and so it is not easy to talk of change here. Urban brotherhood is perhaps the relationship, or really the field of relationships, considered to have changed most.

As Epstein notes, kinship in town becomes synonomous with brotherhood.[1] Home ties or mere ethnic relatedness are emphasized not necessarily with reference to consanguinity. Brotherhood, like kinship, is an ideology used for ordering social relationships. In town this ordering may be quickly followed by a re-ordering, and then by another, so that conflicts and divisions among people may shift rapidly yet still be expressed in the name of brotherhood. The relative constants among Migrant peoples in town are marriage and the status of women. The variables are the relationships of brotherhood, which may be with full or half siblings, cousin, or clansmen. Merging with them sometimes in terminology[2] and very much in practice are ordinary friendships, based perhaps on a common home location or tribe or on chance acquaintanceship at workplace, in a bar, or in the neighbourhood.

Ideology of Brotherhood

The following two detailed cases show how a series of connected disputes among a small network of Luo were manifestly over definitions of brotherhood, but that their latent issues were over the right to act independently in town of those who impose themselves as kin, or brothers.

The first case involves the same Otieno referred to many times already.

A case of kinship 'denial'

Otieno's sister, *Margaret*, as the eldest girl of the family, was the first to be married. She was also the first, by virtue of her marriage, to leave the Luo homestead and go to town. Her husband, *Ogola*, is of Sakwa location. He chose to go to Kampala in 1955 and after spending some time in a suburb managed to rent a Shs. 17/– house in Lower Nakawa. Ogola was a semi-skilled artisan, but in addition to this ran a shop at Kiswa. His shop was not very successful, however, and he was not well off.

In 1956 Otieno, through correspondence, arranged to lodge with his brother-in-law, Ogola, in order to find work in Kampala. He was given food and accommodation free of charge until he found a job after a few months, at which point he began paying his contribution. He had seven years of education, which was a reasonable level in those days, was intelligent and was soon able to find a good job as a clerk. His income was in no time at all much higher than Ogola's. Following a pattern, he shortly moved out and went to live with an unrelated bachelor at Naguru, in a far more expensive house. After a year he himself was able to rent a house back at Nakawa, but this time in Upper Nakawa. His brother, John, immediately junior to him, but some twelve years younger, joined him then, in 1957. He was eleven and had come to receive education at a Kampala school at the suggestion of his father. It fell on Otieno as the eldest son in employment to pay his fees.

Onyango is Otieno's father's sister's son, or, in sociological terminology, his patrilateral cross-cousin. In 1958 Otieno was this time obliged to accommodate Onyango, a sixteen-year-old. Onyango's father, an uneducated man, had refused to continue paying his son's school fees, yet had acquired a fourth wife and shop. His mother had suggested to her brother, Otieno's father, that her son also be allowed to study in Kampala under his cousin's auspices. Otieno was unable to pay any more school fees and advised his cousin to get a job, which he did.

Both cousins were doing well at work and in their personal relationship. They agreed in November, 1959, to go into a partnership and set up a shop at Kiswa, hiring one side of Ogola's shop. Otieno put Shs. 600/– and Onyango Shs. 200/– to make up their joint capital, and it was agreed that Otieno's wife should help in running the shop. They agreed also to pay Ogola Shs. 100/– a month rent, 'because many people used to come'. They sold greengrams, beans, sugar, maize flour, sorghum for *malwa* beer, cooking fat, matches, paraffin, fresh milk, hard-boiled eggs 'for the drinkers nearby', salt, bread and buns.

The whole venture was to provide incomes supplementary to their wages at work. At the end of the first month there was a net profit of Shs. 200/–. Otieno 'borrowed' most of this for an urgent visit home and stocks were not replenished for the following month, at the end of which there was almost no net profit. For the third month Ogola demanded an increase in rent to Shs. 150/–, having seen much of his own clientele diverted to them. Otieno had replaced some though not all of the money borrowed and they managed to make a profit of Shs. 50/– for the fourth month. At the beginning of the fifth month Otieno's mother came to Kampala and demanded that he build her a house at home with a corrugated-iron roof, or provide her with money for the work to be done. She is the only wife, a 'modern' woman, who frequently aspired to such 'luxuries'. Otieno could hardly refuse a request from his mother, who had arrived in person in Kampala and who could see with her own eyes that by local standards he was not badly off. From his own savings and from an unknown profit from the shop at the end of the fifth month he gave her the required amount.

Onyango had been conscious of his juniority in all senses. He was younger, had been entrusted to Otieno by their parents, and lived in Otieno's house. But he made his own investigations and claimed that Shs. 2,000/– were unaccounted for, more or less accusing Otieno of bad management. Otieno, after studying the figures, agreed that this amount was missing from their books, but explained the innumerable pressures he had been subject to. Onyango was not prepared to listen to excuses, legitimate or otherwise, and took the opportunity to air his grievances. He explained how he had often used some of his own monthly salary from work to buy supplies for the shop. He then incensed Otieno with his remark, 'What would you do now if I asked you to give me my share?' Otieno resented this impeachment of his authority and seniority and angrily retorted that Onyango's residence as a 'visitor' in his house did not give Onyango the right to question or charge him like that. Onyango warned that he would not continue to 'work for nothing'. He added also that Otieno's wife would use milk, sugar and bread from the shop for her children while both men were at work. This touched on a sensitive matter between his wife and Otieno, who had recently discovered Shs. 10/– in her possession which she had wanted to send to her mother. Otieno ended the argument by refusing to say more, but the resentment between them remained.

Onyango's position was not a strong one. As he himself put it, he knew very few people in Kampala with whom he could lodge and, anyway, feared very much what the parents would say if he left Otieno, 'for it was Otieno who had allowed me to come here and get a job'. Otieno's many activities in his trade union and other associations allowed him less time than Onyango to mind the shop. Onyango came to be regarded by customers and neighbours around as the sole owner. They expressed surprise that one so young should have done so well, while his 'brother', Otieno, was never there. Otieno got to hear of this and resented it. He accused Onyango of being an upstart.

Midway through the next month Onyango paid Ogola some outstanding rent, and asked Otieno to discuss the business's accounts. A meeting was therefore arranged between Otieno and Onyango, and with Margaret, Otieno's sister, in their shop side. Margaret had asked to be present because she wanted to accuse Onyango of siphoning some of her custom. She, it should be noted, ran Ogola's shop for most of the day. This diversion of custom was perhaps inevitable while Onyango was able to help Otieno's wife in their shop in the evenings. They sold many of the same things, certainly such basics as maize flour, beans and sugar, which bring in most money, and their advantage was that two can serve customers more quickly than one.

Ogola himself was not there 'because he was not concerned with this family matter'. Otieno also accused Onyango of spreading rumours that the shop was his, even though the licence was in Otieno's name and he was the principal 'shareholder'. Onyango claimed that it was necessary to tell people it was his shop because he was the only one of the two men who worked in it. He claimed that his technique was to be friendly with many people and so attract them to 'his' shop.

Otieno and Margaret moved to the point of the meeting and said that if Onyango wanted his original share he had better take it and leave the partnership. Onyango replied that he would leave but would not even bother to take his share. He had been greatly offended by a remark at this point by Margaret that he was 'only a Kabar [his exogamous clan]', which had the meaning, it was explained, that he was unrelated to them [of the Kamagaga clan]. A further explanation was that 'it is very bad in Luo customs to deny a close relationship, and to call a man by his clan name is as an enemy. It means that he [Onyango] can marry Otieno's daughter, but in fact he cannot [because they are already cousins].'[3]

Onyango contacted his mother by writing to a friend at home and told her of this 'abuse' and 'denial'. The mother went to consult her own mother, the only one of Onyango's two real grandmothers then alive, and discovered that Onyango had already written to her brother, Otieno's father. The grandmother 'cried' and said she would have come herself to Kampala but was too old, and Onyango's mother came instead, after expressing her view of the seriousness of the matter to Otieno's father. In Kampala she tackled Otieno, accusing him, not Margaret, of denying he was Onyango's relative, 'and yet you called him here, are living with him and are in business together'. Otieno disclaimed any part in the 'abuse', but his brother, John, and his wife both agreed that there had been bad feeling between them and that references to Onyango's clanship had been made. Otieno, whether in confession or an attempt to appease his aunt, apologized and said that he didn't want Onyango to leave the partnership. However, Onyango refused to re-enter the business, though he was obliged to continue living in Otieno's house. Otieno soon gave up the shop. Ogola followed not long afterwards.

This crisis occurred early in 1960. From then on Onyango made much more effort than previously to cultivate friendships, which tended to be among other Luo. Halfway through the year he managed to lodge with one of these friends, an unmarried Luo of Lower Nakawa, and so took a more positive step on his road to independence. When he left Otieno, he was at pains to point out that he was leaving to allow them more space in the small house, and that he was grateful for two years' lodging. They parted company ostensibly in amiable spirit, though ill-feeling between them persisted.

There are at least three themes in this case. One is of the quest for individual independence. Onyango recognized but resented his urban and kinship minority. As the quarrel between him and Otieno developed, Onyango widened his field of relationships, eventually moving to lodge with a newly made friend.

A second connnected theme concerns actual physical movement as a complement to status differentiation. The movements are of two types: from 'brother' to a friend or another, less closely related 'brother'; and from a lower- to higher-status locality. Otieno had moved from his brother-in-law after improving his job and income. Both themes indicate entry into and participation in the urban status system. Prestige symbols of the system such as renting a house in your own name, the area in which you live, whether you can afford to frequent 'European' bottle-beer bars or drink only traditional liquor (not yet mentioned), and your circle of friends, are important attributes of differences in income, occupation and education.

The third theme concerns the ideological limiting factors of the first two. 'Brothers' are expected to stay together but the status system pulls them apart. Sanctions of disapproval or their threat may have some effect. Onyango was careful to avoid offending Otieno when he moved, fearing the condemnation of home people. Otieno felt the pressures from home severely and was crippled financially. He could not refuse his mother's request after she herself came to Kampala. The 'abuse' of clanship and the 'denial' of kinship or brotherhood had repercussions at home and brought Onyango's mother to town.

The case brings in the first detailed reference to the economic position of Luo in Kampala East. Before Uganda's independence Ganda and Luo were the two main ethnic groups owning or hiring shops, bars, and stalls in the ward. I was unable to get a precise breakdown of all such business and other property in the ward by tribe of owner and/or occupier. But the two areas of Kiswa and Nakawa market, the latter in a Ganda sub-county but socially part of the city ward, can be given as probably good guides of Kampala East generally. At Kiswa 141 houses, bars and shops were owned by Ganda, 44 by Luo, and 38 by other tribespeople. The houses were either four- or six-roomed and were let out at from Shs. 25/- to 45/-, depending on whether the house was mud and wattle or of permanent structure. The two bars at Nakawa and Naguru were owned by the prominent Luo who stood as an independent municipal council candidate in 1962. Most of the shops on the estates were owned by Luo. Reliable figures were difficult to get, one reason being the fear by Kenyans that they would in some way be dispossessed. So widespread was this fear that shortly before and after independence a number of Luo sold their bars and shops, though few, if any, seemed to sell their houses

At Nakawa market, 65 stalls and shops were hired by Ganda, mostly women, except for Ganda Muslim males who operated butcheries, 31 Luo men, though their wives usually ran them, 9 by Luhya, again hired by husbands but in a few cases run by wives, 9 by Toro, including three men, 3 by Nubi males and one by a Gisu male. Ganda were thus numerically dominant, though, before independence Luo owned or ran most of the few lucrative businesses, such as bars and the larger shops. While only these few were economic assets of any significance, it is perhaps obvious though worthwhile to note that the 'big men' in Kampala East, such as the Luo mentioned, certain other Luo, the Naguru Alur councillor, and a few others, constituted the core of owners of such property. It is worthwhile noting, too, that a number of these Luo had positions of leadership in the Luo community, either through the Luo Union or informally.

In the case above, Otieno, Onyango and Ogola typified a fluctuating number of Luo in the years before independence who operated at a much lower profit level than the 'big men'. They either gave up their businesses after a few months or years for lack of sufficient returns or in bankruptcy, or because they felt their futures in Uganda were insecure.

Life histories of Luo in Kampala East reveal a large number who have tried their hands at some type of business, most failing sooner or later. The smaller businesses, such as fish and vegetable stalls, minor shops, 'laundries', and others, frequently depended on an ethnic clientele, not merely Luo, but Luo of a specific location or even clan.

A person of your own home location may be regarded as a type of relative in town if he is linked to you in some activity, such as the inter-location football leagues among Luo and Luhya, or simply as a neighbour-cum-friend. Many clan and location associations have been formed among both peoples for the ostensible purpose of mutual aid or for entering a representative team in the soccer tournament. A number have collected funds and started a business, perhaps a shop, a money-lending syndicate, or a taxi service, with the initial idea of using the ready-made clientele of location or clan, depending on numbers available, and gradually extending it to others. A few have been remarkably successful, while the vast majority fold up after a very short while, to be followed months later by a new group of men acting in the name of the same home area and following a similar policy.

The disputes between members of a failing business of this sort are very frequently expressed in terms of neglected 'kin' obligations. Treasurers run off with the money and are accused of neglecting their clansmen, or 'brothers'. In the case just given the expression was the other way round, that is, there was a denial of kinship recognition and obligations, since the two partners were of different clans. Margaret obliquely appealed to her full brother to help her by eliminating his partner who had stolen her custom.

The basic point here is that most marginal profit businesses fail, much sooner than is anticipated, and that, because relatives are commonly brought in as partners or assistants, the inevitable final dispute is expressed in terms of kinship in a sometimes very extended sense. This is why Luo make remarks to the effect that 'brothers' cannot be trusted and should not be brought into businesses. Yet so many continue to be so, partly because the pressures and common interests of home require it of them.

Kinship is a reference system which operates fairly efficiently for social relationships in the rural area, at least in an area where the basically subsistence economy is no more than supplemented by wage-earned incomes. But in town its looseness for reference purposes has as many disadvantages as advantages. It is useful in shortening social distance by reducing large numbers of people to a vague and variable status of brother. But in the more enduring ties it limits freedom of choice and action. This, I have tried to explain, is much more the case for Migrants than Host people.

Among the Kenyans, and here I must continue to concentrate on Luo, I suggest that urban kinship as an ideology was even more emphasized as a means of maintaining a wide and effective network of associates around any one person. I continue the story of Otieno and Onyango in another lengthy case which shows further how this ideology operates and what the true issues are.

A Luo Network

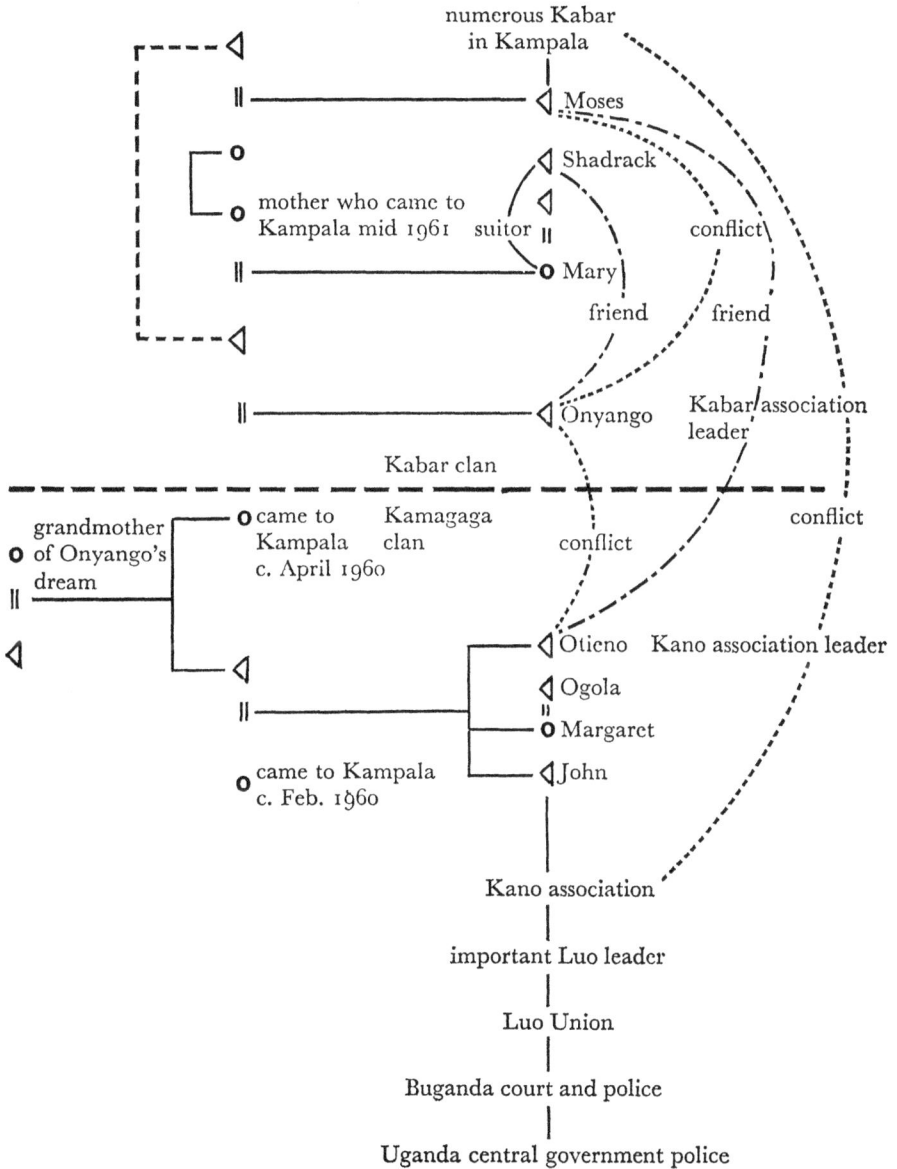

numerous Kabar
in Kampala

Moses

Shadrack

mother who came to   suitor
Kampala mid 1961

conflict

Mary

friend   friend

Onyango   Kabar association
leader

Kabar clan

grandmother   came to   Kamagaga
of Onyango's   Kampala   clan   conflict   conflict
dream   c. April 1960

Otieno   Kano association leader

Ogola

Margaret

came to Kampala
c. Feb. 1960   John

Kano association

important Luo leader

Luo Union

Buganda court and police

Uganda central government police

A case of a Luo network in action

It will be remembered that Onyango left Otieno to lodge with a Luo friend in about the middle of 1960. This friend joined the Kenya police force in October and was sent to Kibuli police training school. Onyango stayed on in his house as 'illegal tenant', paying the rent and pretending to neighbours whom he could not trust to keep a confidence that his friend was on leave. As is usual in such cases he was found out, in March 1961. He believed, again as is usual, that an enemy realized that his friend had moved permanently after such a long time and told the estate manager. Onyango then went to lodge with a clansman, *Moses*, also of Lower Nakawa. Onyango said he would normally have asked this clansman for lodging space the previous year when he needed it, but at that time Moses was 'walking with Otieno' and Onyango feared an extension of his bad relationship with his cousin. But, by this time, Moses and Otieno had broken off their friendship.

During his time with Moses, Onyango came to know a man who was to become a very firm friend. This was *Shadrack*, a Luo of Upper Nakawa, who worked as a survey assistant in a government department and who had acquired local renown for his excellent carpentry which he did as a side-line. Onyango came to order some furniture from him and paid cash in advance. Otieno, whose financial difficulties had not yet left him, happened to be owing Shadrack money for an article of furniture already acquired, and Shadrack mentioned this to Onyango. With common ill-feelings towards him, they had a backbiting session at Otieno's expense, which served as a prelude to their friendship.

Onyango was still lodging with Moses when the latter and Otieno renewed their friendship and started going to bars again, something which Onyango 'had not yet learned'. Onyango had Shadrack's permission to lodge with him in order to escape what he sensed was a conspiracy to discredit him, but hesitated to do so lest he offend his clansman, Moses. Onyango was at the time trying to establish a Kabar clan association and had already put out a few feelers to see what interest there was among Kabar. Moses had been in Kampala since 1952 and had established a Kabar association in earlier years. This had long since dissolved, due to the dispersal of some members to Kilembe mines in western Uganda, but still conferred on him the rights to be consulted and to arbitrate. It was important, therefore, that Onyango should not offend Moses if he was to succeed in setting up the association.

Eventually, with Moses' concurrence, Onyango managed to get

agreement among Kabar in Kampala to start an association, in which he was chosen as initial leader, even though young and unmarried. The basis of the agreement was dissatisfaction among Kabar with the larger location association called Kano. The association nevertheless looked like going the way of most and collapsing before it had really begun. But a dramatic issue arose which not only gave Onyango the opportunity to utilize clan or 'brother' ideology in the interests of the association, but also gave him 'legitimate' reason to break with Moses and lodge with his unrelated friend, Shadrack.

Mary, also of the Kabar clan, was with her husband in Makerere Mjini, a small settlement within the Kampala city boundary and near the university college. Her husband, a Luo from Karachuonyo location, had not paid any more than two cows bridewealth to her parents, in spite of the fact that he had obliged them to return many more cows to Mary's previous husband after 'seducing' her from the latter.

Mary's mother came peaceably enough to make polite enquiries and suggestions regarding the bridewealth. She had been shocked by the abuse she had received. Mary's husband made no attempt to hide his Ganda lovers nor his liking for *mwenge muganda* (a Ganda beer) from his mother-in-law, 'which was a great shame to her'. He evaded discussion of bridewealth money, *pesa keny*, and, when the time came for the mother to leave for home, did not offer money for her fare. He was alleged to have said, 'Take your daughter and get out and go to one of your Kabar relatives'. Mary and her mother therefore came and stayed at Moses' house in Nakawa, the latter then having to lodge with a friend. Moses' mother and Mary's mother are full sisters, and he was the closest relative in Kampala.

During this time Onyango had been at home, having been called by telegram to a funeral, an event which cost him over Shs. 400/– in ceremonial and other expenses. Mary was his 'sister' and though he had heard that her mother had gone on a goodwill visit to Kampala, he knew nothing of the developing drama until he returned to Moses' house in Nakawa. Moses had done nothing about the affair, but Onyango immediately wrote to all the fifteen or twenty Kabar in Kampala, requesting an urgent meeting to which Mary's husband was to be summoned. Within a few days, and two weeks after Mary's husband had dismissed her and her mother from his house, the meeting was held in one of the Nakawa ironing rooms.

Twelve to fifteen Kabar attended the meeting. Present also were Mary's husband and Otieno, 'who had come as the close friend of Moses'. Mary was asked to give her version of what had happened, followed by her mother. The mother made it clear now that she didn't want Mary to marry 'such a bad man', and would refund him his two cows immediately they returned home. The husband asked for forgiveness and said that he didn't want to lose Mary and would send money for bridewealth very soon.

A number of older Kabar spoke first in reply. One told the husband that if he had come to the meeting with money worth two cattle to give them, he would have been forgiven and the whole affair looked on as a common husband/wife dispute, but, as it was, he hadn't even brought the mother's fare for her homeward journey. Another said, 'If you were wise you would have at least given the mother and wife their fares home, but they have had to stay with Moses for two weeks, and he has been supplying their food. You dismissed them as strangers and didn't even go to see how your wife was until today. I am an old man and if Mary was my daughter, I couldn't allow her to be your wife because you are very rough and have no respect. But I refrain from further opinion because I don't really know what is on the mother's mind.'

Onyango then played a useful conciliatory role. He pointed out, 'we have given Mary and her mother help here, because she is related to us and so has this right to Kabar help. If I were Moses I would demand compensation [using the word *faini* or fine] for the expenses and inconvenience you have caused me. The best thing for you to do is to bring their fares and then to go home and discuss the matter with Mary's father. It would be up to you if your parents also attend.' The mother accepted this proposal, and the others consented too. Another man interceded at this stage and suggested a severer requirement, that he should bring money for two cows as well as the fares by a specific date, failing which Mary should be married to someone else. The others stood by Onyango's suggestion and the matter ended there.

Before adjourning the meeting, the present association's first membership dues were collected, a total of Shs. 39/-. The older man who spoke second was made treasurer after agreement that it was too much to expect younger men to take on the responsibility (a reference to the frequency with which treasurers, who tend to be relatively young in urban associations, are accused of absconding with funds).

The husband failed to bring the money for fares within the week allowed him. Mary and her mother stayed for a further month at Moses' until the Kabar association paid money for the mother to be sent home. It was explained that, according to Luo custom, if a mother comes to visit her daughter and both are discharged by the husband, then the mother must leave for home a little while before her daughter. It was agreed that Mary should follow after four days.

But, when Onyango tried to arrange for Mary's departure, Moses declared his intention of finding a husband for Mary in the town. He claimed that, as Mary had no close brothers of her own, he could deal with the matter much more efficiently this way. Onyango angrily retorted that this was contrary to the Kabar agreement, and accused Moses of having been influenced in this decision by Otieno. Moses, to whom had been entrusted the girl's fare, refused to send her, and Onyango in annoyance immediately moved to lodge with his friend, Shadrack.

Onyango called another Kabar meeting. He explained that the conflict was now between Mary's closest relative and the rest of the Kabar community in Kampala. But the Kabar decided that, though they disapproved of Moses' individual handling of the case, simply as her closest relative in the town, he could not really be stopped. During this period of rebellion, Moses had frequently been seen in the company of Otieno and Mary's husband, and Onyango accepted the suggestion by a few Kabar that the three were trying to reinstate Mary with the husband, even though she had 'been moaning and crying in refusal' and wanted to return home to her parents. Onyango was advised by Kabar that if he wanted to help Mary he should do so through the Luo Union, because the Kabar association was 'not allowed' to meddle too much in the domestic affairs of a man and his 'sister'.

Onyango thus had their blessing if no longer their aid, and decided to take the issue up alone. He, too, adopted the policy of trying to marry Mary off in town, claiming that he would get her parent's permission to do this. He asked Shadrack, who had had a series of failed marriages or attempts to marry, if he would take Mary as his wife. By appeasing Moses with a 'gift', Onyango managed to arrange for Shadrack and Mary to meet, and both accepted the idea of marriage.

The arrangement seemed to be developing smoothly until Mary failed to arrive back at Moses' house after an evening out with Shadrack, supposedly chaperoned by Onyango, her 'brother'. Moses was very angry and thought he had been duped by the trio. Otieno, with whom Moses was still friendly, listened to Moses' grievance. Onyango had not after all thought it necessary to contact the Luo Union, as he had envisaged an early settlement of the case. But Otieno saw the latest event as illegitimate interference by Onyango and felt justified in bringing the larger Kano location association, of which he was secretary, into the affair.

Kano is the area of the east and west locations of the same name. Kabar and a number of other clans are local subdivisions, sometimes called sub-locations, of East and West Kano. Some thirty-four locations make up the whole area of Luoland in the Kenya districts of central and south Nyanza. In Kampala and other towns, certain location members form their own associations which acknowledge some subordination to the all-embracing Luo Union. The clan associations are given less official recognition by the Union though they are often quite strong. There is thus a three-tiered pyramidal structure of associations with the Union at the top, the location associations intermediary, and those of clans at the bottom. Some clan associations split into two, forming a fourth level, though instances of this are very few, due, more than anything, to an insufficient number of clansmen in town for this to seem worthwhile.

Kano association itself had had problems of organization, often between certain members of the East and West locations, who had wanted separate associations. But they were united in their opposition to Onyango and his breakaway Kabar association. One of the Kano association leaders was also a leader in the Luo Union, and he echoed disapproval of Onyango there.

The Luo Union, represented by this prominent Kano leader, and Kano association thus supported Moses in his attempt to regain control of his sister. They first deplored that a man should allow his clansman's close 'sister' to be 'seduced' by a complete 'stranger'. They also stated that Mary should not be married to a man such as Shadrack, of Alego location, but 'should be kept for one of themselves to marry' if reinstatement with her husband was not possible. It should be noted here that Shadrack was secretary of his Alego location association, had played in the Alego soccer team, and that Alego and Kano were keen rivals in the Kampala Luo league championship.

Otieno and Moses felt that at least they had the moral support of a large group in opposition to Onyango and his group. They persisted in their attempt to reconcile Mary and her husband. Mary's 'seduction' by Shadrack, aided by Onyango, gave them the opportunity to confront these two openly. They enlisted another Kano man, of Otieno's clan, and marched to Shadrack's house armed with sticks. Mary, Shadrack, Onyango and the latter's Luhya girlfriend, also Mary's friend, were there, but the two men refused to be drawn into a fight. It is not the custom to enter your 'enemy's' house and fight, so Moses, Otieno and their aide left as angrily as they came. During their time at Shadrack's they had warned Mary to get back to Moses' house. Mary's Luhya friend retorted, 'Mary, you are being controlled like a child by your brothers', a remark which undoubtedly settled Mary's hesitancy and encouraged her to answer Moses that she would go back in her own good time.

After withdrawing, Otieno and Moses agreed, reluctantly, to contact the central government police and try to have Shadrack arrested for having 'abducted' another man's wife. Mary's husband, who during this time had been waiting in Moses' house, was required by the police when they arrived to give a statement. The procedure was lengthy and visibly obvious, and Shadrack was able to get clear of his house by the time the police knocked on his door. They found only Onyango and Mary there. Mary explained that she was only visiting her brother, Onyango, and that she had not been 'abducted' or seduced by another man. The police refused to take any steps unless evidence of criminal action was produced.

Onyango had written to Mary's father, explaining that, contrary to the conditions of the original Kabar agreement, Moses wanted Mary to go back to her husband. Onyango and Shadrack sent Mary to her parents the day after the police had come. She returned after three days with a letter from her father giving rights of guardianship over Mary to Onyango, and allowing her to marry Shadrack.

Meanwhile the chairman of Kano association, who was still under the impression that Mary had been 'abducted', had contacted the local Ganda sub-county chief (of Nakawa *gombolola*), 'whom he knew', and had been offered Buganda *askari* or tribal police to arrest Shadrack. Mary had managed to run away, but Shadrack was taken to the *gombolola* court, where Onyango eventually explained that the central government police had dismissed the case. The Nakawa estate manager, a Ganda, confirmed this. Onyango produced Mary's father's letter as additional proof and the charge against Shadrack was dismissed. A copy of the court's judgement was sent to Mary's parents, and Shadrack and Mary were finally allowed to marry on payment of *pesa ayie*, or agreement money, of Shs. 100/– by Shadrack to her parents.

Much later when Onyango had secured his own house in Upper Nakawa, he had a dream in which his maternal grandmother appeared. She was the grandmother who had figured as a strong voice of disapproval in his dispute with Otieno over the shop, but had since died. In the dream she urged Onyango to reconcile his long-standing rivalry with his cousin. She said that it was 'immoral' for Luo 'brothers' to be enemies, and that 'if Luo brothers are not united what will become of the name?' (i.e. of the family, including Onyango and Otieno's two collateral lines of which she was the originator). The dream made a deep impression on Onyango, and the two cousins agreed to settle their differences.

The case illustrates how the ideology of kinship or brotherhood in town is an extremely diffuse system of norms which may be used by an individual to suit his own purposes as the occasion demands. It allows conflicting though not logically contradictory evaluations of the same situation. The main problem is the struggle to acquire legitimacy for a status and line of action. There was no 'right' or 'wrong' in this case. Moses was Mary's closest relative and on this basis had legitimacy for doing what he thought was best. Onyango saw adherence to Mary's and her mother's wishes as the legitimacy for his actions, endorsed even more by an agreement among the majority of Mary's clansmen in Kampala. The Luo Union and Kano association did not consider recognition of the breakaway Kabar clan association as justified, and on this ground felt they had legitimacy for opposing its formation and its leader.

The ultimate source of legitimacy, the State, in the form of the central government police, was called upon as a last resort and answered ineffectively the need for a solution of the crisis. The Buganda *gombolola* court, basically a tribal institution equipped for dealing with such matters, resolved the dispute as a civil case. But it was Onyango's dream which spurred him to end his enmity with his cousin.

All the factions were claiming to support the ideology of dutiful brotherhood, yet it was in the course of the dispute that a number of claims for personal independence were realized. Onyango progressively moved from cousin to friend, to clansman, to friend and finally to his own house. Friendships, that between Onyango and Shadrack, and that between Otieno and Moses, transcended certain obligations of brotherhood, and in reality were another example of the quest for freedom from kin. The Kabar clansmen were able to express dissatisfaction with the larger location association and asserted their own independence, if only temporarily. Even Mary allowed herself to be encouraged by her Luhya friend and took her own stand in the issue.

In a restricted sense the case reasserted the solidarity of Luo in Kampala over the marriages of their sisters, in spite of an appearance of anything but solidarity. The basic desirability that Luo girls should be married by Luo men was never challenged, and was, if anything, underlined. Perhaps more importantly, the dispute, dragging on for months as it did, reaffirmed a wide network of ties, creating loyalties, breaking them again, but at least keeping people in constant contact with each other.

If the spasmodic repetition of such cases among a network roughly of the same people can be imagined, it can be inferred that there is an institutional mechanism at work. The mechanism sustains the existence of a fairly close-knit or effective network of men. The ideological content of the network is brotherhood, while the pragmatic is the struggle for recognition of personal independence, which is part of the general struggle for socio-economic status outlined in earlier chapters.

This close-knit network is larger than the family and, as illustrated in the case, has many links with higher sources of authority in the city. As Bott has suggested for a different situation,[4] it thus mediates between the individual and the wider society, rather in the way that relationships of locality and neighbourhood do. For Host people, a contrasting status of women and a different concept of brotherhood do not provide dramatic issues of this kind around which networks are mobilized. Their whole system of sanctions among kin is diffuse to begin with and allows more individual choice.

NOTES

[1] A. L. Epstein, 1961, op. cit., p. 49 '. . . at its furthest extension kinship becomes synonomous with and gives expression to the fundamental values of brotherhood'.

[2] Among Luo, *omera*, a general term for 'my brother', can be applied to a friend of any tribe, and is distinct from *owadwa*, 'my close brother', where agnatic or collateral ties are recognized, and *ora*, 'someone who can marry my sister'. The Acholi use *omera*, *watta*, and *ora* similarly, and other Nilotes have the same or similar forms.

[3] Luo working in Mombasa express horror at the practice among some coastal peoples of marrying cousins on their mother's side.

[4] E. Bott, 1957, *Family and Social Network*, Tavistock Publications, London.

CHAPTER VII

CHOICE AMONG KIN

Host Society

It is important to observe the different concept of brotherhood among Host people, who do not see it in terms of an ideology involving the same persons over recurring issues of marriage and the status of women. Their special land-tenure systems and established cash-crop economy enable higher status townsmen such as live at Naguru to capitalize within the rural structure. They are less restricted in realizing personal ambitions by an extended family and house/property complex. Brothers can plan their futures, including purchase of land on which they may grow cotton and coffee as cash crops, without reference to each other. Nor do a man and wife's respective families exert strong influence on their relationship as among Migrants. The following are two examples of how people may be affected by these factors.

1. Edward, a Soga of 25, living at Naguru, left school in 1956 after eight years' education. He then attended a technical institute in Kampala East for two years, after which he was employed by the Ministry of Works in Kampala as a vehicle mechanic. Towards the end of his course at the technical institute he came to know a Soga girl through her brother, a friend at the institute. The girl lived with Edward, a child was born, their relationship developed, and five years after they first lived together they had a church or 'ring' wedding. No bridewealth was given to the girl's parents. The couple gave two reasons for this. One was that the girl's brother had considered that his friendship with Edward obviated the necessity for bridewealth, and the other was that the parents professed to have simply come to 'accept him as a son, while he has given our daughter a good home'.

Edward comes from near Iganga in Busoga, but has built a house some six miles from Jinja, the capital town of his tribal district. He continues to work in Kampala and live at Naguru, regarding his house near Jinja as an investment and security for the future as well as currently awarding him prestige. Three brothers have also built houses outside Jinja. But their father continues to live near Iganga.

'He has much land there but it is not known to whom this land will go. Probably the three brothers who are still at school and not yet independent will have the land to help them in case they do not succeed in their education.' Edward expressed the view that since uneducated or semi-educated Soga could earn reasonable money in Busoga on their farms through growing cotton, coffee and bananas, only the 'educated' Soga (i.e. with not less than eight years' education), who could obtain fairly well-paid jobs, found it profitable to have farms near town and grow cash crops as well as maintaining their jobs.

2. Musoke, a middle-aged Ganda and former neighbour of Edward, lives in a Shs. 73/- house at Naguru. His father is a *kibanja* (leased plot) holder in Masaka district, but has only a small plot. Musoke regarded himself as fortunate in having been given eight years of schooling. He left school in 1936 and joined the Uganda police in the same year as a constable. He worked his way up to the rank of sub-inspector, and in 1950 retired from the force. Then he invested the money he had accumulated from his wages in a shop at Nakulabye in Mengo. After initial success with the shop he began to supply more and more customers on credit. This applied especially to a petrol pump which he had had sited outside his shop by an oil company. He referred to the customers as 'big men' since many had high positions in the Kabaka's government or in commerce. His credit accumulated, but so many of his debtors defaulted in payment to him that he became bankrupt in 1956. He now shows a bitter dislike for 'those people at Mengo' on both personal and politico-religious grounds, being an ardent Catholic and supporter of the then opposition Democratic Party. After having to give up his shop he obtained a reasonably well-paid job as a clerk in the city council and eventually moved to his present house at Naguru.

While his shop was still flourishing he had bought fifteen acres of land a few miles from Kampala and now refers to himself as *mutaka* (meaning in this case 'landlord'). He employed labourers and had coffee planted on 3½ acres, reaping a substantial yield five years later. He intends to develop the rest of the land when he permanently retires from urban wage employment and has sufficient capital.

His two brothers are 'just cultivating' leased plots which they obtained independently of each other and of their father at some twelve miles distance from each other and nearer the town of Masaka than their father's plot. Musoke is satisfied at having bettered them.

His wife remains on his land with nine of their eleven children still at school. Of the other two, both daughters, one is a typist in Nairobi and the other a teacher in Kampala. Both are unmarried. Musoke expresses no more than a concern that each of his daughters has 'men friends' from different tribes.

Both Edward and Musoke showed reluctance to settle permanently on their father's land. Indeed, the apprehension of being victims of preferential inheritance precludes this prospect. As members of hierarchical societies, with their division, among others, between large cash-cropping land-holders and subsistence smallholders, Edward and Musoke were able to surpass their fathers. The independent acquisition of land by a son is, of course, much easier in Buganda, where something approaching *de jure* freehold land tenure pertains, but plenty of land changes hands in *de facto* sale and lease among the higher status of other Host peoples.

This individual acquisition of land during a man's successful urban career results not only in the spatial separation of sons from their fathers but also in the spatial separation of brothers themselves, so that ties of common locality loosen. Moreover, for Ganda at least, land boundaries are on the whole indisputable. Landowners have theirs validated by the *mailo* land tenure system Agreement of 1900, and tenants' boundaries are protected by the Busulu and Envujo Law of 1927. Most disputes are not over boundaries but are over land-inheritance, which of course disrupts the unity of the sibling group. This contrasts with the situation among most Migrant societies where major land disputes are usually over a local agnatic descent group's boundaries in face of claims by an adjacent group. Such disputes emphasize the solidarity of each competing group. This solidarity obtains between descent group members in town as much as between those at home, since land is inherited by all sons, who are therefore equally concerned if the dispute and some land are lost.

The possibility of an early dispersion of siblings and their concomitant relative independence of each other among Host people, as illustrated in the above two cases, contrasts with the desire of Luo and other Migrants to build 'permanent' houses on their 'fathers' land'.

Less Effective Agnatic Ties

For Host 'brothers' and agnates living in town, then, the chances of their being united with a common interest in the family or lineage land are relatively small. I do not suggest that 'brothers' are in permanent disunity, since cordial relationships are certainly the norm. But, as Edward, the Soga, put it, 'We do not expect our brothers or relatives to help us get a job, though we know a relative will help us if we are on good terms with him and if we ask for his aid. We prefer to get our job with the education we have and to make our mark independently.' And in the same breath, 'You see we are not like these Kenyans (meaning the Luo and Luhya)'. He observed that the 'Kenyans' and Acholi (including, it seemed, Lango and Alur) accommodated their 'brothers', always if they were unmarried, but often even when they were married. He noticed that even high-status people of these tribes had many 'brothers' in their households who provide domestic help in return for all sorts of aid, whereas 'we Bantu employ servants when we are able. Our brothers cannot expect to come to us just because we have money, and we cannot expect them to be servants.'[1]

Statements of this kind do disclose a difference in values, though they cannot be taken by themselves to indicate a difference in social facts. For instance, Peter's claim that individual progress is achieved 'independently' of relatives is certainly more of a value than a fact at an initial stage of a Host's urban residence and career. He, like any other migrant, is likely to seek relatives living in town as the obvious initial providers of board and lodging. But there are many cases indicating that agnatic closeness alone may be a secondary factor of choice. Many Ganda, in particular, have stressed the high potentiality of fraternal conflict as deterring the choice of residence with even full brothers. In contrast, the Luo and others, while fully admitting the often intense inter-personal rivalry of all 'brothers', stress that a new migrant is under an extremely strong moral obligation to lodge with any close agnates there may be in town, even if other non-agnatic kin are available.

There seem to be a substantial minority of Host people who, during their initial period in Kampala, lodge with maternal kin, and in exercising their greater freedom of choice, may opt to lodge with a mother's kinsman in preference even to a full sibling.[2] This, Luo tell you, would never be tolerated among themselves. They express amazement at this practice and say,

'If your father's sons [and I think this would refer also to immediate patrilateral parallel cousins] are already in town, how can you ever go first to your mother's people there?'

A Multi-tribal Network

This network diagram is intended to provide a convenient reference to most of the persons discussed in the preceding and following cases. Dates and places indicate when and where relationships were established or activated, the details for which are given in the cases.

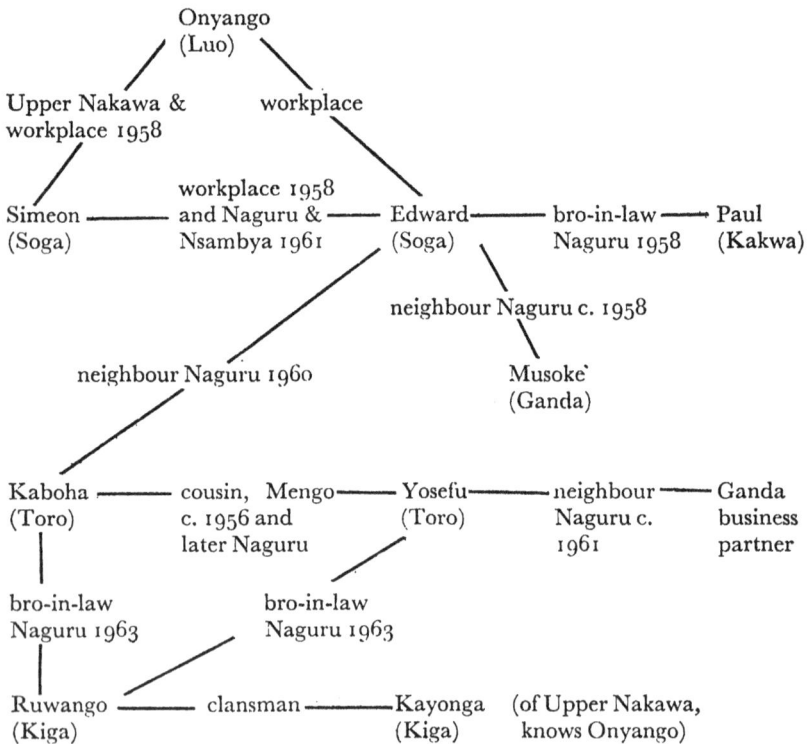

It should be noted that the above network is no more than a mesh of ties, purposive links only involving two or three persons at any one time. It contrasts with the much more *effective* Luo network illustrated in the figure on page 119. *All* persons in the latter are linked with each other through a series of overlapping activities.

Host people do, of course, utilize a large and presumably majority proportion of agnatic ties. But they are less compelled, either by rural common interests or ideology, to utilize them and forsake possibly more profitable and gratifying matrilateral ties. The substitution of some agnatic by matrilateral ties places the townsman at the centre of an urban network of bilateral kin.

Cultural Differences and Conflicts

We can observe this relatively weak emphasis on agnation among Host people, the relatively independent status of their women, and a number of other social factors by tracing the networks of relationships of some of Edward's own associates. Onyango (of the preceding chapter) was a workmate of one of these associates, a Soga called Simeon. It was through Onyango that I came to know first Simeon and later Edward and eventually the overlapping networks of each of them (see figure facing).

Onyango resists assimilation into a Soga network

Onyango and Simeon were neighbours at Upper Nakawa as well as being workmates in the stores department of the Ministry of Works in Kampala. Simeon has more education than Onyango. He had no difficulty getting his present high-grade clerical job in the Ministry of Works. He came to Kampala a year before Onyango in 1957. He spent what he called 'a dreadful year' in a suburb. He has three full brothers and a full sister and two half-brothers and two half-sisters. His father has 'divorced' his second and third wives, the mothers of Simeon's half-siblings. The eldest of Simeon's full brothers, Daniel, has School Certificate and works in the Kampala offices of the East African Railways and Harbours as an accounts clerk, earning 'good money'. This brother came to Kampala some years before Simeon. He lives at the railway workers' housing estate of Nsambya but has spent some time in Nairobi and expects to be transferred in the near future to Dar es Salaam, the capital of Tanzania. He plans to grow coffee on his father's $\frac{1}{2}$ sq. mile of land while continuing in salaried employment. Simeon lodged with a former school friend when he first came to Kampala. He claimed that he was under no obligation to stay with his brother, and provided he visited him there would be no hostility between them.

Simeon's father had sold some of his land and with the capital wished to establish a small shop in partnership with one of his lesser-educated sons in Jinja, capital of Busoga. Simeon had always admired what he regarded as Onyango's skill as a storekeeper's assistant at the Ministry of Works and maintained that it was only the Ganda supervisor's dislike of Luo that had caused him to be dismissed on the 'false' grounds of redundancy. After Simeon had moved to Naguru and after Onyango was dismissed, Simeon suggested to his father and to Onyango that the latter work as 'accounts clerk' in their shop. Simeon himself had wished no part in the business, claiming that unsuccessful, poorer relatives always begged a businessman for financial help.

Onyango saw many personal advantages of employment in Jinja where there are proportionally more Kenyans and where Swahili is more widely spoken. He believed that he could contribute considerably to the success of the business. Simeon and his Soga friends agreed that 'Kenyans' had considerable business acumen. But Onyango's relatives, his Kabar clansmen, and other Luo advised him against a partnership of this kind. They pointed out the difficulties of working among people 'not related' to oneself and of a different nationality. Onyango claimed that they were really jealous and wished they themselves either had the capital to start such a business or could receive a similar offer. Nevertheless, the sanctions of disapproval, whatever their true motives, appeared to have some effect and Onyango did not enter into the agreement proposed by Simeon. Simeon was somewhat slighted, not only at the refusal of his offer but also because he had supported Oyango throughout the period of alleged discrimination by the Ganda supervisor. Thereafter Onyango was too embarrassed to visit Simeon.

But beyond the fact that they had once had common neighbourhood and workplace ties and could reminisce on past incidents, they now shared little in common. Since coming to Naguru Simeon had mixed with a faster and heavier-spending set of friends, mostly Soga. He had also come to know intimately a very attractive Haya girl. This girl's sister was a typist in the Kampala offices of the East African Railways and Harbours and lived at Nsambya. Simeon came to know his Haya girl-friend through his brother, Daniel, who introduced them at Nsambya. The girl came to be known as Simeon's 'temporary wife' and lived with him at his Naguru house. Simeon's eldest sister's son, an eighteen-year-old student at Mengo High School, was lodging with him. Daniel often used to allow Simeon and his 'wife' to sleep at his house at Nsambya 'so as not to disturb the nephew'. Simeon stated that he would probably marry the girl. Neither he nor the girl had contacted her agnates or other kin, though Simeon was proposing to take the girl to his own house to see his parents.

Onyango's resistance to assimilation into a Soga business and social network was clearly not entirely determined by personal choice. He responded to the expectations of 'brothers' in much the same way as he had expected them to respond in his handling of Mary's case. For him, they were viable groups and effective agents of social control.

Neither Simeon, nor Musoke, the Ganda clerk, nor Edward, the Soga mechanic, expected agnates or any 'brothers' for that matter to be mobilized as groups over the social and physical movements of their womenfolk. Musoke, a middle-aged man who may be supposed to be a little more conservative than younger men of his ethnic group, expressed no more than a mild concern that his two independently earning daughters had non-Ganda men friends. He would presumably be equally or more concerned if they married any of them, which, according to the figures given above on inter-tribal marriages at Nakawa and Naguru, was certainly not unlikely. There was no question in his mind, however, of the mobilization of any relatives or others to thwart such a possibility.

Edward's case illustrated the lesser significance of bridewealth payments among Host people. The girl's brother and parents accepted Edward as a brother- and son-in-law not so much in order to fulfil a contractual agreement as to continue a prior, affectively based relationship with him. Simeon's Haya girl-friend lived with her sister. Both girls had independent status. Simeon considered marrying her, but did not consider it necessary to contact either her parents or brothers.

Marriage between a Migrant man and Host woman is one relatively enduring inter-tribal context in which obvious conflicts of values and role-expectations are felt by each spouse. This is especially so if the husband wishes to become assimilated into one of the higher strata of his wife's society but has to contend with resistance from home, and from urban relatives and fellow-tribesmen.

Edward's Migrant friend who became his brother-in-law

As mentioned, one of Simeon's friends was Edward. These two Soga were both employed in the Ministry of Works. Edward knew

Onyango, the Luo, only by sight. The other link between Simeon and Edward was the fact that the latter's wife's brother, a railway station-master, also lived at Nsambya as did Simeon's brother. This man, like Simeon, had a temporary wife, a Soga.

Edward's wife visited her brother and also another close relative at Mulago fairly frequently. But Edward only accompanied his wife on a few of these visits. He had no close relatives in Kampala. Most of his friends were at Naguru. He would go with them to the cinema, or to beer bars at the city centre or at Naguru on evenings or weekends when the wife was at Nsambya. Or he would go to these same places or to the homes of these same friends with his wife on other occasions. He frequently expressed confusion as to how much he should integrate his and his wife's social lives.

Two of his friends were of particular interest. One was Paul, a Kakwa from north-west Uganda. Kakwa share with other Migrants the general cultural characteristics outlined, but they are very few in Kampala. This fact was significant in Paul's urban activities. Paul was educated in a Catholic mission. He spoke good English, had been in Kampala for six years and was an electrician for the Uganda Electricity Board. He married Edward's mother's sister's daughter. Beforehand he had acquired fluency in Lusoga and Luganda. He explained how this process of partial assimilation occurred: 'As you know, there are very few of us Kakwa in Kampala. I had no brothers here when I came and I tended to roam about unchecked. I then came to know a Soga girl. We both used Luganda. This girl wanted to marry me, but I considered her too old and asked her to show me one of her sisters. So she took me to her home and I was accepted by her sister, who joined me in Kampala. During this time her parents asked me for Shs. 400/– dowry [the local English term for bridewealth]. But as I was only earning Shs. 400/– a month, I paid them Shs. 200/– in two instalments of Shs. 100/–. They accepted this. I now have two children. My problem now is when to take my wife to my home as the parents there wish to see her. They do not know how these Bantu girls are and may not understand her, and she is nervous of people there in the north. They wanted me to marry a Kakwa girl they had for me.'

By the time I had left the field Paul had not taken his wife home, though she had by then borne him three children. I sensed more conflict between him and his 'home people' than was immediately evident. Paul's case shows how a man of a very small Migrant tribe in Kampala is unchecked in his assimilation into one ethnic group by the absence of kin and fellow-tribesmen to 'guide' him, yet is unable fully to bridge the expectations of rural and his own chosen urban roles regarding marriage in spite of his above-average education. I give another case shortly of a Migrant, a Kiga, who married into a high stratum of Toro society and had to reformulate kin and tribal ties.

Rural-based Strata Depreciating Wider Kin Ties

Whereas at home the agnatically defined corporate groups of Migrant peoples are never consistently held to be politically and economically superior or inferior to each other, the rural-based status categories of the Host kingdoms may cut across a wider network of kin ties.

Two royal Toro with contrasting backgrounds

Edward's other neighbour and friend of particular interest is a Toro, Kaboha, who also lives at Naguru. Kaboha holds a senior position in a major international concern in Kampala. His father is a *gombolola* (sub-county) chief. His mother is a classificatory sister of the former Omukama (king) of Toro. Kaboha went to a senior secondary school in Toro, but for various reasons was unable to sit for his School Certificate. But his fluent English and royal social contacts have helped him to acquire a very well-paid position. He did not anticipate being the heir to his father's land and expected to 'buy' some himself.

After leaving school in 1954 he lived in an area of Mengo which he disliked intensely because of its 'many thieves'. Some while after he moved to Naguru and now aspires to ownership of a house at Ntinda. His relatives are physically and socially widely dispersed. Two father's brother's sons work in a Toro government ministry, but others 'have no education and are on the land'. His own five brothers have all received or are receiving senior secondary education. His father is able to afford fees for all of them. When I first met him he had not seen any close relatives, including his parents, for 2½ years.

Kaboha used to play soccer, cricket and tennis at his school and met his wife during team visits to her school near Kampala. He married her five years ago. Her father is a Ganda and her mother a Nyoro. Kaboha explained that not only were all members of the 'royal families' of the Host peoples socially very close, but 'commoners' were also, so that intermarriage among these tribes was very common and

137

not at all stigmatized. His wife has three close relatives in and around Kampala who visit them both about once every two weeks.

Kaboha has maintained an intense interest in sport, especially tennis, which he plays and watches often, usually on a weekday evening until 6.30 p.m. His wife is a typist and returns home at about 5 p.m. They have two children, 2½ and 4, who both attend the city council nursery at Naguru and are also looked after by a Ganda woman who is nurse, domestic help and cook combined. She is the 'temporary' wife of a Toro living in Lower Nakawa. Kaboha observed, like Edward, that, unlike Host people, 'the Kenyans, Acholi, and northern people' do not employ servants even when they can afford to, but 'just keep their brothers with them instead'. An interesting sidelight on their notion of status was the manner in which the servant, or *ayah*, greeted important visitors on her knees, whereas Kaboha's wife greeted them by shaking hands. Kaboha and his wife have not met their *ayah*'s husband, nor been to their house.

Kaboha did not feel Edward's dilemma regarding the extent to which his own and his wife's social lives should be integrated. Kaboha earned little more than Edward but his royal, 'élitist' background, his wife's relatively high level of education, and the fact also that she had a prestigeful job, encouraged them to share interests, visits, privileges, and obligations to a considerable extent. They both attended parties at the city centre and brushed shoulders with the capital's élite.

Kaboha had been required to pay the high bridewealth payment of three cows and Shs. 1,000/–, 'compensation to the parents for the loss of a highly educated daughter'. He emphasized that it was not recoverable under any circumstances.

Kaboha claimed not to have seen any close relatives for 2½ years. But he did see Yosefu, a distant matrilateral cousin, and Yosefu's sister, both of whom live at Naguru. Yosefu and his sister are also related to the Omukama of Toro. Their father is one of the Omukama's many patrilateral parallel cousins. But, in spite of the fact that he and his brothers hold 50 acres of land between them, he is not rich, since most of his land is let to many tenants and yields relatively small dues. He has no other occupation than that of landlord. Kaboha's father, on the other hand, not only has enough land available for growing coffee as a cash crop but also has the relatively lucrative post of *gombolola* chief. Whereas Kaboha and his brothers will all have received at least senior secondary education, Yosefu and his nine brothers and sisters have generally much less education. Yosefu has nine years of education, much more than his siblings except his sister at Naguru, who has eight years. Yosefu's adult siblings are, like Kaboha's, physically dispersed. None of them, however, have occupations of any greater standing than that of salesman in a Kampala bookshop.

Yosefu's schooling was stopped through lack of fees. He is an untrained though very competent electrician. He picked up his skills by working as an assistant to two Indians who repaired dynamos and generators. He came to Kampala in 1956 at the age of seventeen. During his early years in the town he struck up an acquaintanceship with an important Ganda, an ex-Katikiiro (prime minister) of the Buganda Lukiko (parliament). Yosefu described the man: 'He had bought shares in a major national enterprise and had a prominent position in the company. Even though I wore only shorts, this man used to give me a lift to my Asian employer's shop. He seemed to like Toro a great deal. My employers went bankrupt but he told me to apply for a job in his company as an electrician. I was given a job, passed an elementary test and received Shs. 150/– a month in the workshops. I was then promoted to sales demonstrator, then to an even better job of travelling sales representative. I reached the salary of Shs. 350/– a month. I owe much to the advice and help given me by that Ganda. I find I get on better with Ganda even than with Toro.'

While canvassing the sale of electricity in Buganda, Yosefu met and fell in love with a Ganda girl primary school-teacher. She then came to work in Kampala. They are now intending to marry. Yosefu stated that though the bridewealth asked is only Shs. 400/– the expenditure on the 'ring' wedding will be Shs. 1,400/– and it is the latter which holds up their plans. He mentioned that his royal status necessitated a lavish 'ring' wedding.

Another of Yosefu's important Ganda contacts was a self-employed man who did electrical installations in some of the many new 'modern' houses springing up in and around certain areas of Kampala. Yosefu met him when he came to buy supplies from the place at which he worked. The Ganda did not speak English but spoke Swahili and had only a few years' elementary education. He felt he lacked administrative know-how and asked Yosefu, an exceptionally intelligent man, to become a partner in his business.

This 35-year-old Ganda's life history reads sadly. His parents separated, and his father, left with some land and three houses in their home district of Masaka, sold all except a single small plot. He and his brothers became dispersed throughout Buganda. They severed relations with their father for having sold 'their' property and lost contact with each other. The Ganda's wife left him for an affluent Ganda clerk some years before Yosefu met him. He has retained his two boys, nine and seven years of age. For at least nine years he has lived at Nakawa, firstly, and Naguru, where he was renting a house when Yosefu became his business partner.

Yosefu sank his few thousands of shillings savings into buying very expensive electrical equipment, leaving himself with very few ready funds. The returns from their business were slow, largely because the amount of work they took on prevented them from completing work on time. Yosefu realized too late that he should have retained capital to employ an assistant or two. He was forced to sell some of his equipment at a rapidly depreciated value, and the business suffered a serious set-back from which it had not recovered when I left the field. With the proposed extension of the railway to Fort Portal, capital of Toro kingdom, Yosefu was considering moving his business, including his 'inseparable' Ganda partner, to this more promising area, where he had many more local contacts.

Though both of royal blood, Kaboha and Yosefu differ markedly in their educational and socio-economic background and present status. Yosefu is an agnate of the Omukama but this fact has not especially helped either himself or his father. His father is a poor 'landowner', receiving moderate dues from his tenants but unable to use his land extensively for growing cash crops. Kaboha's mother is related to the Omukama, but not his father. But his father does grow cash crops and holds the reasonably lucrative and influential position of *gombolola* chief. Kaboha has more effective upper stratum contacts than Yosefu. He received more education. His wife's Ganda father is fairly wealthy and influential. He brought his wife very fully into his social life.

Yosefu has none of these advantages. Except in so far as both he and Kaboha are fond of Yosefu's sister, their relatedness is irrelevant to their respective urban careers. Yosefu did not, for instance, utilize Kaboha's contacts to raise money or find work for his attempt at free enterprise. He established a partnership with a Ganda of relatively low rural status, who, like himself, had no land that could be used for growing cash crops. This may have inspired each of them to establish a private commercial enterprise.

The case of Kaboha's father and of Kaboha himself indicates the possibility of utilizing affinal ties to enter into the social life of both rural- and urban-based upper strata. But social mobility of this kind can only be achieved through high education, a superior occupation, and substantial profit from cash crops.

Between them, Kaboha and his father have these qualities and means. Yosefu has not, and his fairly distant agnatic relatedness to the Omukama is not helpful to him at this stage of his career.

Difficulties of Movement into a Tribal Hierarchy

A Kiga whom I now describe is in a position to utilize affinal links and enter the social life of Toro upper strata. He has reasonably high education, a highly qualified and well-paid job, an acquaintance through school of Toro higher-status life, a whole range of relevant social aspirations, and a partial knowledge of Lutoro, which is close to his own language.

Although he is Bantu and therefore linguistically close to Toro, his rural social structure has more in common with those of other Migrants. He is subject to milder but quite definite sanctions of disapproval as he attempts to rise through another tribespeople's status hierarchy.

Yosefu's sister marries a Kiga

Yosefu's sister is to marry a Kiga, Ruwango, whom she met at the school they both attended in Fort Portal. They have lived together for some time at Naguru. She is now eight months pregnant. Ruwango has School Certificate and is a trained Post Office engineer. He came to Kampala in 1960 after a brief training spell in Nairobi.

Now that his 'wife' is pregnant, Ruwango will approach her parents about bridewealth. He has invited his father to come with him and meet the girl's parents at their home. He did not, however, invite a patrilateral parallel cousin, Kayonga, nor any of the few members of his clan in Kampala.

Kayonga is a clerk in the Police C.I.D. He has much less education than Ruwango, earns much less, and lives in Upper Nakawa. He is a staunch church-goer. He spends a great proportion of his income providing education for his only child, a girl. He knows Onyango through Nakawa tenants' and other association meetings.

Kayonga only discovered inadvertently that the arrangements for his cousin's payment of bridewealth were soon to be made. He had come to Ruwango to try and settle two kinship matters. One was to ask why Ruwango had not visited Kayonga. The other was to discuss what should be done about the Kiga husband of one of their 'sisters' who had not visited either of them. Kayonga had said, 'How can he keep me from seeing my sister?' Ruwango suggested that the man was perhaps busy, as he himself had been. He gave this as the reason for his own failure to visit Kayonga. Kayonga claimed that a man was never too busy to visit his 'brothers'.

When it leaked out in discussion that Ruwango had already decided to visit his 'wife's' parents to discuss bridewealth and other matters, Kayonga was aghast that he should omit to tell him or his clansmen in Kampala and that he should be going without any of them. He claimed that, 'unlike many of our Kiga brothers, I do not oppose marriage with women of other tribes, but we must observe our customs when we do inter-marry. How can we forget our fathers and brothers?'

Kayonga is a great supporter of his tribal association. Its virtues, as he sees it, are in enabling deviant, 'roaming' unmarried and married Kiga women to be repatriated, forcefully if necessary, helping and repatriating the destitute, and sending to their homes the bodies of men who have died in town. He sees another of its values as 'welcoming' newcomers to Kampala and 'guiding' them in the difficult initial phase of adjustment to town life. Kayonga maintains to a considerable extent ties with kin, clansmen, fellow villagers and other Kiga in Kampala.

Ruwango's higher socio-economic status and his marriage 'up' into a royal Toro family, however poor it may be, have widened his social circle to include not only many non-Kiga but also many persons of equivalent status. He sees more of Kaboha, particularly, and Yosefu and his cousins than he does of his own relatives and other Kiga. He knows nothing of the tribal association's activities. Moreover, he is building a 'permanent' house not on his father's but on his wife's father's land. He hopes one day to 'buy' land for growing cash crops in the same or a nearby region. He is thus rapidly becoming assimilated into Toro royalty and the associated high status categories and groups, continuing a process which began with his education in a Toro school. He was sent to the school by a rich uncle, who had himself found success in Kampala.

But even the moderate and understanding Kayonga condemned some aspects of this assimilation. Inevitably Ruwango will 'forget the fathers and brothers' in the figurative sense at least. His children will certainly be Toro first and Kiga second, if at all.

Kayonga is of relatively high socio-economic status for Kiga in Kampala and at Nakawa and Naguru. Most of them are unskilled, short-term workers. But Ruwango is of even higher socio-economic status than Kayonga and is thus part of a very small minority of his tribespeople both in Kampala and generally. Their urban life histories may both be taken to represent opposite ends of a continuum along which a rise in socio-economic status is accompanied by a lessening of emphasis on agnatic ties and all that these imply in marriage and the status of women, land-holding, and the formation of urban kin and clan groups and tribal associations.

Recapitulation

The distinction between Host and Migrant peoples is necessarily crude. That there is a marked cultural division between what Southall and Gutkind have for shorthand convenience called the Interlacustrine Bantu and the rest, is obvious to even a casual observer. To isolate the factors underlying it is more difficult, and runs the risk of over-generalization.

There are firstly special historical and political factors, as well as that of geography, properly awarding the title of Host to Ganda. Other Interlacustrine Bantu often simply found it convenient to attach themselves to Ganda ways of life in Kampala-Mengo, especially in the recent past when Ganda were indisputably dominant. They were similar and the process was fairly easy. Ganda have always encouraged other people to adopt their customs and language and certainly did not resist the assimilation of strangers even though they gave them low status to begin with.

But for many of whom I have called the Migrants, especially Nilotes, assimilation was not desired, even though it provides possible economic benefits. Differences of language are obviously barriers but should not be exaggerated as such. A more important barrier is the existence for each Migrant of a highly effective network of relatives who see themselves as interdependent members of groups based on lines of descent. That they are no longer mutually dependent in their rural homes as they were many years ago when a local descent group had true political autonomy has not completely broken down the ideology of this.

Moreover, certain economic bonds have persisted, if in changed form. The rough relationship between the expectations of valuable bridewealth, frequently of money, and virtuous sisters determines the course of many relationships. Land-tenure and inheritance systems are of similar though more variable significance. Ideas about authority at the small-group level are distinctive. While all peoples in the modern state have government chiefs, elders, thought to represent or know about an agnatic line, even if wrongly, are heeded more in some than other societies. The Luo *jaduong*, or elder, arbitrates or testifies in marriage and land disputes, even in a government court, far more than a person of similar standing among Ganda.

Contrasting laws regarding the social and material value of women is possibly the most important variable of a number making up this cultural distinction, which may be presented in summary form as follows:

Host societies	*Migrant societies*
Traditional authority system persisting in ideology: associational delegation of authority.[3] Low degree of lineage and clan localization and jural, economic and political autonomy. The local authority head is an agent of the kingdom and is unrelated by kinship to the majority under his jurisdiction.	Traditional authority system persisting in ideology: complementary delegation of authority.[3] High degree of lineage and clan localization and jural, economic and political autonomy. There is no single minimal local authority head. Authority roles are ascribed to elder agnates at the lowest levels.
Tribal system of stratification largely based on *de facto* freehold land tenure, tenancy, and widespread cash-cropping.	Egalitarian ordering and conception of clan and lineage groups, with individual access to land vested within such groups, even where cash-cropping has advanced.
Low bridewealth, transferring only sexual and domestic but not genetricial rights to the husband and his group and not generally recoverable. Not regarded as the bridewealth of the bride's brother and not providing a basis for common action among agnates. The genitor may claim a woman's children regardless of whether he or another has paid bridewealth.	High bridewealth, transferring genetricial rights in a woman to her husband and his group and recoverable. Regarded as bridewealth of bride's brothers and providing a basis for common action among agnates.

Relatively independent status of unmarried and married women, and their lesser social and real value to agnates. But wife's ties with her natal group remain strong after marriage. Absence of house-property complex. Women may own property and dispose of it as they please. High incidence of cohabitation without marriage and of separation.

Restricted status of unmarried and married women and their high real and social value to agnates. Married women eventually become fully incorporated in their husband's local descent group. Existence of house-property complex. Low incidence of cohabitation without marriage and of separation.

Inheritance is preferential. Usually the eldest son receives a substantially larger proportion of his father's property than do his other siblings. But the father may choose another son as heir. Daughters and grand-daughters may inherit.

Inheritance is shared more or less equally among brothers, the eldest receiving only a slight advantage. Daughters do not inherit.

I have tried to show that in a sphere of activities stemming from or related to urban domestic life, Hosts and Migrants show certain differences which can be explained to some extent by differences in their rural social structures. While this kind of argument may be obvious, it has to be stated as a preliminary to my next proposition, that distinctive cultural institutions may be used by people to express a type of ceremonial solidarity in the face of political and economic pressure.

Migrants interact fairly frequently with people who are in some way defined as 'brothers'. While this effective network is easily mobilized over a domestic crisis, it imposes sometimes onerous obligations on the individual who is rising in the social scale. The obligations cannot be rejected in any brusque, straightforward manner. How then is the Migrant allowed choice in his relationships?

Crisis situations inevitably produce cross-cutting divisions and alliances among people who are all 'brothers' under the umbrella of a loose urban ideology. The Migrant is thus able to choose which 'brother' he affiliates with in order to pursue a certain course of action. He affiliates in the name of the ideology of good brotherhood, claiming that his opponents are 'corrupting' brotherhood.

His opponents, of course, make the same claim. But, while expressing their differences and going their separate ways, none disputes the value of the ideology itself. Role differentiation (that is, the splitting up of relationships and behaviour one wishes to keep distinct), is thus achieved by an emphasis on the very ideology disclaiming this.

While allowing some choice within a tribal field of relations in town, this mechanism does not encourage enduring inter-tribal ties, where some degree of commitment is expected, as in marriage or a business partnership. The mechanism allows a wide range of choice within the tribal field while restricting choice outside it.

But even this has its advantages. On the one hand members of the network do not want to be restricted, on the other they do not wish to become cut off from 'brothers', for it is these who are useful in providing jobs and accommodation, not only in the same but also in a number of cities. Kenyans in Kampala contact 'brothers' in, say, Nairobi for job possibilities. Some of these brothers may themselves have been working in Kampala previously.

The network has to be both extended and effective for this system to work.[4] It extends among many members both within and throughout towns by the constant making and breaking of relationships: the more 'brothers' you quarrel with the more in the end you get to know, provided there are enough wider issues keeping a large number of you in contact. The issues occur through the ideology described over wives and 'sisters' and domestic crises. This ideology, and leadership and activity in ethnic associations, sustain the network's extensiveness and enable dyadic relationships within it to be singularly effective in providing employment and accommodation opportunities. I believe that the Kenyans, especially Luo, gained a certain protection of their economic and political interests in Kampala through this mechanism. Briefly, Migrants share a distinctive institutional complex, which proved to have a valuable latent function for Kenyans.

Host people are undoubtedly less preoccupied with an ideology of incorruptible brotherhood. Patterns of ideal behaviour are more easily seen as emanating from the fairly clearly defined status divisions of land, wealth and office in their societies. There are not normally urban networks of relatives comprising a hard core who are regularly mobilized over a domestic crisis. Choice in country is complemented by choice in town. With little appreciable difference in emphasis on mother's or father's side, a Host network of kin is more 'bilateral' and can include many people whom he person knows or is in contact with. It may thus be highly extended without being effective.

It remains a matter of speculation as to what would happen if Host people (say, Ganda) were very numerous in a foreign town like Nairobi and, due to political changes occurring in the wider society, felt that they were exposed to a loss of economic privileges. If the State would not allow them to organize as a political force to protest against new legislation, or if they found it inexpedient to do so, within what framework of home institutions would they acquiesce and turn their attentions homeward in a gradual and orderly manner, as did Kenyans in Kampala? While this is no more than a hypothetical problem, it can serve as a point at which to pull together the threads of an argument centred on Kenyans, particularly Luo.

In recapitulation, the estates of Kampala East provided Migrants with an opportunity to work and live outside the main jurisdiction of Ganda society. In earlier years it was less useful to be a Ugandan than a Ganda, since they were dominant, even in the municipality of Kampala as well as Mengo. Migrants did not make the distinction among themselves of Kenyans and Ugandans. Migrants above the average in socio-economic status and length of urban residence came to the estates. There they felt secure, both as a distinct urban category and, by dint of their scarcity value in skills and education, in employment.

Based on income differences and a prestige ranking of occupations, an urban status system typical of many towns was bound to make its impact on people of this category. Involvement in the system and the influence of a rising wave of political nationalism produced and strengthened a sense of community. Leaders arose and a type of middle class became more clearly defined, among whom status differences were seen to be increasingly more important than tribal membership. Kenyans did not therefore dominate tenants' and other associations, in spite of being in a numerical position to do so.

They were active, however, in trade unionism. In this they provided the initial drive in Uganda and, while they never acted out of specific tribal or national interests, became discernible as a dominant national group, numerous in employment as well as unions. With independence Uganda's leaders were obliged to try to alter this picture of dominance if citizenship rights of priority were to have meaning. But, in fact, before independence there had been apprehension among Kenyans. In earlier years it was expressed as rivalry with Ganda on the job market, with the colonial government holding supreme power. With the approach of independence the apprehension was that they would be made redundant for not being citizens.

Ties were maintained among Kenyans in Kampala, in other towns and at home. One way in which this was done was through the persistence of highly effective networks of relatives recruited and exhorted in the name of a flexible ideology of brotherhood. Another was in the constant proliferation and fading away of numerous associations, whose membership and leadership frequently overlapped, so that a large number of people were in fairly regular contact with each other.

While the manifest aims of the associations might be mutual aid, recreation, or political support, the latent were the maintenance of a long chain of communication among leaders of many levels, from the Kenya capital in Nairobi, from the Luo capital of Kisumu, from 'big men' in Kampala, to the ordinary men and their families making up this expatriate group. It was this link with the ultimate source of authority which was an important factor enabling the Kenyans to be in a position to undertake a phase-out from Kampala without too much personal and social dislocation, if this became necessary.

NOTES

[1] Cf. A. W. Southall (ed.), 1961, *Social Change in Modern Africa*, O.U.P. for I.A.I., p. 24, where Luo and Ganda notions regarding 'servants' are contrasted: ' . . . in Kampala wealthy Ganda employ servants of other tribes or quite unrelated Ganda, because it would usually be shameful and embarrassing for status reasons to employ a relative. But wealthy Luo, with an egalitarian traditional system and very strong agnatic ties which transcend modern status differences, employ servants who are usually relatives. For a young Luo does not mind assisting a relative informally, but would often be ashamed of open employment as a servant by a member of his own tribe.'

[2] H. C. A. Somerset, 1964, 'Home Structure, Parental Separation, and Examination Success in Buganda', a paper presented to the Faculty of Social Sciences, Makerere University College, in which he reports the frequency with which many Ganda schoolchildren appear to prefer to live with matrikin after parental separation.

[3] From Southall, 1965, 'A Critique of the Typology of States and Political Systems', in A.S.A. Monographs, No. 2.

[4] Cf. A. L. Epstein, 1961, op. cit., p. 55.

CHAPTER VIII

LUO UNION AND OTHER ETHNIC ASSOCIATIONS

Structure of Luo Associations

Of the eight most important full tribal associations in Kampala, all but one of them have their headquarters and most executive and general meetings at either Naguru or Nakawa, and mostly at the latter. Nearly all the associations' leaders or elected officers live in either of these two estates, again, mostly Nakawa. In occupational skills, education and length of urban residence the leaders are above the average for Kampala as a whole.

All these associations are of Migrants and thus signify even further the special position of Kampala East, where most of their activities are. Host people's associations are much less in evidence. A Bika (clans) football association is open to Ganda in and around Kampala. Its aim is recreational and the association was started, an official implied, in imitation of the football competitions organized by the Luo and Luhya. A Nyoro association was established by a handful of men and became defunct within a year. A few Soga claimed that a Soga association used to meet every April in celebration of the Kyabazinga's (the Soga form of king) birthday, but, due to some dispute within the organization, did not meet in 1963. No Toro association exists.

Among some of the Migrant associations there are two or three levels. At the lowest level are clan associations. At the next level are, for Luo and Luhya, the location or subtribe associations. The final level is that of the whole tribal union or association. Only the Luo and Luhya have all three levels. The Acholi and Lango have the two levels of clan and tribe, but less extensively. The Kiga have coalesced with the Ankole to form their only association, the the Banyankole/Banyakigezi Association. The Lugbara have an association and branches, but the branches are not differentiated from each other according to home divisions of lineage or clan and subtribe, but each comprises a heterogeneity of Lugbara.

While contrasting in their strength, these associations have fairly similar aims, in every case expressed in a constitution in both English and the vernacular. While it is quite clear to members what the association's manifest functions are, they are not normally aware of unintended social consequences which derive from an association's mere existence as well as its activities. These latter latent functions are of special relevance in understanding the Luo and Luhya organizations.

The Luo is by far the most viable, followed by the Luhya, and is properly to be understood as a node in a network of such associations established in many towns in East Africa. The English copy of the Luo Union constitution runs to eight foolscap pages, which includes the following information.

'The Union's headquarters shall be at Kisumu, the capital of the Luo country . . . The Union shall have branches anywhere the Luo are residing permanently, working or otherwise . . . The aims and objects of the Union shall be: . . . To promote and maintain mutual help and understanding among the Luo wherever they are . . . To find ways and means of improving the Luo country generally, socially, educationally and economically . . . To encourage and put into practice the Luo customs which are conducive to and compatible with modern civilization . . . To look into and to object very strongly to those foreign customs which may be detrimental to the Luo people . . . To look into and safeguard the welfare of the Luo people wherever they are . . . '

The constitution also states the intention of owning and operating printing presses, bookshops, libraries, reading-rooms, magazines, and even hospitals and dispensaries. And, indeed, though the Union has not yet been able to fulfil all these aims, it has sponsored the building of the Ofafa Hall in Kisumu and the Ofafa Makingo centre in Nairobi, both named after a Luo Mayor of Nairobi who was assassinated during the Kenya Emergency. In addition, it has offered financial aid to the KANU party and government, has periodically given men the opportunity of overseas education, and at the headquarters of Kisumu and every branch puts on dances and organizes inter-location football competitions.

Membership qualifications are relatively liberal: '. . . Membership of the Union is open to . . . all adult Luo men and women . . . any other adult person other than Luo who lives within the Luo community and agrees with Luo customs and traditions and with this constitution.'

In Kampala, and in Nairobi and Kisumu too, the extent of the Union's size and aims has to be considered together with the existence and proliferation in the town of small location and clan associations of the tribe. The following is a partial view of the structure of Luo associations in Kampala. The diagram is not exhaustive and for purposes of clarity and space deals with the clan associations of only one location or subtribe association.

The Structure of the Luo Union and Some Affiliated Associations

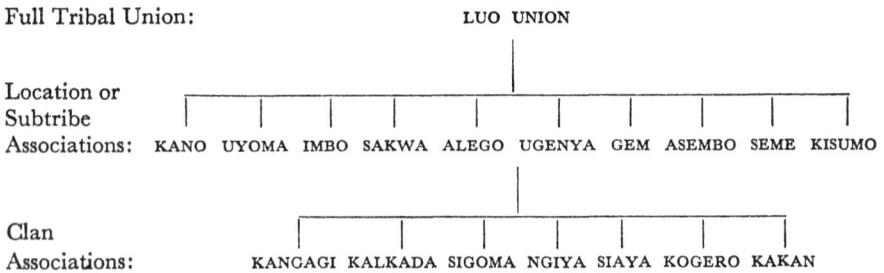

Full Tribal Union: LUO UNION

Location or
Subtribe
Associations: KANO   UYOMA   IMBO   SAKWA   ALEGO   UGENYA   GEM   ASEMBO   SEME   KISUMO

Clan
Associations: KANGAGI   KALKADA   SIGOMA   NGIYA   SIAYA   KOGERO   KAKAN

The Union has established schools and nurseries in Kampala as well as organizing the Luo inter-location soccer competitions and occasional dances. But it is unable to deal with the more frequent and commonplace urban problems directly affecting the individual. There was, it would seem from the constitution, a belief that this would not be beyond its capacities: '. . . The Executive Council alone shall have the power to establish or recognize or ratify Branch(es) and also to delimit Branch boundaries . . . Any fifty or more members may form a Branch of the Union and send their request to the Executive Council for recognition. In one town or village there shall not be more than one Branch. Any members numbering less than fifty in any one town or village may form a Division of the Branch nearest them . . . A Division or Sub-division of a Branch shall not proceed to hold any meetings or form any associations unless such has (have) been permitted or authorized by the Headquarters or by the Executive Council.' This prohibition of the formation of branches indicates that the Union felt itself able to deal with all the problems likely to be experienced by all minorities.

But, by looking at the diagram and gaining even an incomplete picture of the Luo structure of associations in Kampala alone, it is clear that, approved or not, members of smaller groups within the tribal collectivity have had recourse to self-help and mutual aid. Location associations are, it is true, primarily concerned with inter-location soccer, which, being organized by the Luo Union Sports Club, awards them recognition. But their activities are not confined to this field and as is shown in the appendix to this chapter (pp. 203–14), membership of a location or similar division counts for something at the annual election of executive officers to the Union.

It is the clan associations, however, which are most concerned with mutual aid. They may consist of anything from ten to thirty, or at the most forty members. These members, if not directly related, are drawn from the same local home area, and in some cases this appears to reinforce the efficacy of the clan association's structure of authority with regard to individual behaviour. Each member is aware that there is a constant inter-communication of people in the town and at home, and that those at home will quickly hear of any deviant behaviour and may voice their disapproval of the offender when he returns. Nevertheless, clan associations are still prone to the fluctuating existences typical of others. They may die away through lack of enthusiasm, to be revived by different clansmen at a later time.

The outstanding distinguishing feature of clan associations, and this applies to the clan or comparable small associations of other tribes, is that their leaders and most regular and active members are below the socio-economic average for the tribe's urban population. Members of these small associations are brought together, initially at least, on the basis of a common need of economic and social security. Thus, clansmen who regard themselves as above the socio-economic average may feel no compulsion to be regularly active or even join the association, though they may show nominal interest.

Whereas neither the Luo Union nor the location associations are consistently concerned with affairs of the individual, except in some cases of death, when they may organize a collection of money to send the corpse home, the clan association tries to be much more so. In addition to the repatriation of deceased clansmen it may collect for a number of purposes; help in cases of trouble with the police or local *gombolola* court; help in sending a destitute, unemployed member home; personal intervention in some disputes between members; the obligation to send home any unmarried or unattached girl of the clan who is found 'roaming' in Kampala (though sometimes the major Union or location association attempts to act upon this matter and there may be a conflict of expectations of responsibility between it and the clan association as in the case given in chapter five); and the obligations among clansmen to visit each other and to sit and drink together on festive and other occasions.

The large Luo Union and the location associations are basically community-oriented in their activities. The major purpose of each location association is to play soccer against other location teams in Kampala. This activity has a more social flavour. For instance, during Christmas, 1962, seven Kampala location associations hired ten buses in order to take members home to Kenya to play soccer with their Kisumu counterparts.

The realized objectives of the Luo Union itself have already been summarized and relate to the development in a variety of spheres of the Luo collectivity. The aims of the clan associations are clearly to help the individual townsman in personal hardship, and people join or form them on this basis, though most are usually disillusioned before long.

Some go beyond their original aims. One Luo clan association started a money-lending business. Loans were only made to persons, of any Luo location or subtribe, who had been vouched for by a member of the association. Though there were constant organizational difficulties, the business eventually showed good returns and the mutual aid function of the association became subsidiary, especially after money was invested in the purchase of a shop. Similarly, another clan association, under inspiring leadership, saved enough money to buy a car to be used as a taxi. Business flourished and in a short while they had a fleet of three taxis. A Luhya clan association also saved enough money to buy a shop. It was stated that this would enable an out-of-work member to run the shop and take a compensatory greater share of the profits. This same association has opened its membership ranks to three fellow-tribesmen not of the founders' clan in the hope of attracting the clientele of friends and clansmen of the latter. These three members and any clansmen willing to join will receive a scaled-down share of the profits until they have contributed as much in capital towards the shop as the founder members. This measure has, perhaps unwittingly, maintained power of the administration of the business in the hands of the original clansmen. These highly successful clan associations are not to be regarded as typical. They have exceeded the bounds of their original objectives. Most continue as individual clan welfare societies, with a high turnover of membership resulting in dissolution.

Most clan associations ask three or five shillings a month from each member, in addition to 'emergency' collections, and the imposition of fines for absence at meetings or unjustifiably late payment. By contrast the Luo Union has relatively few fully paid up members. On the other hand, at the annual Luo Union elections there is always an attendance of some hundreds of Luo, when money can be collected and when, as on other occasions, the collectivity is urged to sponsor a 'national' cause.

Members of the location associations pay a shilling a month, the regular and majority proportion of which goes towards the hiring of city council soccer pitches and referees, and the purchase of jerseys and footballs. The Luo location championship is at the Lugogo stadium, almost adjoining Naguru in Kampala East.

We must keep in mind the fact that only a minority of townsmen are members of associations at any one time. But the high turnover of interest and participation means that a larger number are at some stage connected with them. The history of the Luo Union in Kampala suggests a few facts about the developments of the Kampala Luo community. No consistent historical accounts were given and the following is a brief version of points which were agreed on.

The Luo Union in Kampala was established in 1947. It was regarded as a strong organization approved of by the government for its primarily welfare activities. In those days it concerned itself with more than just 'big enterprises', i.e. nursery schools, primary schools and community halls and centres, but also took care of the affairs of the individual. If a Luo was arrested for not having paid his poll tax, the Union would come to his aid. Similar action would be taken with regard to errant unattached women and in helping a family send a member's corpse home. But during 1954–6 [*sic*, though probably meant during 1956–8], the numbers of Luo coming to work in Kampala increased considerably. The Union found itself less able constantly to attend the individual needs of its poorer members and inclined to a greater interest in larger-scale projects. Dances, parties, rallies and meetings were held with the intention of raising funds for community centres, schools, and one single major project—the Ofafa Hall at Kisumu.

With a much greater Luo population in Kampala and with a parallel growing inability to heed to individual problems, the Union became less centralized in its influence and control over the tribal collectivity. In response to a need for individual welfare, and unrestricted by a virtually decentralized Union (according to the constitution the formation of branches in the same town was illicit), location associations came into being. These were immediately strong and after about a year were 'recognized' by the Luo Union in Kampala and were affiliated to it.

However, a number of disputes occurred after a while within the organization of some location associations. These disputes centred around what may be called 'clan nepotism'. Each location at home consists of a number of territorially distinct clans. A keen, often sporting rivalry exists between members of such clans in town as well as at home. In some Kampala location associations, clansmen attempted to help each other into office, often by first trying to impeach non-clansmen officers. How much accusations of clan nepotism reflected not reality but simply intense inter-clan rivalry is not known. The fear by some clansmen, anyway, that one or two clans might dominate proceedings was enough to bring about their withdrawal of participation. A location association might then cease to exist or might carry on lamely, still expecting subscriptions from the defaulters and condemning them as such. In response to the breakdown of some location associations and to a still unsatisfied need for individual welfare, clan associations were established.

In the late fifties, an entirely novel factor re-established and reaffirmed the location associations. This was soccer, or rather the introduction of an inter-location soccer competition. The idea stemmed from the Luo Union, and their sports club is at present in charge of organizing the playing of matches in the competition. Soccer is the major form of public recreation in Kampala East. The intense popularity of the game and the desire to do well in the competition knit interested members of each location together in a new solidarity. At the same time, because they recognized the need in such a competition for a neutral overruling and organizational body, location associations paid greater deference and allegiance to the Union than had existed for some time. This in turn reaffirmed a type of tribal solidarity, as evidenced when two very high-status Luo gathered around them a small number of 'highly educated' fellow-tribesmen, who had become dissatisfied with the administration of the Union by what they were alleged to have called 'illiterates', and established the East Uganda Luo Branch for 'educated men'. They were severely condemned by very many Luo through the Union and, in fact, unceremonially disbanded the Branch.

The accuracy of dates and certain facts in this account may be in question, but what does emerge clearly is concern with what I have earlier called the ideology of brotherhood, or, by extension in the present context, the ideology of being a Luo. The underlying theme is that the Luo Union was under some moral compulsion to prevent the Luo community losing sight of itself. When it allegedly failed to provide for individual needs it paid the penalty and saw location associations come into office. These faded away and the blame was put on clan nepotism, though, as shown in an earlier case, the basic conflicts are little to do with clan or other descent ties. With more Luo in Kampala it was realized that the existence of strong location associations under the paternalistic wing of the Union was in fact an effective way of keeping people in contact, of maintaining some kind of chain of communication. The Luo Union was thus credited with the idea of introducing the football league championship among location teams, so reviving their associations.

It is significant that this is said to have been introduced in the late 'fifties, since it was during this period that the Kenyans, mostly Luo, became a proportionally larger element in the labour force while Ganda became less. The same period saw an acceleration of the earlier development of nationalism among both Ganda and Kenyans. The widely ramifying organization embracing the Union leaders at the top and 'subordinate' location and clan association leaders undoubtedly provided a viable system of communication among people at different levels in the Kampala Luo community.

Business Interests

Because the number of Luo in Kampala grew so large it was inevitable that status groups should not only develop but become much more obvious. Higher-status people tended to take the positions in the Luo Union, less well off but perhaps aspiring men would assume leadership of location associations, and leaders of clan associations tended to be poorer. Numbers of people available are very important in the development of this ranked structure. Thus the number of Luo in Kampala of a specific location might be too small to segment into clan associations and their location association might have more in common with those of clans of other more represented locations.

This point may be obvious but serves to emphasize how important status considerations were in forming these associations which purported to represent a home area. An even more important elaboration of this is that a large proportion of leaders in the Union and some location associations were 'businessmen', especially in Kampala East. The Luo were the only tribe other than Ganda to own property and run businesses on any scale in Kampala East.[1] Some hired out houses at Kiswa, others owned or hired shops and bars, ran taxi services or merely had wives working at market stalls earning a useful supplementary income. Though it is not suggested there was a conscious manipulation, the structure of leadership and system of communication did have the result that a leader would soon become known as a 'prominent' Luo, might become popular and might find his bar, shop or taxis patronized more than if he did not enter the public eye. The Luo community, after all, was the largest tribal group in Kampala East, able to provide abundant custom.

Another attribute of the organization was its potential as a forum of leadership. One Luo candidate at the 1962 municipal council elections was a secretary of the Luo Union. An appointed Luo councillor for Kampala East played an important part in certain of the Union's activities and frequently addressed meetings. Other prominent Luo were directly associated with it in observable capacities. All were property-owners in Kampala East and sometimes elsewhere in the city. As leaders of the Kampala Luo community they were in constant contact with developments in Kenya, especially during the period when fears regarding employment were being expressed. They were able to reassure the many Luo who attended general meetings that they would speak with the Uganda government on the status of Kenyans in Uganda. They were able also to intervene in a number of disputes in political organizations in Kampala which came into being with the approach of Kenya's own independence.

Their roles were thus conciliatory, rarely being recognized as such, and were also those of pacifiers. The existence of subordinate associations meant that people could rise in positions of leadership and aspire to office in the Luo Union. The correlations between rise in leadership, status and business success are illustrated in the following case of a man, from East Kano location, who was mentioned in the case in chapter six involving Otieno, Onyango, and Mary, the 'sister'.

Rise and fall

It will be remembered that this office-holder in the Kano location association was also a leader in the Luo Union. This man, whom I shall call Jeremiah, was literate in Swahili and Luo but not in English, which he did not speak well. He came to Kampala in 1953 to work as a cook for a European. After some years the European left the country, depositing what was to Jeremiah a large sum of money in the bank for him. Jeremiah used the money to hire a vegetable stall at Nakasero market, in the city centre, which is patronized by many of Kampala's European and Asian population.

He was soon well established in his business. He would order vegetables from Kikuyu growers in Kenya and sell them at his stall in Nakasero. He landed a very profitable contract with an educational institution. People claimed that he was favoured by a prominent Luo on the staff. He also began supplying some African and Asian retailers. Many of the Luo stall-holders at Nakawa market bought from him. He moved to a Shs. 72/- house at Naguru, furnishing it with a suite and other pieces left him by the European. As one informant saw it: 'Mr. Jeremiah fitted everything in his house and it was marvellously fashioned in European style. It had four rooms, for resting, sleeping, visitors, and as a kitchen, in which there was a cooker [the house was wired for electricity]. He had a carpet in the resting-room and the sofa set was arranged suitably. In his house he was living like a minister who has been in the National Assembly for four years.' He later moved to a Shs. 140/- house.

He was able to dress well, and people began to respect him as a successful businessman. Some claimed that it was this respect which enabled him to be elected chairman of the Kano association in 1957 'even though he could not read and write English'.

In 1955 he set up home with a Ganda woman whom he had met in a Kampala hospital. 'Brothers and parents' had advised him against the union, saying that the woman would not stay with him and would just waste his 'energy' and money. He had resisted their wishes because he loved her, and pointed out that the woman had already borne him children. He maintained that only barren women (of the Host tribes) leave their 'husbands', but that his had no 'need' to. His parents angrily broke off relations with him and he did not go home for a long time. They mellowed after a while and visited the couple by way of reconciliation, inviting them back home.

In 1958 it was agreed at a meeting of Kano association to have two sections, one each for East and West Kano. There was no dispute, but with a growing number of Kano people in Kampala it had been thought appropriate to have separate treasurers collecting separate funds, in order to avoid any disputes over use of the money. Jeremiah remained chairman of the whole Kano association, which continued to function as one. His industry enabled Kano to enter an excellent team in the Luo football league and they won the championship that year. They did very well in all championships and other competitions until 1962.

A complementary activity of the association was money-lending. Applicants for loans were vetted by the committee beforehand to decide their suitability. Loans could be made for the inevitably high expenses incurred by a funeral at home, or to help start a new 'business'. Money could then be given to cover the cost of, say, hiring a market stall and an initial purchase of vegetables or fish, though rarely more than this.

Interest was payable on loans and until 1959 the system worked well. But then Jeremiah lent Shs. 500/- from the funds to a shop-keeper at Kibuli suburb whom he knew and trusted but who had not been vetted by the committee. Nevertheless the committee approved of the loan when Jeremiah told them immediately after-wards. The man did not repay, claiming that as his name was not in the book usually signed by borrowers, his debt could not be proved. The alleged debt reached Shs. 1,000/- with interest. Jeremiah told the committee that he himself would replace the money. The committee had already accused him of collusion with the man and did not believe that this promise would be honoured. A number left and the association lost much of its former strength.

The association flourished as a football club and members kept in contact with each other through a shared enthusiasm in the team's successes. Money continued to be collected for football expenses, though only a few subscribed money for the traditional welfare purposes. Altogether fifty to sixty people were actively concerned with the football club, and many more from other towns were occasionally brought in either as players or to provide help.

Jeremiah branched out in a different direction of business in-terests at about Christmas, 1960. He was by then an organizer of football for the Luo Union. He arranged to take the 'star' Kano team 'home' to Kisumu, and hired buses from Kampala. He also hired the Ofafa Hall in Kisumu from the Luo Union for 'dances', and the stadium from the municipality for a football competition. Luo from many locations attended this major function and the proceeds more than covered the costs involved. Jeremiah presented a cup bearing his name as the prize for this football competition. It was the same success story in 1961 and 1962. He organized a similar event for Easter, 1963, but sustained a heavy loss, which he had to bear.

This latter had been an especially expensive venture. He had ordered a Congo jazz band from Kampala for Shs. 900/– and had also paid Shs. 3,000/– for the hire of a bus to take footballers and traditional dancers free of charge to Kisumu. He had posters printed advertising the event, costing Shs. 1,000/–. In the end the proceeds did not cover these costs, let alone the hiring of the hall and stadium.

Jeremiah returned to Naguru, opted out of his leadership both of Kano and in the Luo Union sports club and concentrated again on his business at Nakasero. Within a few months he had recovered poise and proposed to hold a dance at Naguru, not, as he himself emphasized, in the name of the Luo Union or any other Luo association this time. It did transpire, however, that those who helped him organize the dance and nearly all those who attended were Luo, and it is quite clear that the event was made possible because of his standing in the local Luo community.

He hired an excellent Kampala band and the dance went well, many people attending. He collected the money personally this time, because on his previous venture he had entrusted the job to others, with the result, he claimed, that many people were admitted free. He continued to wait for people until four in the morning on the reasonable assumption that a number could come even at this late hour. He had not had the money deposited anywhere but had it with him in the cash-box he was using. A gang of thieves snatched the box from him and it was never recovered. The hiring of the hall and the band had been agreed on credit terms, as his success as a businessman and therefore his credit worthiness were widely recognized. He could barely scrape together enough money to pay for these costs and was left a poor man.

To add to his troubles, a little while afterwards he lost his major contract with the educational institution in Kampala. His Luo 'contact', who with the approach of Kenya's own national elections had left his job and Uganda to stand as an M.P. for his home constituency, was, it was claimed, unable to protect Jeremiah's interests. The reason given by the institution for the termination of the contract was that he made too many late deliveries. In any event an Asian who bought produce from small-scale farmers in Kigezi, south-west Uganda, was awarded the contract instead.

Jeremiah's unhappy plight inevitably had an effect on his relationship with his Ganda wife. They quarrelled and she left him. Many Luo somewhat gleefully pointed to this as proof of what they had always said would happen. But, reduced as he was to living in a Shs. 36/– Naguru house, strain between them was unavoidable. Jeremiah had seven children by her at that stage, but she took all of them with her. He was well liked by her parents, having been a helpful son-in-law to them, and when he went to see them about his wife and children, they successfully urged their daughter to allow him at least the four eldest children. Jeremiah did not wish to take the matter to court and was satisfied with this settlement. The Luo Union contributed towards his and his children's fare home to Kenya, as he was too badly off even to afford this. Thus, like other Luo leaders at this time he left Uganda for good and settled in Kenya. The story has a happier ending. He contacted some of his former Kampala Luo associates and established another business in Nairobi. His wife joined him and he was reunited with her and his children.

More examples could be given of Luo in business, whether bar-shop- or taxi-owners, who became 'prominent' men of their tribe in Kampala. The fact that many of the leaders in the Union and in some location associations were businessmen of this or humbler categories cannot be put down to chance. The unconscious benefit of being in the public eye through leadership of this sort is in attracting popularity and with it custom. It is doubtful if leaders think in such instrumental terms. An important personality factor is that the more successful businessmen are in any case talented administrators, whether or not they have an education or knowledge of English. They are often attracted by the prestige reward of leadership of the Luo community, in which a knowledge of English is not particularly important. Admittedly, most top leaders do know English, but at least men like Jeremiah can exercise influence and gradually acquire respect without it.

I have relegated a detailed account of the Luo Union general election of officers in October 1963 to an appendix (page 203). It is too long to include here and cannot conveniently be condensed. But from it the argument that there is a correlation, though not necessarily a conscious one, between leadership in the Kampala Luo community[2] and business activity is confirmed. The outgoing chairman had property which he hired out at Kiswa. A previous secretary, who played an important part in the proceedings and was the more successful of the independent candidates at the 1962 council elections, owned bars. The outgoing acting secretary was a trader with a shop on Nakawa estate. The new chairman was for many years a 'trader' but was now recognized parish headman appointed by the Buganda government for the suburb of Nyamwongo, where many Luo live. He owned and let houses at Kiswa and owned a 'club' in Nyamwongo. One of the unsuccessful nominees for the post owned a shop and also had a full-time job as a mechanic. The new secretary was a 'medical dresser' at Mulago hospital but was able to apply his skills in an unofficial self-employed capacity, dispensing injections and tablets among Luo for certain common ailments. The new assistant treasurer ran a shop at Nakawa full-time and also undertook to deliver goods on his scooter to certain customers. Like most he had started his shop on capital saved from earnings from a previous job, in his case that of clerk. The chairman of the sports club, not present at the election, also owned a shop.

In addition to these there were a number of other prominent Luo in Kampala who, while they never stood for office, nor were expected to, frequently addressed meetings and were certainly regarded as leaders. They, too, were property-owners.

It is not intended to create a picture of an emerging capitalist class occupying all or most of these positions of ethnic influence. Many of these people ran businesses as a side-line, often at only marginal profits. Most were certainly small-scale and were no less vulnerable to failure than Jeremiah. Even the few very top businessmen who operated at a secure profit level disclosed misgivings about the future of their jobs and business interests in Uganda at independence. None felt wholly secure, and it was one of the themes of the 1963 Luo Union annual election address, before some 500 Luo, that the Premier of Uganda be urged 'not to forget the Luo', as they had helped Uganda on its road to independence and as they, too, were Nilotes (i.e. like the Premier).

Many other Luo who did not exert influence on this scale had business interests. On both Nakawa and Naguru there were forty-one Luo household heads who relied exclusively on 'self-employment' for their incomes. They included businessmen of the type described as well as a smaller proportion of tailors and launderers, or *dobi*. There were twenty-four Ganda self-employed, sixteen Nubi, and nine Luhya and Samia. No other tribespeople provided more than two or three. Proportions of self-employed within each tribe were Luo 12 per cent, Ganda 14·6 per cent, Nubi 21·3 per cent, and Luhya 4·6 per cent.

It is not surprising that many Nubi, who lack tribal lands, have directed their resources into private enterprise. Even so, the proportions for Luo and Ganda are high. Many of these Ganda household heads are women, of unmarried or 'independent' status. But Luo wives who sell at market stalls and earn incomes supplementary to their husbands' are not household heads and so are not included in these proportions. Therefore the figure for Luo involved in some way in business either themselves or through their wives is higher than the proportion given suggests.

We may distinguish four categories of Luo business interest: where the man depends exclusively on the enterprise; where he has wage employment but additionally either hires out property or employs others to run his business; where his wife works at a market stall or in his shop but contributes her income to the common domestic budget, most of which depends on his wage employment; and where husband and wife work together at a market stall or in their shop.

The latter two categories require the strict control over wives' status exerted by Luo and other Migrant males. The often wholly independent status of Ganda and other Host women does enable them to set up businesses more freely and extensively but serves also to entrench their independence economically. The extent to which a wife then contributes with her husband, if she has one, to a common domestic budget depends on their personal relationship and is not dependent on the husband's insistence as a matter of right.

Ceremonial Institution

The obvious Luo acumen for private enterprise, in Kampala East and elsewhere, depends basically on three securities. One is political non-interference. Hence the locus of Kampala East as probably the best area for Luo businesses, followed by other areas in the city, such as Nakasero market and, to a less extent, special 'Luo' areas outside the city, like Kibuli and Nyamwongo, where a parish headman is Luo. Another is the avoidance of strong competition by other Africans, principally Ganda, and the creation of an alternative non-Ganda clientele, which, because of their large numbers, is conveniently Luo. The third is the preservation of jural and conjugal control over their womenfolk, who, with subordinate status within the family, may definitely help a man keep a foothold in business, without necessarily requiring him to sacrifice wage employment.

The system of communication within the Luo Union and affiliated associations was one way of guaranteeing these securities as much as was possible. It provided a ready pool of leaders who were in constant contact with each other and with other Luo, through the complicated, popular and well-patronized soccer programmes, or by attendance at public meetings over matters seemingly totally unrelated to those of an economic or political nature. These leaders were able to report on the problem of political interference when it came, and though they had no power or legitimate authority in the eyes of the Uganda government, they were able to represent the interests of Luo by appeals which undoubtedly did have some influence.

Secondly, the very existence of a constant coming-together of Luo, however irregular and for whatever purpose, enabled the public recognition of leaders of all levels. Since many of these leaders had business interests of some kind, any popularity in leadership could be translated into at least a temporary upsurge in custom. The bigger the leader the larger tended to be his business interests and the greater his gain from this process.

Thirdly, the various levels of association were all in agreement over the desirability of continued control over their womenfolk, however much they might differ in their ideas as to how this might be done. All deplored any possible development of status among their women on the Ganda pattern.

I must repeat again that these latent economic and political functions were rarely consciously regarded as such. To most people the Union and associations helped people in trouble, might even set up a business in their own names, and provided much enjoyment through their soccer competitions in which spice was added by a fervent allegiance to one's own location team and hostility to others. Few people were consistently members of such associations. But there was always some activity in the name of the Luo Union or other association, frequently involving a hard core of the same people. The well-attended public meetings of the Union were really communal ceremonies in which latent themes were the expression of economic ties and political solidarity.

If one could regard the Union as in some respects a ceremonial institution, its leaders must be regarded as guardians of custom or proponents of morals. These were roles which were distinct from their roles as political representatives to the government or as businessmen, but they served to reinforce each other in practice, as is illustrated in the following case.

Guardians of custom

Henry, a Luo of Kisenyi, ran off with an older Luo's young wife whom he had known before she married. The girl was from Nyakach location while both Henry and the older man were from East Kano and of the same clan as Otieno, who has figured in previous cases. The older man was at home in Luoland when his wife was 'taken'. He reported the matter to his local chief, who wrote a letter to Otieno, as the leader of Kampala Kano association most closely related to the man. Otieno approached Henry, now in Kisenyi with his lover, and gently suggested that he send the girl back home to her husband. Henry refused and so Otieno felt it his duty to inform the Kano association committee and then to inform the Luo Union in the association's name.

After informing the Union, Otieno was advised to refer the matter to the Ganda chief of the Nakawa *gombolola* or sub-county, who, although he operated outside the city boundary, had the power to arbitrate in matters of tribal customary law if called upon. The Union quite frequently had matters of this sort referred in its name to the Ganda chief. An *askari* was sent, and Henry and the girl were arrested and remanded for five days, at the end of which the Luo Union obtained formal permission to submit the couple to 'trial' by their committee and some other selected Luo.

At the 'trial' were some fifteen officers and members of Kano association, all the Luo Union officers and some other men. Also present were three women. Two were wives of the chairman and secretary of the sports club. The third was the wife of an Alego man who was not a Union officer but had acquired renown by establishing a clan association and turning it into a flourishing business with three taxis in service and a shop at Kiswa.

Henry admitted his 'sin' almost immediately and claimed that the girl had said she was unmarried. Now that he knew she was

166

married he was prepared to abide by the Union's decision. The assembly did not trust the girl to go home by herself and so delegated the task of accompanying her to one older man who was an out-of-work relative of the husband, and to a *gombolola askari*, whose services had to be hired. The Union paid for this and for their fares by steamer to and from the husband's home. Otieno was given the task of writing to the chief in East Kano who had originally contacted him, telling him of the result of the case.

Sometime afterwards Henry's mother, perturbed that her son should run after a clansman's wife, sent a girl, whom he knew and liked, to him in Kampala as a wife. Henry was only labouring and did not earn much money, and after a few months decided, in 1963, that he and his wife should return home. After a short period at home he was able to get work as a porter on the railways in Nairobi through a Luo contact who, somewhat ironically, had himself been prominent in the Luo Union some time previously.

While 'sons' must not be allowed to err, they must also be looked after and 'guided'. This eventual peaceful settlement of conflicts among Luo over wives is not unusual, even if much anger is expressed beforehand. While Ganda legal institutions may be resorted to for legitimacy, Luo still prefer to settle the matter among themselves. The arbitrators and conciliators are the leaders of the community, and though cases of this kind do not often reach the level of the Union these days, even their spasmodic settlement at this level reimpresses on people's minds the real sources of influence in the Luo community.

The inclusion of women at the meeting would be defended on the grounds that the girl needed some of her kind to sympathize and put her point of view, and indeed their presence did give the girl confidence even though it made no difference to the wider implications of her 'elopement'. There is in general no objection to women being brought into certain Luo association affairs, and at least two wives of prominent Luo in Kampala occasionally addressed Luo Union meetings, one even becoming treasurer one year.

This integration, while due partly to demands made by a few wives and partly to a desire for this to happen by certain 'enlightened' male Luo, in many ways strengthens male authority by seeming to lend female support to institutions which males dominate. Thus, the women present at Henry and the girl's 'trial' did not dispute the undesirability of girls running away from husbands or of men stealing other men's wives. Females want conjugal stability and for the most part do get it, but the complementary implication is a continuation of their own fairly restricted status, except for those who are educated enough either to earn good money in a secure job or to demand in an articulate and effective manner some degree of emancipation. The latter are still very few.

Kisumo location association held a meeting in September 1963, at which a major proposal was to establish a women's branch. Thirteen men and three women attended. The chairman and outstanding leader was a man in his forties who had an affectionate but strongly authoritarian relationship with his wife. She ran a very successful vegetable stall at Nakasero and helped swell their domestic budget, which was severely strained by their eleven children, all living at their house at Nakawa. He worked long hours in a bakery. By their expectations the relationship was a mutually satisfying one. It was he who proposed this rather revolutionary departure from established association procedure among Luo in Kampala. He even proposed a women's football club as a subsidiary of the association which, having just won a championship, was in its heyday. Others pointed out that no other association had done any of this, though some had mooted the possibility. They liked the idea but felt that the matter should be given consideration. The proposal never took effect but was interesting in itself as an indication of the desire of at least some men to bring their wives into spheres of activity which remain under their control.

The exhortations of brotherhood, of observing Luo propriety, and preserving virtue among their women inevitably take on the shape of a special urban ethnic moral system. Special because in town it must constantly be emphasized to withstand the 'dangers' and 'corruption' believed to be inherent in the type of life found there. This moral system is the ideology expressed in any Migrant's network of 'brothers', described in a previous chapter. For Luo it is seen to operate effectively from the ego at the centre of any such network to the ethnic associations with which he is connected directly or indirectly, regularly or spasmodically.

The underlying common interests go far beyond the ideological and are of a many-sided economic and political nature. Luo have jobs which they feel have been threatened by the new tide of events which independence in Uganda seems to have brought. Those who have businesses are also threatened. If other Luo lose their jobs and leave Uganda then they will lose much of their clientele. Communication must be maintained in the growing competition for fewer jobs and fewer customers. Reassurance must be sought, as in religion, and what better than to obtain this through demonstrations of solidarity at well-attended meetings of the Union or through the collective enthusiasm of the soccer championship? The leaders are not gods but they are seen to have succeeded where others have failed and their links with both the Uganda and Kenya governments are very real and possibly not without influence.

Diversion of Interests to Politics in Kenya

The second strongest tribal association, that of Luhya, caters for a much smaller number of tribespeople, but in certain respects is similar to the Luo Union. It runs soccer league championships and tournaments and is part of a three-tiered pyramidal structure of associations. It consists of people and leaders at all levels either interested or active in small-scale commercial enterprises. It heads a scale of leaders from the 'big men' in touch with national governments to the central figure of an ordinary clan association. Though far fewer than Luo, the Luhya probably provided as many, even more, prominent trade unionists in Kampala. There was a similar overlapping of personnel in political, trade union, and tribal association leadership. It was mostly in the political field that Luo and Luhya were to establish jointly the acceptance of their expatriate status, doing so in what was another ceremonial show of alternating conflict and unity.

Their leaders did this in a general process involving three stages. The first was to move towards a policy of non-interference in Uganda politics and by implication to emphasize the neutrality and 'respectability' of tribal association leadership, so enabling them to retain a public platform. The second was to divert public attention to the political party division within Kenya on the eve of national elections there seven months before independence. The third was publicly to banish tribal and political conflict in favour of Kenyan unity only weeks before independence. The process made possible a public definition and acceptance of national identity during a period of political and legislative change, while at the same time allowing economic ties and interests to continue much as before.

Up until the national elections held in Kenya in May 1963, Luo and Luhya in Kampala were fairly clearly discernible as opposed in their support for the two Kenya political parties, KANU and KADU.

The conflicting policies of these two Kenya parties to a limited extent arose from a fear on the part of the smaller and politically weaker tribes making up KADU of domination by the larger Luo and Kikuyu. The KADU supporters wanted something of a federal structure for Kenya when she became independent, while KANU, consisting of most Luo and Kikuyu, the two largest tribes, wanted a more unitary state and opposed regionalism on the grounds that it would merely entrench problems of tribal difference.

While in Kampala there were a few Luhya who did support KANU, though no Luo to my knowledge who supported KADU, most Kenyans expressed the party conflict in these tribal terms. Certain issues seemed to confirm their impressions. A notable one was when a Kenya minister, who was a Luhya and member of KADU, came and addressed a political meeting at Naguru early in 1963. A large crowd was gathered. Possibly not realizing so many Luo were present, he addressed the crowd in a Luhya dialect and was angrily called upon by Luo to talk in Swahili, which he did. The Kenya national elections were due in a few months and undoubtedly there was considerable feeling over the division between the parties. Politically active Kenyans in Kampala, when asked at the time if the threat of Kenyans in Uganda losing their jobs did not allow them to forget their differences and close ranks, if only temporarily, always answered that the 'bitterness' between KANU and KADU and between Luo and Luhya was as strong as it was in Kenya. They claimed that their common interests as expatriates did not transcend their home political differences.

Yet there was an undercurrent of feeling among ordinary Kenyans that they should be non-political. They believed that the organization in Uganda of Kenya political party branches drew too much attention to their expatriate status and might in some way be regarded as irresponsible and bring about their eviction from Uganda. In October 1962, a short while after Uganda's independence, a number of Kenyans, mostly Luo, drawn from Nakawa and Kiswa met at the latter to protest at a KANU branch meeting held at Naguru, ostensibly to celebrate the anniversary of Mr. Kenyatta's release. The core of the organizers at Naguru were officers in the Luo Union and the effect of the protest was to impeach them in their capacity as tribal association leaders for 'interfering' in national politics.

In February 1963 the Luhya Association was involved in a controversy in which the association's leaders were accused of interfering in a Buganda by-election in Naguru, of the same name as the estate but outside the city. It was alleged that they had urged Luhya to vote for the DP candidate, who emerged victorious. The accusation appeared to come from UPC supporters. It transpired that only one member of the Luhya Association was guilty of this charge. He promptly had his membership of the association suspended. The president went to the extent of advertising this penalty in the national daily newspaper in order to show publicly that the association's policy was not to meddle in Uganda political affairs.

These and other cases demonstrate a growing sensitivity of Kenyans to involvement in Uganda politics. Nevertheless, many of the very leaders in the tribal associations had already been involved, either through Uganda trade unionism or ward or constituency elections. Disfranchisement and attacks on Kenya trade unionists now made it expedient for these leaders to emphasize and draw attention to different roles, one of which was leader of tribal association, publicly proclaimed to be nonpolitical. By remaining tribal leaders they continued to be known and regarded as representatives of their people in Kampala.

Having thus established the legitimacy of their standing as tribal leaders who would no longer participate in Uganda politics, at least to any observable extent, they then turned to the political affairs of their own country and established a KADU and re-established a KANU branch in Kampala. Both were located at Naguru estate and both included prominent members of the Luhya Association and Luo Union in their respective leadership. With KANU victorious in the Kenya national elections in May 1963, the KADU branch at Naguru disbanded almost immediately. From then on began a period in which a number of associations sprang up, involving the same small cliques of leaders, who now, however, proclaimed a policy of anti-tribalism and the political unity of all expatriate Kenyans.

This development involved three organizations, one the KANU association referred to, another the Uganda Kenya African Union, and the third the Kenya Independence Celebrations Committee.

The Uganda Kenya African Union (U.K.A.R.) had existed since 1959, when it was formed by an unemployed Luo who had been searching Kampala for a job as office messenger. Some time afterwards a number of prominent Luo are said to have complained that this man was too 'unknown' to lead such an organization, and three of them took it over. They apparently soon lost support, firstly because they did not fulfil the association's original objective to cater for individual welfare needs, and secondly because 'they used it as a platform for KANU speakers'.

The U.K.A.R. was re-established in June 1963, at Lugazi, where many Kenyans were employed on the sugar estates. Lugazi is a few miles from Jinja, the second largest town in Uganda and forty-eight miles from Kampala. Jinja has had a large proportion of Kenyans in its labour force since shortly after the Second World War. Most protests organized by Kenyans were held at Jinja, though many of the leaders involved were from the Kampala group. Most Kenyans in Uganda are located in either Kampala or Jinja, and the protests were publicized in a daily newspaper to appeal to as many as possible. In the *Uganda Argus* of July 13th, 1963, immediately following the new franchise regulations, the following appeared: 'Three meetings are due to take place in Jinja this weekend and during next week. The topics will be the alleged discrimination against Kenya workers and the effect of being a non-citizen of Uganda on Kenyan and African communities.

'A meeting of Kenya workers will take place in the Walukuba Community Centre this afternoon. It will be attended by delegates from Jinja, Kakira and the Lugazi sugar estates.'

The KANU branch in Kampala also entered the controversy on voting rights at that time but immediately withdrew on the principle that this was 'interference' in Uganda politics, or at least would only make Kenyans' position worse. The Luo secretary-

general of the branch who had issued a press statement condemning the new franchise system was immediately replaced by
the wife of the fairly well-off Luo who had stood as an independent
candidate for Kampala East in the 1962 council elections. These
kinds of action usually only involve a small number of leaders or
committee members, but they percolate to a wider public and in the
absence of anything more definite are taken as pointers in the
developing situation.

There was a final attempt by the UKAR at Lugazi to deal
with the anxieties over employment. A meeting with the Uganda
Prime Minister was advertised for the 28th July but never came
off. What went on in the corridors of power may never be known.
But it is clear that if employment opportunities continued to
decline as they had done up to the time of independence, and that
if there were Uganda citizens able to fill the jobs remaining, then
the Uganda government could hardly be expected not to give its
own citizens preference. The Kenya leaders in Kampala and Jinja
sensibly appreciated this, and saw their role not so much in
making militant protests that 'discrimination' should cease forth-
with, but in gently requesting that any possible redundancy among
Kenyans should be gradual so as to avoid a major social upheaval.
Their request was granted before it was made. Skills are scarce
and large numbers of men cannot summarily be dismissed over-
night to be replaced by new workers in the morning. Any redundancy could only be gradual, for the sake of Uganda's
economy as much as of Kenyan workers.

The other mediating role played by these Kenya leaders was to
pacify their own people, to suppress any show of militancy, as in
the instance mentioned above. Leaders, as minor property-holders
in many cases, as well as higher-grade workers and the ordinary
rank and file as employees in government and private industry, all
stood to lose by any rash outbreak of demonstrations incurring the
wrath or even anxiety of the Uganda government. Feelings did
indeed run high at times but the situation was delicate and most
leaders and ordinary people realized this. What they needed was
reassurance that the right course of action was simply to accept
their expatriate status without undue protest and to make their
own arrangements regarding a return to Kenya if this became
necessary.

This collective consciousness was achieved in a few weeks by a series of disputes occurring in the leadership first of the KANU branch and then in the Kenya Independence Celebrations Committee. As usual, there was considerable overlapping in the leadership of both.

There were many strands to these disputes and for clarity and brevity I give only the broad outlines. The KANU branch split into two during October 1963. It had been revived in July in order to prepare Kenyans in Uganda to celebrate Kenya's own independence due on December 12th.

The 'original' branch was the one already mentioned in which a Luo secretary-general was dismissed from office in July for issuing a hostile statement about the new voting rights. The Luo woman who replaced him, wife of the Luo notable who failed to become a municipal councillor, soon launched into an attack on the chairman, a Kikuyu, accusing him of embezzling the club's funds. He replied that he had used the money to make a necessary trip to Nairobi in connection with the proposed independence celebrations. He angrily called an *ad hoc* meeting which agreed to suspend the woman. A Luhya was elected in her place. A third Luo member of the committee left, after experiencing what he felt was opposition to his activities as press officer for the Youth Wing of the Uganda Democratic Party. Again, the opposition here was presumably based on the principle of non-interference in Uganda politics by Kenyans.

The dismissed Luo woman's husband, whom I shall call Michael, formed a Kenya Independence Celebrations Committee on the 10th October. Representatives from all Kenya tribes in Kampala were included on the understanding that each, however small, would be able to play its part in arranging tribal dances which were to be an important feature of the celebrations. Michael was made treasurer, another Luo chairman, and a Luhya secretary.

On the 19th of the month, these three, dissatisfied with the inactivity of the KANU branch, became part of a group which established another 'breakaway' KANU branch. The rather large committee consisted of twelve Luo and only the one Luhya, who was incidentally previously treasurer of the now disbanded KADU branch. The representatives of the other Kenya tribal groups claimed that this was 'tribalist domination' by Luo and dissociated themselves from both the KANU branch and the

Celebrations Committee, turning instead to the Kikuyu chairman of the original KANU branch.

This Kikuyu responded readily to the situation and re-established his own branch to include two Kikuyu, two Luo, a Kamba, a Luhya and a Kisii in its leadership. Those leaders of the Luo Union who were not part of Michael's Luo-dominated 'breakaway' branch condemned it and made known their support for the more obviously tribally representative one. The original and resuscitated branch then requested four men, two Luo, a Luhya and a Kamba, to head a Celebrations Committee. One of the Luo was Otieno, who thus again found himself confronting Michael, as he had over a year earlier in the municipal elections.

Both claimed legitimacy for their own Celebrations Committees and, as well as calling numerous meetings within days to prove their point, carried on a type of impersonal dialogue in the press, denying rights of recognition to the other committee and in one case mentioning its members by name, but stressing their intention to hold celebrations for all Kenyans regardless of tribe and political affiliation.

Crucially important was that though Michael had erred in setting up an almost entirely Luo committee in his breakaway KANU branch, he had been informed 'officially' by politicians in Nairobi that he should assist in organizing the Celebrations Committee. He had no legitimacy in his capacity as KANU branch organizer but he did in his Celebrations Committee. Otieno had been asked among others to run a Celebrations Committee in response to popular local demand among certain Kenyans in Kampala. But could popular appeal be regarded as more legitimate than 'orders' from Nairobi, the Kenya capital?

This problem of defining legitimacy was in the end decided by the arrival in Kampala of the assistant executive officer of the celebrations directorate in Nairobi. This officer, a Luo, had only a few months previously left Kampala, where he had been an appointed city councillor. He now successfully urged a re-election of a new committee from officers of the two old ones. Michael, much more influential and more widely known than Otieno and in spite of his connection with the breakaway KANU branch, was easily elected chairman, while Otieno was not elected into any office. As if to emphasize even more the new ideal unity of all Kenyans in Uganda, the official address of the committee was given as Jinja as a gesture to Kenyans there, although most members lived in Kampala.

In addition to Michael, the new officers included two former members of the dissolved KADU branch who were also leaders in the Luhya Association, the Luhya president of the also now defunct Uganda Kenya African Union, and a Kikuyu and three Luo who had not figured in the preceding association wrangles.

The result of these eventual settlements was that with only five weeks remaining before Kenya's independence day, the two groups of leaders in the KANU branch and Celebrations Committee were drawn from all the major Kenya tribal groups in Kampala. People like Michael with effective contacts with the real sources of power in Nairobi strengthened their positions while those like Otieno failed in the end to achieve any. The symbolic non-tribal unity included also the ending of dissension between KANU and KADU supporters and, in the eyes of many, between Luo and Luhya.

It is not suggested that all grievances and rivalries immediately ceased. What is significant is that an important Nairobi official, who had himself been a prominent Kenyan in Kampala, appeared personally to confer de jure status on certain of the disputants. The act had symbolic value not only in expressing a need for unity among all tribes and political parties, but also in impressing upon both participants and ordinary observers the need for a centralized arbitrating mechanism. The whole affair fitted in a practical manner into the ideology of nationalism.

In face-to-face communities symbolic acts of this sort can reach down to the ordinary man and help express identity of common interests. While there were important divisions, the Kenyans in Kampala had many of the attributes of a face-to-face community. Leaders had very little authority but could in crisis situations exert influence and were the only political representatives available to expatriate Kenyans. They existed at all levels of status grouping so that, even though top leaders might be out of personal contact with the bulk of the people, they constituted part of an informal chain of communication reaching down to them. They all had economic interests in common, either through continuing employment, and/or through small or large private enterprises and the maintenance of a largely ethnic clientele.

The series of disputes, occurring over a short period, involved a large number of associations: the Luo Union and Luhya Association; the KANU and KADU branches; the celebrations committees, and even, through indirect connections, the D.P., U.P.C. and certain trade unions. A breakdown of most of the leaders or committee members involved, however periphally, reveals this constantly shifting overlap in association leaders.

Information on the numerous positions occupied by thirty of them is that they include four full-time trade unionists, two ordinary trade union committee members, a shop steward, fourteen present or previous Luo Union leaders, five Luhya Association leaders, at least ten Luo location association leaders and one of a clan association, chairmen of two very small Kenya tribal associations in Kampala, a D.P. Youth Wing press officer, three officials in the former KADU branch, and three former leaders in the defunct Uganda Kenya African Union. All were at some stage holding office in one of the KANU branches and/or celebrations committees. Most lived in Kampala East, especially at Nakawa and Naguru, and about thirteen of them had small business interests of some kind here and elsewhere in Kampala.

The only constant organizations in this effective system of leadership and public communication were the Luo Union and Luhya Association and their subordinate associations. They had existed for years, adapting to demographic and socio-economic changes and giving way to decentralization but enabling the almost corporate Luo and Luhya communities in Kampala to continue as such by introducing the very popular soccer programmes. The ideology of brotherhood at the personal level, a structure of associations at a wider level, and the underlying economic and political common interests entrenched their ethnicity but, when the need arose, facilitated their adaptation to a necessarily precise definition of national status.

The other, non-Kenyan Migrants also had associations and were in this way distinct from the Host peoples. For most of them their associations' manifest aims had much in common with those of Luo and Luhya, but they affected proportionally fewer people and were weaker. They did not organize soccer programmes. In their current forms they were relatively recent creations. Their people were generally far fewer in Kampala than the two Kenya groups and this factor of numbers available to form associations must partly explain their lesser significance. However, there were peoples such as the Acholi, Kiga and Ankole who were probably as numerous or nearly as numerous in Kampala as the Luhya, and their associations did not match the Luhya Association in the extent of their activities. Many Kiga, Ankole and a much smaller proportion of Acholi are short-term, low-grade workers who are not attracted to membership of an association for the limited period they are in town, and this, too, is a factor in the development of ethnic associations.

Numbers in town, urban socio-economic status and length of residence, and type of rural social structure are certainly important variables in the formation of tribal associations.[3] But so also is the value of the tribal group in town as an economic and political clientele in trade unions, commerce, and in local and national politics. The Luhya were less numerous than Luo in Kampala and had fewer private business interests while being every bit as active in trade unionism. The Luo were numerous, were concerned with many private enterprises, and had entered trade unionism on a large scale. Both were expatriate groups who had been conscious of their exposure as such to any vagaries in employment. Before independence their apprehension was of Ganda, while after independence it was of the less easily delineated Uganda state. During this period of transition their ethnic associations played an important if indirect part in enabling their basic economic and political ties to be expressed first as ideological tribal, then as national bonds.

NOTES

[1] As mentioned earlier, of 223 properties at Kiswa, Ganda owned 141 and Luo 44. At Nakawa market Ganda hired 68 stalls and Luo 31 out of a total of 121. The bars and most shops at Nakawa and Naguru were owned by Luo. Outside Kampala East but in the city, Luo hired many stalls at the profitable Nakasero vegetable market.

[2] To avoid detailed references every time, I have used the term 'Kampala Luo community' in a general but loose sense. The many Luo, and Luhya, working for the East African Railways and Harbours are sufficiently distinct to be regarded as constituting a community in their own right. R. D. Grillo has confirmed my impressions in this regard. Most of them in Kampala live on the Nsambya railway workers' housing estate. Many are liable to sudden transfers to almost anywhere in East Africa. They are definitely townsmen but have strong links with many towns. They even have a language or at least a system of idioms of their own. They have a strong trade union and

secure jobs and in these respects are often the envy of other townsmen. Few figured in the Kampala ethnic associations I describe. Objectively they cannot be said to be as exposed politically and economically as non-railway Kenyan workers in Kampala.

[3] In D. J. Parkin, 1966, 'Urban Voluntary Associations as Institutions of Adaptation', *Man*, Vol. I, No. 1, I have discussed some of these variables in the context of the urban status system, concentrating on the variable of rural social structure. See also A. C. Cohen, 1966, 'Politics of the Kola Trade', *Africa*, Vol. 36, No. 1, in which he rightly suggests there has been an over-concern with the culture variable in J. Rouch, 1956, '*Migrations au Ghana*', *Journal de la Société des Africanistes*, Vol. 26, Paris, and M. P. Banton, 1957, *West African City*, O.U.P.

CHAPTER IX

CONCLUSIONS

Process

I have described the interaction of three types of variable relationship. Firstly, townsmen forge ties on the basis of status grouping in the Weberian sense of a distinct style of life. Secondly, their cultural links as members of an ethnic group or tribe persist in varying degrees of complexity. Thirdly, national affiliations emerge as a crucial factor requiring adjustment in all relationships.

The special local contexts of the situation described are important. Like most towns, Kampala-Mengo has distinct residential zones. Most such zones in Britain are appropriate to specific status groups, while many suburbs in the U.S.A. are parcelled out not only on this principle but also according to membership of religious and/or ethnic categories.[1] Kampala-Mengo perhaps more closely approaches this simple model of American suburbia.[2]

Southall has distinguished towns in Africa into two types, the 'old-established, slowly growing towns' and the 'new populations of mushroom growth'. This contrast was intended to be broad and recognized the overlap of criteria on which it was based.[3] Kampala-Mengo falls clearly into the older established type of town, yet an important part of it, notably Kampala city, is a modern enclave of the established Ganda-controlled municipality of Mengo. Those who least prefer or are unable to become assimilated into Ganda society live here. They include Europeans, most Asians, and better-off Africans, especially those whose home culture and language are in striking contrast to Ganda. Kampala East has only existed in its present viable form since the end of the Second World War and has seen the rapid growth of an incipient middle class and considerable local political and commercial activity.

Ganda have always predominated in the Kampala labour force but their position has been challenged if not superseded by increasing numbers of those whom I have called Migrants. The Kenyans emerged as by far the most effective group in this challenge, providing the impetus for trade-union development and

180

numerically increasing their hold on employment opportunities. The challenge has to be seen in the context of a rising tempo of nationalism both for Ganda and Kenyans, beginning in the mid-fifties. Ganda were undoubtedly the dominant power group in Uganda as a whole and this position was mirrored in their preponderance in the Kampala labour force, while Kenyans were effective through new ideas and organizational skills.

The Kenyans in Kampala are divisible into two main tribal groups, the Luo and Luhya. Both countered Ganda power in the manner described and at the same time continued to emphasize their individual identities as distinct ethnic groups and sub-groups. The more involved they became in the urban status system, the more certain of their leaders developed vested interests and encouraged tribal association, having become partly dependent on an ethnic clientele for economic and political purposes.

This structure of ethnic leadership and consciousness facilitated a timely expression of national identity among Kenyans in Kampala after Uganda's independence. It enabled leaders firstly to demonstrate Kenyans' 'voluntary' extrication from Uganda politics and secondly to acknowledge publicly their acceptance of expatriate status by an exaggerated what I would regard as ceremonial interest in their own country's politics.

They were undoubtedly anti-militant, preferring a policy of acquiescence to the new changes. Economic ties, either through private enterprise or wage employment, were not suddenly disrupted, though a 'state of readiness' was maintained in case they should be. At the egocentric level effective kin or 'brother' networks[4] continued to operate through an ideology mostly expressed over the status of women. At the categorical or tribal level the organization primarily of soccer and secondarily of other activities among fellow-tribesmen allocated leadership roles which were seen to reach in a chain from ordinary townsman to incumbent of high office.

Such tribal interests and ties had to be expressed subtly in order that they should not conflict with the exhortations for 'non-tribalism' at national and neighbourhood level. Tribal leaders tended to occupy other leadership roles and this helped to negate impressions of parochialism.

In summary, the whole process described is of tribal ties, ideology, and ceremony being used to express an acceptance of national political change while enabling the status system and certain common economic interests to continue relatively unaltered.

Kinship and Tribe as Variables

Max Gluckman's now famous statement is that 'The tradition of anthropology is still [i.e. 1959] "tribalistic", and with it goes a tendency to make the tribe and the tribesman the starting-point of analysis . . . it seems to me apparent that the moment an African crosses his tribal boundary to go to the town, he is "detribalized", out of the political control of the tribe.'[5] The point of this approach was to react against earlier studies which emphasized an urban migrant's tribal background as a crucial factor in what was believed to be a painfully slow process of 'detribalization'. As Mitchell has urged, an urban system of relations must indeed take priority over tribal origins as a starting-point for analysis.[6] It should be emphasized that neither author proposed that tribal factors were irrelevant in the form and content of urban relations. Epstein has pointed out that, though useful at an earlier time, Gluckman's firm formulation oversimplifies the complex interplay of factors, including those of tribe, in urban social systems.[7] If applied to Luo in Kampala the formulation would hide the possible utilization of the tribal category by townsmen as an instrument to preserve economic and political interests which are specifically urban.

Many scholars have emphasized the continuing importance of tribal factors in the sphere of domestic relations, in choosing a wife, or in finding employment or someone to lodge with.[8] Few have stressed that the sanctions and restraints involved in this enduring system of relations may vary considerably among different groups.[9]

I have shown how two 'supertribal'[10] categories do differ markedly and that the differences have relevance not only in domestic relations but also for the town's residential and status structure and may even be used as an initial basis or springboard for expressing national political affiliations.

It is likely that in other tribally mixed African towns the cultural contrasts of supertribal or ethnic groups may become convenient vehicles of expression for underlying political and economic conflict. As Banton points out,[11] the pre-independence 'structural opposition' in the Central African Copperbelt urban areas was based on 'a clear-cut racial division of labour'. Europeans were opposed by Africans, a unitary opposition which subordinated the expression of divisions within the African population itself.[12] With political independence and eventual greater economic self-sufficiency one might expect the latter to emerge at some stage in one form or another.

In Freetown, Sierra Leone, a long-standing structural opposition was between Creoles, the 'host' people, and immigrant tribespeople, with Europeans an insignificant element. Creoles have since lost their political power and the conditions are set for oppositions to arise within and between ethnic groups. At least this is a possible development. Banton sees this as part of the problem of alternating alignments and identities of tribe and class in social change. Competition for the inevitably scarce economic resources has always been a major factor of integration and opposition and will continue to be so, and the realities of recent political independence in many African nations add a new dimension to this process.

Ethnic cultural differences are infinite and their possible social significance is very much related to the local situation. In Kampala-Mengo highly contrasting differences in kinship structure are important. It is a truism that the value of kinship relations in African towns persists. In a general sense it changes to accommodate emerging 'class' differences,[13] yet specific differences between ethnic groups may remain constant within this general change. There is no evidence that a universalistic 'non-tribal', class-differentiated kinship structure will emerge in Kampala-Mengo, or in other African towns.

For a tribally heterogeneous town it may be possible, on the basis of empirical data, to construct a continuum of differences in kinship network effectiveness coinciding with broad ethnic differences. Hosts and Migrants in Kampala would occupy opposing halves of the continuum, with Ganda and Luo at the extremes. The factors underlying the differences in urban kinship effectiveness, that is the extent to which an ego mobilizes and recruits 'kin' for whatever purposes, may perhaps be seen to vary more by tribe than 'class', though there will be some overlap. 'Traditional' systems are not always completely dead and may have variable relevance for urban life. Other factors are a tribe's distance from town, its historical and cultural relationship to it, its proportion of the urban population, its socio-economic span and extent of urban role involvement.

Data is insufficient but West Africa may provide parallels with Kampala. Thus, in Monrovia, Liberia, a contrast is noted between Vai, who at home were traditionally hierarchically organized, and Kru, who, like Luo, are decentralized and segmentarily organized. Fraenkel notes that young Kru try to avoid the onerous expectations constantly made of them by kin and there is no suggestion that Vai are subject to the same extent to this system of sanctions and restraints by kin. She says, '. . . Kru households, compared with those of other tribes, contained few children who were not related by kinship to the household head. In fact, the Kru criticize other tribes, notably the Vai, for their practice of sending children away to be brought up by strangers . . . ',[14] a striking parallel of criticism on similar issues made by Luo and other Migrants of Ganda and other Host peoples in Kampala.

Banton tentatively ventures an explanation for the difference between Mende and Temne migrants in Freetown, Sierra Leone, partly in terms of differences in rural social structure. The Mende have never formed tribal associations while among the Temne they have developed rapidly and widely. He says, '. . . it is not easy to see why the two tribes should differ in this way, for the social circumstances of Temne and Mende immigrants in Freetown are very similar'. He suggests that there may be 'greater scope for private initiative in the traditional social structure of the Temne and more devolution of authority'. The Kru, like Temne, form many associations. Banton notes 'that before the end of the nineteenth century the Kru brought with them to Freetown from Liberia the basic notions of a contractual association. From what we know of the traditional Kru social structure it was of the decentralized segmentary type with age grades, resembling that of the Ibo and Yakö. A working hypothesis may therefore be advanced that, other things being equal, the more devolution of authority there is in tribal societies the more rapidly contractual associations emerge.'

This hypothesis was based on the fact that the Mende chief exercised personal rule and had clearly defined secular authority, while the Temne chief was traditionally no more than a semi-sacred figure. 'The Mende look to the chief to deal with problems which the Temne, thinking them alien to the chief's duties, attempt to solve by their own activities.'[15] Fraenkel uses the hypothesis in an attempt to explain the formation of associations among Kru in Monrovia and their absence among Vai. The examples of strong association development given by Little include Ibo and Ibibio, who are culturally similar to Kru and Temne.[16]

Piecing together these items of evidence one might suggest a distinction between those societies in which, in the traditional absence of specialized authority roles, there is a relatively strong persistence of effective kin relations in town and among whom there is a tendency to create ethnic associations, and those in which kin relations are much looser-knit, less restrictive and more open to choice, there is more reliance on a traditional but continuing system of secular, full-time chiefs, and less tendency to establish urban tribal associations. The Host and Migrant peoples in Kampala might fit into this distinction quite well except that the former figuratively 'owned' Kampala and so had little need to form associations, while the Migrants were 'foreigners' and might in any event be expected to form them. Additionally, both tribal and non-tribal associations in Kampala East have to be seen as an expression of the overall status system, with 'big men' leading the higher-ranked associations and lower-status men running the smaller, less prestigeful associations. Luo and Luhya associations had the further economic and political significance already discussed. The straight relationship between rural structure and urban tribal association formation is thus better regarded as simply a possible variable though by no means a crucial one. This is the line taken by Cohen[17] and is implied in Banton's qualification of his hypothesis, 'other things being equal'. Evidence from pre-independent Zambia where tribal associations were of very limited significance supports this view. Here the racial cleavage of African and European may have been crucial.[18]

What is perhaps more useful is to consider the distinction between these societies in so far as their urban kinship networks are highly contrasting. 'Other things being equal', societies among whom even nowadays much of rural social life is mediated through extended families or local descent groups, especially agnatic ones, tend to provide the best conditions for the existence of effective kin networks in town. Societies which generally lack these rural features and mediate many of their social relations through patron-client relationships, often of a non-kinship nature,[19] allow for the existence of extensive urban kin networks which are not, however, so consistently effective for an ego and which are rarely mobilized over issues to do with family life at home. What might be called the property of group mobilization is stronger for Migrant than Host kin networks in Kampala.[20]

This is a rough distinction and obviously tautological. Its importance for the Kampala situation is in demonstrating the existence for Migrants of a pool of people within the tribal category who can in some way be regarded by a man as his 'kin' or 'brothers' and who interact frequently on the basis of this shared ideology. The making and breaking of relationships beyond the extended family has little to do with the domestic issues suggested by the ideology but does enable a core of the same people to maintain constant contact. The successive overlapping of these networks means that the bulk of a man's role-relationships are within the tribal category, that is, with fellow-tribesmen, while the looseness of the ideology enables a man to claim legitimacy for many courses of action and so be allowed considerable choice within the tribal field.

Among Luo conflict within this field has been a focus of considerable co-operation. Ogot has spoken of the 'migratory vein' among Luo as an historical and modern cultural trait.[21] Ever since the extension in 1901 of the railway in Kenya from Mombasa and Nairobi to the Luo capital of Kisumu, the Luo have spread far and wide as artisans, clerks and unskilled workers to towns throughout East Africa. While they have become increasingly differentiated by status or 'class' they have maintained over this period a strong ideology of 'brotherhood' which has been sustained by its flexibility and usefulness. In earlier years its usefulness was in providing the distant links prior to urban migration necessary for accommodation and employment. In later years, as numbers swelled and some accumulated a little capital, it provided a ready clientele in private enterprise. In Kampala and elsewhere, it provided an additional springboard for entry into trade unionism and politics, many of the leaders in which first operated in the Luo Union.

The Luhya did not regard themselves, nor did they interact as a single cohesive ethnic group until recent years and their links were less tenuous and their urban migration less penetrating. But they have shown similarities of the same process.

None of this is to suggest that the 'cause' or 'explanation' of widespread urban migration by Luo lies ultimately in their ideology of brotherhood. Indeed no 'cause' is postulated at all. What is suggested is that this ideology has been of functional significance during their economic and political development in towns. That is to say, it was and is 'useful' in maintaining a system of communication, in providing an initial forum for leadership, and in the development of common economic interests. Yet it is sufficiently flexible to allow conflicting but not contradictory evaluations of behaviour. It thus confers legitimacy both on the ordinary man who wishes to loosen though not sever ties with a senior kinsman and on the local leader who alters his role for appropriate situations, tribal leader in one context, but trade unionist, 'businessman' or entrepreneur, or political leader in others. In general it enables the rationalization of a rapid but continual circulation of role-relationships among the same people.

Urbanism

For Africa there has been considerable literature on urbanization, the process of becoming a townsman, more than urbanism, the way of life in town. 'When is a townsman not a townsman?' seems to be the question in some of the studies of urbanization.

But, in structural terms, the bald notion of 'townsman' is unhelpful, even meaningless. So, for that matter, is the notion of 'town'. They are unhelpful because they have to be defined by reference to a particular town and to a particular regional context. Thus, Schwab expresses difficulty as to whether Oshogbo, a lineage-based Yoruba township, is in fact urban, and seems to imply, rightly, that this label does not really matter.[22] After all, if Oshogbo and huge, industrialized, pluralistic Johannesburg are both classed as urban, then the notion ceases to have much value. This is an obvious point. We can, of course, draw up various measureable criteria and then classify this wide range of social entities into ideal types, as has been done in distinguishing 'urban' from 'rural'. This is an interesting exercise and certainly has value, especially in making statements about variations in role structure generally, though, as Hilda Kuper says,[23] this classification of ideal types, if it continues as no more than a classification, can become too out of touch with reality and lose sight of empirical social process. I shall return to this problem.

The point I want to make here is that the notion of 'townsman', because it is tied to a particular local or ethnographic context, is essentially a cultural one. Thus, Wilson and Mafeje's three-fold classification of migrant, semi-urbanized, and townsmen, only has meaning in the context of Langa township, near Cape Town.[24] Philip Mayer's Red and School migrant types are, also, as he points out, culturally defined.[25] But the process of 'incapsulation', and its opposite, is a structural one, because it can be seen to operate not just in towns but in any single system of relations in which cultural differences are articulated to express and even manipulate socio-economic status differences, or economic and political divisions.

Putting it crudely, 'structure' is based on such divisions, while 'culture' includes the ideas people have of this distribution of power and authority and their modes of expressing these ideas in behaviour and conversation. Certain attempts at structural-role analysis have gone beyond mere classification and demonstrate the different patterns of key variables. Southall proposes six aspects of role change involved in the transition from 'rural' to 'urban'.[26] Frankenberg incorporates these in his own rural-urban continuum of role types and activity.[27] Basically both Southall and Frankenberg explain the process whereby urban roles have become more highly specialized, more highly differentiated or marked off and observable, and tend to occur among a larger number of people than in a rural or tribal area. They do this with sophistication and in detail, which need not be dealt with here. These are primarily attempts to define town and country in structural terms, though each author is aware, and indeed suggests, that his role theory or continuum might be used to analyse the *internal* processes of an urban, rural, or any community, as well as simply distinguishing between them. Certainly, as fewer studies in future deal with urbanization and more concentrate intensively on urbanism, we can expect these ideas to be applied in the analysis of the structurally differing groups and sub-groups *within* a single urban system of relations.[28] In this way a use may be found for classifications, and a possible tendency to over-classify and lose sight of empirical process, of which Hilda Kuper warns us, may be avoided.

The trouble with the conventional notion of 'urbanization' is that it assumes that there is a final stage to be reached. Mitchell has warned us not to confuse people's commitment to a town with their involvement in its system of relations:[29] long residence and the need to work in a town do not necessarily imply support for and participation in all its institutions. One suspects that in many African towns the maintenance of two systems of relations, town and country, may be a virtually permanent feature of their working populations, even where they are highly involved in the urban system of relations. Far from being incompatible, economic and social interests in town and rural home area may complement each other. This does seem to be the case in Kampala-Mengo.

The need for ultimate social security is one of a number of reasons for maintaining strong links with the rural home and, by way of reinforcing these links, for adhering to customary expectations in urban domestic life. This at least is a stated reason. But it is not only the poor people in towns who stress custom in order to maintain rural links. Well-off urban leaders who are supported by fellow tribesmen in town, whether or not this support is openly admitted to be tribal, also need to keep open chains of communication with their supporters, and what better way to do this than by emphasizing the highest common factor in their cultural attributes—namely, the propriety of their own customs.

There are a number of factors to elucidate here. The cultural factors are of two broad types: those values and modes of behaviour which ostensibly derive from the town's social relations and which are not associated with any particular tribespeople or ethnic group—simple examples are the use made of prestige-awarding situations and status symbols, as for example in moving from Nakawa to Naguru in Kampala East, or in visiting 'bottle-beer' bars rather than traditional ones; then there are those values and modes of behaviour which *are* associated with a particular tribespeople or ethnic group and which directly affect domestic relations and family life—examples are the differing conceptions of the status of women between Hosts and Migrants, and more specifically, a man's choice of a wife not only from his own tribe but also from his own home area where she will be married in customary manner, as among Migrants, or the differing notions among Ganda and Luo regarding the employment and status of servants to which Southall drew attention (see footnote 1 on page 148).

Complementing these cultural features of urban life are structural ones, which derive from the distribution of jobs and economic opportunity and of power and authority. Some of the 'external determinants' and 'extrinsic factors' described respectively by Mitchell[30] and Southall,[31] and referring in summary to administrative, settlement, demographic, mobility, and stratification patterns, seem to me to have been much more 'external' or 'extrinsic' in the colonial than in the post-colonial era. Since independence, decisions relating to the control and planning of these factors are taken by persons who are inextricably involved in the long-term system of relations in a way that colonial administrators were not.

The description in chapter two of the municipal council elections in Kampala East showed this inextricable chain-like involvement of remote party leaders, intermediary local and not-so-local candidates, and the ordinary voter. Though they clearly differ in the scale of their applicability, these 'external' factors are structural ones, in so far as they relate to positions of power and authority. Any planned alteration of these factors through legislation or inducement necessarily has implications for and is affected by the ethnic composition of, say, urban councils and the types of support relied on by their members.

The transition from colony or protectorate to independent nationhood is, after all, a political transformation, however strong the old economic grip remains, and it would be surprising if this were not reflected in an alteration of relations at many levels of society, urban and rural.

A crucial problem in urbanism is the interplay of these structural and cultural factors both synchronically and over time. Cultural factors are only sociologically significant if there are mutually observable cultural differences. That is to say, among different groups involved in a single system of relations, cultural differences express their positions in the social structure, or, more importantly, offer them possibilities of articulating their positions in the structure. I have tried to show in this book that, before independence, the cultural division of Hosts and Migrants broadly expressed and coincided with a political and economic cleavage. With the approach of and after independence, Kenya Luo and Luhya among the Migrants 'used' their cultural distinctiveness and their common language of custom and belief to express at a public level an acceptance of their expatriate status and, at an egocentric level, continued as before to mobilize networks of kin and fellow tribesmen as possible sources of aid and support.

These comments give the impression that cultural factors have no 'reality' of their own, that they are simply customs and beliefs used with great fluidity as situation demands to mark up changes in the wider politico-economic structure. In fact, as is well known, people do not 'slavishly obey the dictates of custom', values and beliefs, and there must be 'real' structural relations underlying them in turn, however much divergence between action and ideal there is. Where, then, do these *second-order* structural relations lay? They lay in urban domestic life—that is to say, in marriage and family patterns and the system of kinship obligations. And urban domestic life, as I hope I have shown in this book, derives much of its form and content from the respective rural social structures of urban groups. Obviously, new and specifically urban patterns are emerging, but, as is shown by evidence from urban populations which maintain strong rural links, expectations deriving from rural social structures remain important in urban domestic life.

It follows, therefore, that in a single system of relations such as characterizes a town, and in which there are (1) strongly maintained rural links by the majority of the urban population, and (2) ethnic diversity, contrasting rural social structures will entail contrasting patterns of urban domestic life among ethnic groups. The significance of this tautology is in explaining the existence of diverse cultural ideologies which may be utilized in contexts other than that of urban domestic life.

The suggestions contained in this section may be summarized in the form of an ideal paradigm: Kampala-Mengo's population is both ethnically diverse and does maintain strong rural links; the contrasting rural social structures of Host and Migrant groups within the urban population define structurally their contrasting urban domestic and kinship systems; though structurally defined, these contrasted urban domestic and kinship systems constitute founts of ideal norms and beliefs, in short an ideology of kinship, the use of which may sometimes be drawn beyond the 'pragmatic' requirements of domestic life and kinship; this elasticity of the ideology of urban kinship, and, by extension, of traditional custom generally, enable it to express, and to be articulated to express, positions held by groups in the first-order structure of power and authority; as an ideology, or a way of expressing ideas about structure, it is cultural, yet rests 'basically' on the 'real', second-order structural relations of urban domestic life and kinship.

There are thus two 'structures': a first-order one of the widest level concerning the distribution of power, authority, and economic opportunity in the single urban system of relations; and a second-order one of the urban domestic life of individual ethnic groups whose rural home systems of land tenure, marriage, residence and descent have great relevance.

There are also two 'cultural' systems: an ideology of kinship and traditional custom which emanates from urban domestic life but which becomes a diacritical and syncretic characteristic of individual ethnic groups and tribespeople in political and economic contexts; and a collection of notions centring on a common pursuit of prestige and status symbols, and reinforced by values set on 'non-tribalism' at neighbourhood and national level.

The second of these cultural systems derives from and is permanently associated with the first-order structure of power, authority, and wealth. The first of these cultural systems, the ideology of kinship and custom, does derive ultimately from different rural structures, but alternates between being associated with urban domestic life and with the first-order structure. That is to say, in one situation, activity justified in the name of 'proper Luo kinship and customs' has relevance for settling ordinary domestic problems. Yet it may also be the idiom through which people are kept together and in a constant state of communication during what is believed to be a period of political exposure.

If the ideology of kinship and custom, as a cultural system, is so flexible, then it must surely be of prime analytical importance in towns of ethnic diversity and characterized by strong rural links among its population. Admittedly, not all African urban populations are either ethnically mixed or simultaneously involved in a home rural system of relations. But those of the newer towns distinguished as Type B by Southall, and also some of Type A, tend to be. In such towns, an important variable worthy of attention is *the degree of ideological commitment to a kinship-tribal role structure as a reservoir of urban economic and political roles.*[32] Strong ideological commitment of this kind does not preclude 'full' participation in urban institutions, as is illustrated by the Luo, Luhya and other Migrants of Kampala East.

The case of Luo, in particular, suggests that members of an urban ethnic group can be highly involved in the wider urban status system—that is to say, can become fully-fledged townsmen, yet at the same time can preserve considerable ethnicity by emphasizing a diffuse kinship-tribal role structure. The diffuseness of the structure allows conflicting evaluations of individual courses of action while enabling a blanket cover of ideology and ceremony to be utilized for more concerted activity as occasion demands. While the underlying bases of such ethnicity are common economic and status interests, the occasions demanding concerted activity are political, especially of a national kind since independence.

Other tribespeople may use different rural cultural idioms. The virtually non-corporate Ganda kinship system would not be a good idiom for expressing underlying economic or political solidarity, because it does not normally provide issues around which people, exhorted in the name of kinship, descent or affinity, may be mobilized. The Kabakaship, or features of rank and nobility, deriving from the centralized state structure, would possibly provide more viable cultural idioms.

The variable I have put forward is part of a wider sociological phenomenon. In a plural society, for example, cargo cults among indigenous people 'expressed their political mood neatly'.[33] The parallel is a loose one, but 'activist' cargo cults and 'passivist', secular emphasis on tribal ideology in plural social situations may have similar latent functions.

NOTES

[1] Such as Italian or Irish Catholics, Jews, Negroes, and white Protestants of 'Anglo-Saxon origin', the now proverbial 'Wasps'. A. C. Cohen discusses such similarities of ethnicity in a forthcoming monograph.

[2] M. P. Banton touches on similarities and contrasts between Freetown, Sierra Leone and American cities. 'Social Alignment and Identity in a West African City' in Hilda Kuper (ed.), 1965. *Urbanization and Migration in West Africa*, University of California Press.

[3] A. W. Southall (ed.), 1961, op. cit.

⁴ These would be called action-sets in A. C. Mayer's terminology, 1966, 'Quasi-groups in the Study of Complex Societies' in A.S.A. Monograph No. 4, *The Social Anthropology of Complex Societies*, Tavistock, London. I have used network in Bott's and Epstein's senses of ego-centred entities. This is different from J. A. Barnes' use of network as a general mesh of ties not centred on an ego. J. A. Barnes, 1954, 'Class and Committees in a Norwegian Island Parish', *Human Relations*, Vol. 7.

⁵ M. Gluckman, 1961, 'Anthropological Problems Arising from the African Industrial Revolution' in A. W. Southall (ed.), op. cit.

⁶ J. C. Mitchell, 1966, 'Theoretical Orientations in African Urban Studies' in A.S.A. Monograph No. 4, op. cit.

⁷ A. L. Epstein, 1967, 'Urbanization and Social Change', *Current Anthropology*, Vol. 8. No. 4.

⁸ P. Mayer, 1961, op. cit. J. C. Mitchell, 1957, 'Aspects of African Marriage on the Copperbelt of Northern Rhodesia', *Rhodes-Livingstone Journal*, No. 22. A. L. Epstein, 1958, op. cit. pp. 232 et seq. M. Wilson and A. Mafeje, 1963, *Langa*, O.U.P., Cape Town. A. W. Southall (ed.), 1961, op. cit. pp. 31 et seq. J. A. K. Leslie, 1963, *A Social Survey of Dar es Salaam*, O.U.P. for E.A.I.S.R. p. 33.

⁹ P. Mayer, op. cit., does bring out clearly the relationship of differing social networks and degree of 'incapsulation' within an ethnic group. See footnote 12 below.

¹⁰ J. Rouch, 1956, op. cit. Here the concept of supertribalism is introduced.

¹¹ M. P. Banton, 1965, in Hilda Kuper (ed.), op. cit.

¹² Deep divisions within the African population are subordinated to the general racial division in South African towns, but different cultural patterns emerge. In the all-Xhosa town of East London, immediately adjacent to Xhosa reserves, Phillip Mayer, 1961, op. cit., shows that pagan 'Red' contrast with Christian 'School' migrants in remaining 'incapsulated' in home-based groups while School migrants express urban-status consciousness in different styles of life and are less 'traditional'. In Cape Town, which is tribally mixed but still predominantly Xhosa and more distant from tribal reserves, a tripartite division of the most to least 'incapsulated' is of paramount significance, so that even at the lowest level Red and School mix in common home-based groups. M. Wilson and A. Mafeje, op. cit.

¹³ For an analysis of how lineage relations may retain strength in the face of status differentiation in a Yoruba town, see W. B. Schwab, 1965, 'Oshogbo—an Urban Community?' in Hilda Kuper (ed.) op. cit.

¹⁴ M. Fraenkel, 1964, *Tribe and Class in Monrovia*, O.U.P. for I.A.I., p. 116.

¹⁵ M. P. Banton, 1957, op. cit., p. 195.

¹⁶ K. Little, 1965, *West African Urbanization*, Cambridge U.P., pp. 34 and 162.

Apparent similarity in certain respects between Ibo and Luo is worth noting. The Ibo of Nigeria have migrated widely to work in other regions of the state. Like the Luo, they are highly individualistic and successful in private enterprise, yet they maintain highly effective links with kin and other fellow-tribesmen (see S. Ottenberg, 1959, 'Ibo Receptivity to Change', in W. R. Bascom and M. J. Herskovits, *Continuity and Change in African Cultures*,

University of Chicago Press). It is remarkable that, after the massacres and expulsion of Ibo from the north of Nigeria in 1966, two million of them were somehow absorbed into Ibo society through extended family links, even though many had lived outside Iboland all their lives.

[17] A. C. Cohen, 1966, op. cit.

[18] A. L. Epstein, 1966, op. cit.

[19] Note here Southall's comment, 'Kinship roles are the fundamental matrix from which other roles emerge, and there is an inverse relationship in any society between the political aspect of kinship roles and the level of political role differentiation', A. W. Southall, 1965, op. cit., p. 124. While this is intended as an ideal formulation of the interplay of the kinship and political role variables, it is of relevance for domestic relations among those townsmen whose local authority systems retain some 'traditional' characteristics in spite of subordination to the modern State. In this regard Luo and Ganda contrast strikingly at the home local group level and will continue to do so for years, a factor in their more general contrast in Kampala.

[20] Reverting again to A. C. Mayer's terminology, op. cit., this would mean that Migrant kin networks consist much more of frequently superimposed action-sets and would thus be classed by Mayer as quasi-groups.

[21] B. A. Ogot, 1966, *History of the Southern Luo*, East African Publishing House, Nairobi, p. 239.

[22] W. B. Schwab, 1965, op. cit.

[23] Hilda Kuper (ed.), 1965, op. cit., pp. 12 et seq.

[24] M. Wilson and A. Mafeje, 1963, op. cit.

[25] P. Mayer, 1961, op. cit.

[26] A. W. Southall, 1959, 'An Operational Theory of Role', *Human Relations*, Vol. 12.

[27] R. Frankenberg, 1966(a), 'British Community Studies', in A.S.A. Monographs No. 4., op. cit., and 1966(b), *Communities in Britain*, Harmondsworth, Penguin Books.

[28] As an example, the quasi-corporateness of Luo in Kampala East, deriving from their putative political exposure and expressed in certain traditional idioms of descent and fraternity, made them more 'close-knit' as a grouping than others. Following Southall's terminology, we can say that they showed a 'lower density of role texture' (i.e. had more multiplex relations) than other co-resident urban groupings. At a more general level, this is a characteristic of 'rural' as opposed to 'urban' relations, as suggested by Southall, 1959, op. cit.

[29] J. C. Mitchell, 1956, 'Urbanization, detribalization and stabilization in Southern Africa', in *Social Implications of Industrialization and Urbanization in Africa South of the Sahara*, (ed.) D. Forde. UNESCO., Paris.

[30] J. C. Mitchell, 1966, op. cit., p. 49.

[31] A. W. Southall, 1961, op. cit., p. 5.

[32] I should like at this point to acknowledge my indebtedness to A. C. Cohen for much stimulation regarding these ideas, both in discussion and in his written work. See his 1968, 'The Politics of Mysticism in Some Local Communities in Newly Independent States', in M. Swartz (ed.), *Local*

Level Politics, Aldine, Chicago, and 1967, 'Stranger Communities: The Hausa', in Lloyd, P., *et al.*, (eds.) *The City of Ibadan*, Cambridge U.P.

[33] P. Worseley, 1957, *The Trumpet Shall Sound*, p. 44, Macgibbon and Kee, London.

ADDITIONAL DETAILS ON THE MAIN TRIBES
REPRESENTED IN KAMPALA-MENGO

The Ganda are the tribe local to Kampala. Buganda is one of
the four provinces of Uganda. But only about two-thirds of the
people in Buganda are Ganda. Most of the non-Ganda are immigrant labourers who have either come to work for Ganda landlords or have been given permission by them, in return for a fee, to
occupy and work land themselves. But the Ganda themselves
number over a million. Their kingdom has always enjoyed a
considerable degree of autonomy even under British rule. At
independence its internal autonomy in the Uganda state posed a
difficult and delicate problem for this nation. A symbolic gesture
towards mitigating this problem was made in 1963 when the
Kabaka or king of Buganda was given the title of President of
Uganda, which was withdrawn in 1966. Afterwards there were
constitutional amendments effectively eliminating the status of
this and other kingdoms and bringing them more into line with
other provinces.

Under the British, Ganda autonomy derived from the recognition by the colonial power of the relative political advancement
of the kingdom when F. D. Lugard first made his claim over it in
1890. Considerably modified, though in many ways even more
institutionally entrenched, the Ganda kingdom endorsed its
political and social complexity under the British. The traditional
system of land tenure had been at the basis of the feudal-like
system of social stratification. There were various legal enactments
with regard to land tenure at intervals from the beginning of the
twentieth century onwards. There was also the introduction of the
cash-cropping of cotton and coffee and immersion in a cash
economy. These innovations put even higher material and status
value on individual land tenure, to some extent ownership. The
resultant factors of individual and *de facto* freehold land tenure,
more or less so in different regions, more individualistically based
and achieved social strata, and the subsequent physical dispersion

of people made the system of stratification more class-like and less based on, among other things, agnatic kinship affiliations.[1] The situation now is that, though the Ganda are still referred to as 'patrilineal', the transmission of property, including land, authority and status, is sometimes passed down through women as well as men. Women may own and dispose of property as they please. Patriliny is a relative concept and, compared with certain tribes of East Africa, Ganda kinship affiliations may nowadays be regarded as bilateral in many respects, not only in the transmission of property and rights, but also in situations of expressive and instrumental coactivity. Lineages and clans are generally not localized.

The Toro[2] in particular, and, to lesser extents, the Soga[3] and Nyoro[4], share many characteristics of present-day Ganda social organization.

The four tribes fall into what are called the Interlacustrine Bantu, all of which have been referred to as patrilineal. The Toro and Nyoro are two tribes of the Western Province. Like the Ganda, they had a supreme tribal ruler or king, called the Omukama. Both tribes have until recently preserved, or have been encouraged to preserve, their traditional fairly highly centralized political systems. The Soga of the Eastern Province consisted of a number of petty kingdoms, each highly centralized. There was no supreme Soga ruler. The Kyabazinga was a modern constitutional head of the whole Soga tribe and district and from 1963 to 1966 was Vice-President of Uganda.

Among these tribes there have been few legal enactments over the years relating to land. But cash-cropping has developed on appreciable scales, particularly in Busoga. *De facto* freehold land tenure, or at least the acquiring and holding of land by individuals rather than minimal lineages, has developed in some areas, particularly those close to towns. 'Tithes' payable to village head-men or chiefs for the use of land are in many cases considerable sums of cash. Kinsmen, including agnates, are commonly physically dispersed. Aspects of a more bilateral kinship system have emerged. Lineages and clans, like those of the Ganda, are generally not localized.

The Ankole were also traditionally politically centralized. They had a supreme ruler, the Omugabe. The traditional caste-like division between ruling pastoral Hima and agricultural, serf-like

Iru has not broken down completely. Unfortunately little is known about the present-day kinship and local organization of the Ankole.[5] But the Iru appear in some cases to be settled in patrilineage-based local communities and do not as yet seem to have acquired the characteristics of the centralized tribes above. In other cases, descent groups have become dispersed and other local groups have emerged with a consolidated interest in bananagrowing. It is only the Iru who are significant in Kampala's labour force, according to the statements of Kampala Ankole themselves. For these reasons it would be unjustifiable to regard the Ankole who work in Kampala in quite the same light as the Ganda, Soga, Toro and Nyoro. Moreover they are numerically insignificant in Kampala East.

The Ankole Iru seem to share much in common with the Kiga. The Ankole and Kiga are adjacent tribes of the Western Province. Like the four tribes described above, the Ankole and Kiga speak Bantu languages which, in their case, are mutually intelligible. The Kiga appear to be organized similarly into localized agnatic lineages and clans, though the genealogical depth of these units is still not known.[6] Kiga traditional society was politically uncentralized. Modern Kiga society has none of the stratification of the Interlacustrine Bantu kingdoms.

The Ruanda do not originate from Uganda, though a number have settled and in some cases were born in Buganda, where they have migrated in large numbers to work for Ganda landowners.[7] The one-time kingdom of Ruanda lies to the south of Uganda. Its system of stratification was caste-like, consisting of a division between pastoral Tutsi and agricultural Hutu, and was thus more similar to the Ankole system than that of the other Interlacustrine kingdoms.[8] Most of the Ruanda who have migrated to work in Kampala itself are said to be Hutu, though the fact that a significant though small minority of Tutsi are in the town is suggested by the alleged sometime existence of individual and separate Hutu and Tutsi Kampala tribal associations, though I have no personal evidence of the latter.

The Haya, or Ziba as they are alternatively known in Kampala, were also traditionally politically centralized. Their language is similar to the dialects of the Nyoro, Toro, and Ankole, though their political organization into autonomous petty kingdoms was similar to that of the Soga.

An impression is that most of the Haya who have migrated to Kampala are self-employed and unskilled workers. Many of the migrants are unattached women who are widely reputed to be traders, market-stall-holders, and, especially, prostitutes. Like the Ruanda, most of whom are also unskilled, the Haya assume many Ganda characteristics of behaviour and, to some extent, have entered the lower cadres of Ganda life and even of the Ganda population. A feature of Ganda rural society is its easy assimilation of strangers. There are very few Haya in the housing estates of Kampala East.

The traditionally uncentralized Nilotic Kenya Luo have linguistic and cultural affinities with the Uganda Acholi, Alur, Jonam, and Padhola. All are highly patrilineal.

In their ideology and systems of genealogical articulation, the Kenya Luo most closely approach the 'classical' uncentralized, segmentary lineage society as instanced among the Nuer, another, more distant, Nilotic tribe, and as described by Evans-Pritchard.[9] But it must be remembered that Nuer lineages are not localized. Among the Luo, localized lineages of increasingly wider levels are numerous. Sometimes they are not localized. Very frequently they are all highly corporate. Clans and maximal lineages are also generally localized and exhibit a relatively high degree of corporateness.[10]

The Acholi were also traditionally an uncentralized segmentary lineage society based on strong principles of agnation. But aristocratic lineages developed among and coexisted in the same 'domain'[11] with common lineages. In the existence of these very slight aspects of centralization over and above agnatically defined local groups they had something in common with their western neighbours, the Alur and Jonam.[12]

The Lango were also traditionally uncentralized. There are local agnatic descent groups, but clans are not generally localized though clan sections may be. The Lango were once Nilo-Hamites who assimilated Nilotic speech and customs during the southward migrations of the Nilotes, but who have nevertheless retained many Nilo-Hamitic customs.[13] They are now reasonably well-off cotton-growers. The Padhola, or Dama as they are sometimes called by neighbouring Bantu, were also uncentralized and based on a localized segmentary lineage system, possibly having much in common with the Kenya Luo.

In Kampala, these Nilotes come to understand each others' dialects. A loose super-fraternity exists between them, especially since Interlacustrine Bantu until recently referred to them all as 'barbarians'or 'foreigners', using the Luganda word *abanamawanga*. Nowadays such terms as 'Northern people', 'Luo', 'Lwoo' or 'Acholi' are used in the collective sense, though increasingly people have come to discern different tribespeople more accurately.

The Lugbara were also politically uncentralized. They are organized into relatively shallow but local and corporate patrilineal descent groups and have been designated as one of at least three types of segmentary lineage society.[14] Except for the Madi, the Lugbara in Kampala are unable to establish a wider fraternity of tribes speaking similar languages. They are not a large category of Kampala's population and are somewhat isolated in many respects from other tribespeople. They are perhaps the most inward-looking of all major tribal groupings in the city.

Little is known about the Teso in their home country. They stress the existence of 'clans', that is, exogamous units, which are not localized, however. The Teso are certainly strongly patrilineal and are organized into local descent groups.[15] As Nilo-Hamites, it may be supposed that the Teso had a dominant age organization, but, nowadays, age organization is not especially significant. The Teso, almost certainly once pastoral, are now settled agriculturalists with a continuing high interest in cattle. Teso District favours the growing of cotton as a cash crop. The district enjoys a high *per capita* income from its yields.

The Bantu Luhya of Kenya were uncentralized and, at clan and lineage levels, still have much in common with the Luo. They are said to have a localized segmentary lineage organization within each of the component Luhya subtribes.[16] But beyond the level of subtribe, there is no tradition of the past fission of larger groups. The Luhya have come to be regarded as a single tribe with internal subtribal divisions only in recent times, and mostly for administrative and political purposes. The Luo, on the other hand, conceive of their respective subtribes as related in some way and as deriving from the fission of a smaller number of groups. Their myths of origin refer to the migration from the north, that is, from the Sudan, of the Luo as one people. For all this, at the local lineage and clan level and, superficially, at the tribal level, the Luo and Luhya share structural similarities.

NOTES

[1] M. Southwold, 1960, *Bureaucracy and Chieftainship in Buganda*, East African Studies No. 14, Kegan Paul, Trench, Trubner, London, and L. A. Fallers, 1964, *The King's Men*, O.U.P. for E.A.I.S.R.

[2] B. K. Taylor, 1962, *The Western Lacustrine Bantu*, African Ethnographic Series, O.U.P. for I.A.I.

[3] L. A. Fallers, 1956, *Bantu Bureaucracy*, W. Heffer & Son for E.A.I.S.R., Cambridge, and 1959, 'Some Determinants of Marriage Stability in Busoga', *Africa*, Vol. XXVIII.

[4] J. Beattie, 1960, *Bunyoro, An African Kingdom*, Henry Holt, New York.

[5] K. Ogberg, in M. Fortes and E. E. Evans-Pritchard, 1940, *African Political Systems*, O.U.P. for I.A.I. The late D. J. Stenning had done considerable fieldwork among the Ankole, but was unable to publish all his findings.

[6] M. M. Edel, 1957, *The Chiga of Western Uganda*, O.U.P. for I.A.I., and P. T. W. Baxter, in A. I. Richards (ed.), 1959, *East African Chiefs*, Faber for E.A.I.S.R.

[7] A. I. Richards (ed.), 1955, *Economic Development and Tribal Change*, Cambridge, Heffer & Sons for E.A.I.S.R.

[8] J. J. P. Maquet, 1961, *The Premise of Inequality in Ruanda*, O.U.P. for I.A.I.

[9] M. Fortes and E. E. Evans-Pritchard (eds.), op. cit.

[10] E. E. Evans-Pritchard, 1949, 'Luo Tribes and Clans', *Rhodes-Livingstone Journal*, and A. W. Southall, 1952, *Lineage Formation among the Luo*, I.A.I. Memorandum No. XXVI, Oxford.

[11] F. K. Girling, 1960, *The Acholi of Uganda*, H.M.S.O., London.

[12] A. W. Southall, 1954, *Alur Society*, Cambridge, Heffer & Sons for E.A.I.S.R.

[13] A. G. Tarantino, 1949, 'Lango Clans', and 'Notes on the Lango', *Uganda Journal*, Vol. XIII, Nos. 1 and 2, and P. H. Gulliver, 1951, 'The Name Lango as a title for the Nilo-Hamites', *Uganda Journal*, Vol. XV, No. 1.

[14] J. Middleton and D. Tait (eds.), 1958, *Tribes Without Rulers*, Routledge and Kegan Paul, London.

[15] A. C. Wright, 'Notes on Iteso Social Organization', *Uganda Journal*, Vol. IX, No. 2. J. C. D. Lawrence, 1957, *The Iteso*, O.U.P., London. P. N. Wilson and J. M. Watson, 1956, 'Two Surveys of Kasilang Erony, Teso, 1937 and 1953', *Uganda Journal*, Vol. XX, No. 2.

[16] Gunter Wagner, Vol. 1, 1949, and Vol. 2, 1956, *The Bantu of North Kavirondo*, O.U.P. for I.A.I.

APPENDIX II (to Chapter VIII)

LUO UNION GENERAL ELECTION OF OFFICERS, OCTOBER 1963

In the following description of the Luo Union 'annual' general elections, voters' affiliations of location or subtribe and wider tribal area become apparent. So, too, do some of the properties of tribal association leadership.

The general meeting was arranged rather hastily. Some Western Luo, comprising members of Gem, Ugenya and Alego locations, had complained that the Luo Union team which plays in the Kampala and district football league was suffering too many defeats. Members of these locations are the most numerous in Kampala. They suggested that a reason for the Union team's defeat was the small number of Western Luoland players in the team. They suggested, too, that the union as a whole had become inactive. They proposed that this general lethargy might be further related to the fact that the then members of the Union's and Sports Club's executive committee were from East and South Luoland.

Easterners and Southerners argued that Westerners had never bothered to attend meetings and never made the effort to get their own people elected into office. The Westerners replied that they were not asking for a change of all officers but only for the replacement of the chairman. The chairman, K.O., however, stated that in view of the complaints and suspicions of nepotism, it would be better to have a new regime, and accordingly called a meeting for the election of all officers. The chairman had held almost uninterrupted office since 1950, not long after the Union was established. Now, he said, he was tired of the complaints made about him and wished to retire. Someone commented that recently his power had dwindled because the Westerners had relentlessly opposed him.

The meeting was held on the piece of spare land outside Naguru Community Centre. About 500 people were in attendance. A few of them were from other tribes. Since the meeting was to be held

203

in DhoLuo, they would not all be able to understand proceedings. A number of notables were there, including P.A. from Nairobi, then the Kenya Independence celebrations officer, who had a short while before been working in Kampala. *Ker* (a Luo of high rank) had come to represent the Kisumu chairman of the wide-scale Luo Union, East Africa.

The two introductory speakers were O.O., the acting secretary, a trader with a shop at Nakawa estate, and M.A., an executive and a teacher, who was the previous secretary of the Union. He owned a couple of bars in Kampala East.

O.O. gave a progress report of the Union since the last elections in 1961. There were frequent interruptions from the audience as to how the Union's money had been spent. He brushed aside their questions and called upon *Ker* to speak. As *Ker* stood up, an *abu* (like a trumpet, and made from a large gourd and attached to bamboo) was sounded. People were very impressed by this and waited expectantly for *Ker* to speak. *Ker* was dressed in European clothes but 'with a hat like Oginga Odinga's', and with a fly-whisk. He greeted the people and called upon the departing chairman, K.O., to speak.

The chairman gave his swansong. Not long after the Luo Union was started in Kampala in 1947, he was its chairman. He was elected out of office a year later. His successor found the job a difficult one and K.O. was called to serve again within a year. He said that he had made the Union strong and effective in those days, but now he felt weak and unable to lead it well. He said he had always been anxious to protect Luo in Kampala from discrimination and intimidation by the people of Uganda. He explained that the kings of Nyoro and Toro were 'both Luo', and that the Kabaka of Buganda was related to them, and that in view of this there was no reason for Luo to feel they were foreigners. A retracing of Luo history revealed that they came from South Sudan, through north, east, south and west Uganda, to Nyanza Province in Kenya, and that, throughout this path, people were basically one. He emphasized that this gave Luo the moral right to live anywhere in Uganda. In order to show his good faith in the fact that the people of Uganda and the Luo of Kenya had common affinities, he had invited Dr. Milton Obote for the Uganda Independence celebration at Naguru Hall in October 1962, 'as he was a Nilotic'. He had wanted to urge the Uganda Premier not to forget the Luo, as they had done a lot in achieving Uganda's independence and as they, too, were Nilotes. Unfortunately, he said, the visit had been unable to take place.

The outgoing chairman finished his speech by putting forward some proposals he had had in mind concerning the buying of taxis or a bus in the name of the Union for repatriating the bodies of persons who had died in Kampala, for social visits home, and for fulfilling soccer teams' travelling obligations. Clans and locations, he claimed, were wasting money in having to hire 'these Ganda vehicles'. He hoped that now that he was retiring, these proposals would still command attention.

Further discussion centred on the question of why the Union had in fact become weaker. The chairman was eventually called upon to speak again and he suggested that the Union had lost its influence during the Kampala municipal council elections of September 1962, when three high-status Luo, one the previous secretary of the Union present at the meeting, had fought against each other for the council seats. The previous secretary was alleged to have neglected his work for the Union in his municipal council campaign, and each Luo candidate, in stressing the contradictory policies of opposing political parties, had divided Luo against Luo, so that both the administration of the Union and the solidarity of Luo in Kampala had suffered. Furthermore, he claimed that at this time ordinary Luo themselves lost interest in the Union and continued to devote all their time, energy and money to clan and location associations.

Each of the other notables spoke again, urging the people to vote not according to a man's clan or location but according to his value, past and future, to the Union. *Ker* noted that very few present had paid their subscriptions and asked whether the votes of the majority might not be invalid since, according to the constitution, only paid-up members were entitled to vote. This suggestion was hotly contested amid a shower of light abuse at *Ker*, and it was agreed that all Luo present should vote, as was the perennial practice. Nominations for offices, starting with that of chairman, were then invited.

At this point the grouping and affiliations of voters according to location and wider tribal area should be indicated. The wider tribal areas are West, East and South, and the locations constituting them are referred to by name. It must be remembered

that there were more workers of the western locations, particularly
Ugenya, Gem and Alego, in Kampala and at the meeting than of
other locations.

West	*East*	*South*
Ugenya	East Kano	Karachuonyo
Gem	West Kano	East Nyokal
Alego	Kisumo	West Nyokal
Sakwa	Nyakach	Kamunga
Asembo		Kadeni
Seme		Kamagambo
Imbo		Kindu *et al.*
Uyoma		

Nominees for the post of Chairman (Jakom) and Vice-chairman (Jalup Jakom) in order of nomination:

(1) A.   (Gem)
(2) Os. (Uyoma)
(3) Od. (Ugenya)
(4) Ad. (Alego)

(1) A. is a *muluka* chief appointed by the Kabaka's government
for the Kampala suburb of Nyamwongo, where a large proportion of Luo reside. He owns and lets some houses at Kiswa
temporary housing area, and owns a club in his own village of
Nyamwongo. He has 'many wives'. He is greatly respected for his
position as chief and for the fact that he represents the 'foreigners',
mainly Luo, in his area. He is 45 and has been over 20 years in
Kampala. Before becoming a *muluka* chief he was a trader. He
speaks no English but good Swahili and some Luganda. He is now
a rich man 'mainly through bribes' (i.e. gifts or tribute not
interpreted as such by Luo). It is said that he has already built a
permanent house at his home in Luoland.

(2) Os. is a storekeeper in a private firm and earns about Shs.
350/–. He has eight years of education and speaks English well. He
is 38 years old and first came to Kampala in 1950, joining his
present firm in 1951. He began then as a store's messenger and
went to evening school to learn accounts and bookkeeping and so
secured promotion. In 1952 he was elected to the post of Luo Union
secretary, in which he worked hard and helped extend the Union's
influence. He it was who eventually instigated the Union's

sporting activities and so brought the location associations together under the Union. He has continued to support the Union as
an active member.[1] He is married with five children and lives in a
Shs. 39/– house at Naguru. He keeps his wife at home in Kenya
'so that she may dig', and he is recognized as a Luo who refuses
to neglect his land, whereas others in town do. His children are
also kept at home so that they may undergo their schooling
there.

(3) Od. also has eight years of education, works as a clerk and
is referred to as an 'educated man'. He is extremely popular with
people of his own location (Ugenya) and is well known by most
Luo. He wears expensive clothes and has a forceful personality. In
this particular election, he was never cat-called by members of the
crowd, though others, even successful nominees, were. He is a
'young man' of 30, is married with three children, and has been
five years in Kampala, having previously worked in Nairobi. He
lives at Naguru with his family in a Shs. 52/– house.

(4) Ad. has four years of education, does not speak English and
is a mechanic of experience rather than training. He also owns a
shop at Nyamwongo, where he lives. He is well known by
members of his own location, Alego, and has been actively concerned with the sporting affairs of the Luo Union for some time. He
is 35, and married with six children, has been in Kampala since
1949, joining the Union when it was first established.

At these nominations for the office of chairman, Easterners and
Southerners shouted and claimed that the fact that three of the four
nominees were Westerners, and of the most closely allied locations
at that, proved that the people of Ugenya, Alego and Gem had
prepared their nominations before the meeting and had campaigned for them. They claimed that they themselves had been
given too short a notice of the elections to consider their own
nominations. Whatever the truth of these allegations, it was clear
from the applause that greeted the introduction of each nominee
that the crowd was divided at this stage between support for A.
and Os., with the balance in favour of the former. M.A., the previous secretary, who seemed to be handling matters at this stage,
called for those people who supported A. to raise their hands.
Most hands went up. He called Os.'s name. Again, most hands
went up. M.A. Claimed that a lot of people must have voted twice
and that this was not permissible. The voters shouted, 'Shame.

You should count the exact number.' He replied, 'That is not the system.' They retorted, 'Don't speak English.' M.A. then suggested setting A. and Os. apart and letting their respective followers go to them. He called A.'s name, and a large body of people went over to where A. had moved, bringing a hesitant stream of persons in their wake. Os. was left with an obviously smaller number of supporters who whistled and booed and claimed that 'the illiterates' had moved over to A. because they were confused and had just followed those who had moved first.

Meanwhile the votes were counted: A. had 195 and Os. had 105, The same system was employed for Od. and Ad. and again there was a mass movement of people, so that Od. received 175 votes and Ad. none. Amidst much grumbling, complaining, and even some threats at private re-election, A. was declared chairman and Od. vice-chairman.

The *Ker* intervened and said, '*Piny ok ong'e*', literally, 'the world is not known', a plea for tolerance,[2] and urged people not to base their voting and acceptance of leaders on their membership of locations, but to co-operate with each other in choosing the most suitable person for the job. There were further claims from the crowd that 'it was all arranged', and *Ker* was accused of being in league with the organizers and of 'consuming our money', but the declaration of the two new officers was eventually generally accepted.

Nominees for the post of Secretary (Jagoro), and Assistant Secretary (Jalup Jagoro) in order of nomination:

(1) Owi. (Ugenya)
(2) Owa. (Alego, but living in Kisumo)
(3) Aj. (Karachuonyo)

(1) Owi. is a 'medical dresser' at Mulago hospital. He is only 28 but has been in Kampala since 1954. He is referred to as a 'doctor', since he is well known by Luo for his 'private' work of giving people injections and tablets for the relief of ailments. He is popular with members of his own location for his sociability and eagerness to help any of them with his medical knowledge and appliances, often free of charge. He is an active man with nine years of education and a good speaking knowledge of English. He is married with two children.

208

(2) Owa. is now an invoice clerk, 32 years of age, in the city council. He came to Kampala in 1949 and in 1950 got a job as a cashier at the Speke Hotel. He was discharged, however, because it was decided to employ a European as a cashier. He then got his present job and, instead of the car he once had, acquired a bicycle. On getting this job 'he became a simple man and started to wear simple clothes'. He also began attending Luo Union meetings, but did not mix with members of the executive committee and was not very active in it.

Recently, in 1961–2, when people were suspecting him of 'aloofness' and self-importance, he changed his manner and began to participate fully in the Union. He had always managed to be sociable with people on an individual basis, but kept apart from Luo Union meetings and activities, and persons directly connected with them. He has a flair for gathering small informal groups of people around him and talking politics or current affairs. He is married with three children and lives in a Shs. 36/- house at Naguru estate, but only has inexpensive chairs in it now, whereas formerly he had a big sofa. He used to wear a beard 'to look political', but has since dispensed with it. He doesn't tell people how much money he has, but it is thought that he must have a healthy bank account. If this is so, he keeps it quiet, for fear that 'people will run after him and kill him'.

(3) Aj. is 36 and works as a copy-typist in the Department of Education in Parliament Buildings. He has seven years of education and is fairly fluent in English. He has been in Kampala twelve years. He has two children by his first wife, who died in 1959, and has remarried. He regularly attends all Luo meetings, including those of his location association.

After these nominations, the same procedure of calling a name and having people vote for it, this time by raising of hands, was continued. And again, the first called, Owi. of Ugenya, and the second, Owa. of Alego, were elected secretary and assistant secretary respectively, recording 176 and 165 votes. These two are of the majority Western locations, whereas Aj., who was last called and recorded 95 votes, is of a Southern location. Large numbers of Southerners and some sympathetic Easterners again complained that the election was being rigged and many left the meeting in dissatisfaction.

Nominees for the post of Treasurer (Jakeno) and Assistant Treasurer (Jalup Jakeno) in order of nomination:

(1) Ok.   (Seme)
(2) J.A.   a woman (Ugenya)
(3) P.O.   (Ugenya)
(4) S.   (Kisumo)

(1) Ok. is the acting secretary referred to in the beginning of this account of the Union election. He is a trader, owning a shop at Nakawa, and delivering some of his goods by scooter. He seems to be doing well and is able to afford Shs. 120/- a month for his excellent shop plot. He had only had his shop at Nakawa for three months at the time of the elections, having lived and traded at Nyamwongo before. He established his shop from capital realized through savings from a former job as a clerk.

He is regarded as 'polite' and humble' and 'talkative', and is recognized for his active support of the Union. (He is chairman of Seme location and an official of the 'breakaway' KANU branch). During the previous secretary's municipal council campaign (see above), he became acting secretary and appeared to do the job well. He is 34 and has been in Kampala ten years. He lives with his wife and three children in the back room of his shop at Nakawa. He speaks good English.

(2) J.A. is the 30-year-old wife of a Luo machine operator working in Kampala who, though now fat and forty, was a celebrated Union and location soccer player. They have no children. J.A. herself has eight years of education, which is two more than her husband. Her mother had married a second time and had come to Kampala with her husband. J.A. used to visit her in the town and eventually met her own husband there. While in Kampala she had become interested in teaching children and came to do this under the auspices of the Union. She began to attend Luo meetings, voiced her opinions occasionally, and tried to persuade women to participate in its activities, especially that of teaching in one of the Luo schools in Kampala.

(3) P.O. is particularly noted for his productive efforts at strengthening his clan and location associations and participating fully in the Union's activities. He is a typist and has held the same job since coming to Kampala over seven years ago. He wears

'superior clothes, including suits', is only 28, and lives at Nyam-wongo with his wife and two children.

(4) S. is a clerk and has been in Kampala over six years. He was accepted by the city council as soccer referee and has worked hard as such for the Luo Union's inter-location competition. It was on this basis that his name was nominated, though he did not other-wise seem to be a popular choice. He is 32, married with five children, and lives at Naguru in a Shs. 39/– house.

The only reaction to the nominations themselves was the ap-parent outright rejection of a woman as treasurer. It was pointed out that the previous treasurer was also a woman, the wife of the departing chairman, who, they claimed, had not done her job well. This woman treasurer was at the meeting and spoke to defend herself. She apologized to all concerned if they had felt that she had been a bad treasurer. She pointed out, however, that she had been elected to her position and had done her best. She knew, she said, that those who complained about her were the people who had not wished to subscribe funds and who had made it their business to dissuade others from contributing. To act like this was to act as though the Luo were not a tribe, and it made her feel she herself was not a Luo. She assured whoever might succeed her that he need have no fear, since he would be elected to his position, and, provided he did his best, would, like her, be guilty of nothing.

Ok.'s name was called first. The claim that those whose names are called first get the most votes, appeared disproved here, since he was awarded only 105. He was, however from a minority Western tribe, whereas P.O., who was called third, and who was awarded 176, the highest number of votes, was of Ugenya, one of the majority Western tribes. The woman J.A. recorded only four votes, during which banter was exchanged to the effect that to give a woman the post of treasurer was to tempt someone into carrying her and the Union's money off and 'marrying them both'. It was also stated as shameful to have to take a woman to court if she embezzled the funds, whereas a man would have to pay up or be jailed. S. received no votes, since, by this time, the Kisumo and other Eastern location members had refused to raise their hands to vote, in protest against the alleged rigging of the election. S. had even been told by then not to bother to stand.

The Westerners were clearly very satisfied at the results of the election and they left the area blowing their *abu*, while their women gave out a high-pitched, tongue-flapping form of ululation known as *sigalagala*, and moved off in a shuffling dance.

The Easterners and the few Southerners who had remained were disgruntled, and continued in their complaints. Many of them wanted to know why buses had not been provided to take them home. The outgoing committee was blamed for not being able to organize a collection of money for this purpose. They said it was no wonder that the location associations had looked after their own interests, since no one could have faith in the Union.

The previous secretary, M.A., retaliated by stating that Shs. 1,500/– had been sent to the headquarters at Kisumu, that this represented the money collected from 1961 to the present time, and that there were still Shs. 231/– left in the Kampala Union's funds. Invitations were then extended for membership for Shs. 5/–, to which some people retorted, 'Let the Westerners pay and become members. Let us continue to strengthen our location associations.' A shabbily dressed man, whose location had not succeeded, said, 'I don't dress well, but I can fight anytime because these are good clothes for fighting [i.e. rags]. Nor am I being fed by you. If I am dismissed from work, I shall just go home.' He then left, not having had much effect on the crowd. An 'educated clerk' said, 'The Luo Union should be dead. I earn a lot of money and spend it well and as I please. People should know what the Union had done with its money. I shall not be a member.' This man, too, was virtually ignored. People felt their feelings had been expressed too strongly and amounted to little more than abuse.

At about this time, anyway, *Ker* was called upon to be greeted by his people with money. He placed his *kofia* (beaded cap) on the table in front of him, so that anyone who came up to greet him might put money in it. The money was to go to Kisumu, capital town of Luoland. *Ker*, who was regarded as occupying the seat in the Union that Oginga Odinga once had, closed the meeting.

The proceedings may be summarized thus:

As a reaction to apparent inactivity and lethargy by the Union, many Kampala Luo called for a change of chairman. The protests appeared instigated, in fact, by men from Western Luoland, who saw only Southern and Eastern Luo in office and attributed the Union's inadequacy to this. When the election itself got under way, the affiliations of location as well as area became evident.

In particular, members of the three Western locations of Ugenya, Gem and Alego, who are the most numerous in Kampala and were so at the meeting, acted and voted as a close-knit, almost exclusive group, to the extent that, of the eleven nominations, seven were of these three locations. Of the other four, two were Westerners, so that the transfer of power from the executive committee composed of Southerners and Easterners to one composed of Westerners was dramatic.

All officers elected were Westerners, and all but one were of the three closely interacting locations.[3] The organizers of the meeting were even accused of rigging the elections and there was so much growing feeling against the Westerners that, for the election of the final pair of officers, many non-Westerners refused to vote, so that the number of voters dropped from a previous 475 and 436 to 285.

In view of this factionalism and of the numerical imbalance of the voting population's locations, it is difficult to assess clearly the qualities thought necessary in a leader by the electors.

However, certain impressions may be drawn. Only four of the eleven candidates were regarded as particularly wealthy, though nine were regarded as having prestigeful occupations and were also distinguished in this respect by their dress. Eight spoke English.

Nine of the eleven candidates had been in Kampala for seven years or more, which immediately accords them urban seniority. Urban seniority may be distinguished from biological seniority, since only four of the candidates were 35 years of age or over, though most were married, a fact indicating the continuing importance of one aspect of traditional social majority.

Ten candidates were already renowned for their interest and participation in Luo Union or location activities. None of the current candidates were renowned for non-tribal association activities, though in most years, for instance the previous year, there are usually one or two officers who are.

Location membership particularly favoured by the voters, I have illustrated, is that of either Gem, Ugenya, or Alego.

Peripheral criteria of candidature are prestige of residence, oratory, and forcefulness of personality, while preserving humility and a general absence of 'pride'.

Thus the impressions are that a certain length of urban residence is required before a man can be expected to be nominated, since all but one of the nominees had resided in Kampala for seven years or more; that a nominee is likely to have a relatively prestigeful occupation and, to a lesser extent, is likely to have a knowledge of English; and that he will very probably have been active in the Union or his location's activities. The membership or otherwise of a 'favoured location' has already been discussed in the description of the voters' factionalism.

NOTES

[1] The Luo Union Sports Club is a sub-committee of the Luo Union proper and has separately held annual elections of executive committee officers. However, it defers in nominal allegiance and subordination to the Union.

[2] This phrase is used by Luo elders and notables in many contexts to warn people of the vicissitudes of life. In the present context it was an appeal for unity, for, as one informant said, 'You never know what may come next,' referring to the position of Luo in Uganda.

[3] Alego, Gem and Ugenya are part of an administrative 'division'.

APPENDIX III[1]

TABLE VII(a). NAGURU ESTATE RELIGION (1962)

Tribe	Roman Catholic	Church Missionary Society	Other Protestants	Muslim	Bahai	Pagan	Unknown	Total
Luo	50	69	23*	–	2	1	1	146
Ganda	62	53	1	10	–	–	2	128
Luhya	19	34	13	–	–	–	2	68
Toro ⎫ Soga ⎬ Nyoro ⎭	23	28	1	2	–	–	–	23 ⎫ 18 ⎬ 54 13 ⎭
Nubi	1	–	–	48	–	–	–	49
Acholi	23	12	–	–	–	–	–	35
Samia/Gwe	10	15						25
Teso	7	7	–	–	–	–	1	15
Lango	5	8						13
Lugbara	7	5	–	1				13
Others	53	32	6	5	1	–	2	99
TOTAL	260	263	44	66	3	1	8	645
Total per cent	40·31	40·78	6·82	10·23	0·47	0·15	1·24	100·00

*Including 20 Seventh Day Adventists.

Others

	Roman Catholic	Church Missionary Society	Other Protestants	Muslim	Bahai	Pagan	Unknown	Total
Ankole	3	6	–	–	–	–	–	9
Gisu	4	1	1	1	–	–	2	9
Ruanda	6	3						9
Kiga	4	4						8
Padhola	7	1						8
Madi	7	1						8
Alur	6	1						7

[1] Though Muslims occupied a very special position, other religous affiliations were not consistently evident as important bases of urban status systems in Kampala East. This does not mean that they were sociologically insignificant. They showed themselves sporadically in urban and national political contexts. A more extensive study might well show how church and sect membership is reflected in status systems of the wider society, especially among Ganda, as Fraenkal has shown for Monrovia.

Tribe	Roman Catholic	Church Missionary Society	Other Protestants	Muslim	Bahai	Pagan	Unknown	Total
Gwere	2	3	–	–	1			6
Kamba	1	1	3					5
Jonam	3	1						4
Kakwa	2	2						4
Kumam	2	–						2
Nandi	–	1	–	1				2
Hororo	–	2						2
Chagga	1	1						2
Bemba	2							2
Haya	–	1	–	1				2
Kisii	–	1						1
KiKuyu	–	1						1
Meru	–	–	1					1
Nyasa	–	1						1
Comorian	–	–	–	1				1
Mjita	–	–	1					1
Mfipa	1							1
Zarai	–	–	–	1				1
Swahili	1							1
French (missionaries)	1							1
TOTAL	53	32	6	5	1	–	2	99

TABLE VII(b). NAKAWA ESTATE RELIGION (1962)

Tribe	Roman Catholic	Church Missionary Society	Other Protestants	Muslim	Pagan	Total
Luo	79	78	21*	2	3	183
Acholi	62	39	–	2	5	108
Luhya	30	34	9	3	3	79
Lugbara	33	28	–	–	4	65
Kiga	34	25	–	–	2	61
Samia/Gwe	18	18	1	1	3	41
Ganda	10	17	–	7	2	36
Lango	15	16	1	1	–	33
Nyoro ⎫ Toro ⎬ Soga ⎭	15	16	1	–	13⎫ 13⎬ 32 6⎭	

* including 18 Seventh Day Adventists.

216

Tribe	Roman Catholic	Church Missionary Society	Other Protestants	Muslim	Pagan	Total
Ruanda	25	5	1	—	—	31
Nubi	1	2	—	22	1	26
Madi	21	3	—	—	—	24
Jonam	17	7	—	—	—	24
Teso	9	15	—	—	—	24
Ankole	7	3	—	—	—	10
Others	26	15	1	4	—	46
TOTAL	402	321	35	42	23	823
Total per cent	48·5	39·00	4·25	5·10	2·79	99·99

Others						
Alur	6	1	—	1	—	8
Padhola	6	2	—	—	—	8
Kakwa	2	4	—	1	—	7
Gisu	1	2	—	1	—	4
Kumam	2	2	—	—	—	4
Nambo	3	—	—	—	—	3
Hororo	1	1	—	—	—	2
Kisii	1	—	1	—	—	2
Nyamwezi	—	1	—	1	—	2
Kamba	1					1
Shona	1					1
Ziba	1					1
Nyasa	—	1				1
Unknown	1	1				2
TOTAL	26	15	1	4	—	46

REFERENCES

Abbreviations: I.A.I. International African Institute
     E.A.I.S.R. East African Institute of Social Research
     O.U.P. Oxford University Press

Banton, M. P. 1957 *West African City*, O.U.P.

— 1965. 'Social Alignment and Identity in a West African City', in Kuper, Hilda (ed.) *Urbanization and Migration in West Africa*, University of California Press.

— (ed.), 1965. A.S.A. Monographs No. 2. *Political Systems and the Distribution of Power*, Tavistock, London.

— (ed.), 1966, A.S.A. Monographs No. 4. *The Social Anthropology of Complex Societies*, Tavistock, London.

Barnes, J. A. 1954. 'Class and Committees in a Norwegian Island Parish', *Human Relations*, Vol. 7, No. 2.

Baxter, P. T. W. Chapter on Kiga in Richards, A. I. (ed.), 1959, *East African Chiefs*, Faber for E.A.I.S.R.

Beattie, J. H. M. 1957. 'Nyoro Kinship', *Africa*, Vol. 27, No. 4.

— 1958. 'Nyoro Marriage and Affinity', *Africa*, Vol. 28, No. 1.

— 1960. *Bunyoro, An African Kingdom*, Henry Holt, New York.

Cohen, A. 1966. 'Politics of the Kola Trade', *Africa*, Vol. 36, No. 1.

— 1967 (a). 'The Politics of Mysticism in Some Local Communities in Newly Independent African States', in Swartz, M. (ed.), *Local Level Politics*, Aldine.

— 1967 (b). 'Stranger Communities: The Hausa', in Lloyd, P., Mabogunje, A. L., Awe, B. (eds.), *The City of Ibadan*, Cambridge University Press.

Edel, M. M. 1957. *The Chiga of Western Uganda*, O.U.P. for I.A.I.

Elkan, W. 1960. *Migrants and Proletarians*, O.U.P. for E.A.I.S.R.

Epstein, A. L. 1958. *Politics in an Urban African Community*, Manchester University Press for Rhodes-Livingstone Institute.

— 1961. 'The Network and Urban Social Organization', *Rhodes-Livingstone Journal*, No. 29.

— 1964. 'Urban Communities in Africa', in Gluckman, M., and Devons, E. (eds.), *Closed Systems and Open Minds*, Oliver and Boyd, London.

— 1967. 'Urbanization and Social Change', *Current Anthropology*, Vol. 8, No. 4.

Evans-Pritchard, E. E. 1949. 'Luo Tribes and Clans', *Rhodes-Livingstone Journal*, No. 7.

Fallers, A. L. 1956. *Bantu Bureaucracy*, Cambridge, Heffer for E.A.I.S.R.
— 1957. 'Some Deterimants of Marriage Stability in Busoga', *Africa*, Vol. 27, No. 2.
— (ed.), 1964. *The King's Men*, O.U.P. for E.A.I.S.R.
Fortes, M., and Evans-Pritchard, E. E. 1940 *African Political Systems*, O.U.P. for I.A.I.
Fraenkel, M. 1964. *Tribe and Class in Monrovia*, O.U.P. for I.A.I.
Frankenberg, R. 1966. 'British Community Studies', in A.S.A. Monographs No. 4. *The Social Anthropology of Complex Societies*, Tavistock, London.
— 1966. *Communities in Britain*, Penguin Books, Harmondsworth.
Girling, F. K. 1960. *The Acholi of Uganda*, H.M.S.O., London.
Gluckman, M. 1950. 'Kinship and Marriage among the Lozi of Northern Rhodesia and the Zulu of Natal', in Radcliffe-Brown, A. R., and Forde, D. (eds.), *African Systems of Kinship and Marriage*, O.U.P. for I.A.I.
— 'Anthropological Problems arising from the African Industrial Revolution', in Southall, A. W. (ed.), 1961. *Social Change in Modern Africa*, O.U.P. for I.A.I.
— (ed.) 1962. 'Les Rites de Passage' in *The Ritual of Social Relations*, Manchester University Press.
— and Devons, E. (eds.) 1964. *Closed Systems and Open Minds*, Oliver and Boyd, London.
Gulliver, P. H. 1951. 'The Name Lango as a Title for the Nilo-Hamites', *Uganda Journal*, Vol. 15, No. 1.
Gutkind, P. C. 1962 (a). 'Accommodation and Conflict in an African peri-urban Area', *Anthropologia*, *N.S.* Vol. 4, No. 1.
— 1962 (b). 'African Urban Family Life', *Cahiers d'Etudes Africaines*, Vol. III, No. 10.
— 1963. *The Royal Capital of Buganda*, The Hague, Mouton & Co.
Kuper, Hilda (ed.), 1965. *Introduction, in Urbanization and Migration in West Africa*, University of California Press.
Lawrance, J. C. D. 1957. *The Iteso*, O.U.P., London.
Leslie, J. A. K. 1963. *A Social Survey of Dar es Salaam*, O.U.P. for E.A.I.S.R.
Little, K. 1965. *West African Urbanization*, Cambridge University Press.
Maquet, J. J. P. 1961. *The Premise of Inequality in Ruanda*, O.U.P. for I.A.I.
Marris, P. 1961. *Family and Social Change in an African City*, Routledge, London.
Mayer, A. C. 1966. 'The Significance of Quasi-Groups in the Study of Complex Societies', in A.S.A. Monographs No. 4.
Mayer, P. 1961. *Townsmen or Tribesmen*, O.U.P., Cape Town.

Mboya, T. 1963. *Freedom and After*, Andre Deutsch, London.

Middleton, J. F., and Tait, D. (eds.), 1958. *Tribes Without Rulers*, Routledge and Kegan Paul, London.

Mitchell, J. C. 1954. 'African Urbanization in Luanshya and Ndola', *Rhodes-Livingstone Communications*, No. 6. Rhodes-Livingstone Institute, Lusaka.

— 1956, 'The Kalela Dance', Rhodes-Livingstone Papers, No. 27.

— 1957. 'Aspects of African Marriage on the Copperbelt of Northern Rhodesia', *Rhodes-Livingstone Journal*, No. 22.

— and Epstein, A. L. 1959. 'Occupational Prestige and Social Status', *Africa*, Vol. 29.

— 1966. 'Theoretical Orientations in African Urban Studies', in A.S.A. Monographs No. 4.

Mphahlele, E. 1962. *Down Second Avenue*, Seven Seas, Berlin.

Ogberg, K. 'The Kindom of Ankole in Uganda', in Fortes and Evans-Pritchard (eds.), 1940.

Ogot, B. A. 1966. *History of the Southern Luo*, East African Publishing House, Nairobi.

Ottenberg, S. 1959. 'Ibo Receptivity to Change', in Bascom, W. R., and Herskovits, M. J., *Continuity and Change in African Cultures*, University of Chicago Press.

Parkin, D. J. 1966. 'Urban Voluntary Associations as Institutions of Adaptation', *Man* (N.S.) Vol. 1, No. 1.

— 1966. 'Types of Urban African Marriage in Kampala', *Africa*, Vol. 36, No. 3.

Perlman, M. L. Dec. 1960 and Jan. 1962. 'Some Aspects of Marriage Stability in Toro, Uganda', 'Land Tenure in Toro', *E.A.I.S.R. Conference Proceedings*.

Richards, A. I. (ed.) 1955. *Economic Development and Tribal Change*, Cambridge, Heffer for E.A.I.S.R.

— (ed.) 1959. *East African Chiefs*, Faber for E.A.I.S.R.

Rouch, J. 1956. 'Migrations au Ghana', *Journal de la Société des Africanistes*, Vol. 26, Paris.

Schwab, W. B. 1965. 'Oshogbo—an Urban Community'?, in Kuper, Hilda (ed.).

Scott, R. 1966. *The Development of Trade Unions in Uganda*, East African Publishing House for E.A.I.S.R., Nairobi.

Somerset, H. C. A. 1964. 'Home Structure, Parental Separation, and Examination Success in Buganda', *E.A.I.S.R. Conference Paper* (MS.).

Southall, A. W. 1952. 'Lineage Formation among the Luo'. *I.A.I. Memorandum No. 26*, Oxford.

— 1954. *Alur Society*. Cambridge, Heffer for E.A.I.S.R.

— 1956. 'Determinants of the Social Structure of African Urban

Populations, with Special Reference to Kampala (Uganda)', in *Social Implications of Industrialization and Urbanization in Africa South of the Sahara*, I.A.I. for UNESCO.

— Southall, A. W., and Gutkind, P. C. 1957. *Townsmen in the Making*, East African Studies No. 9, E.A.I.S.R., Kampala.

— 1959. 'An Operational Theory of Role', *Human Relations*. Vol. 12.

— 1960. 'On Chastity in Africa', *Uganda Journal*, Vol. 240.

— 1961 (ed.) *Social Change in Modern Africa*, O.U.P. for I.A.I.

— 1965, 'A Critique of the Typology of States and Political Systems', in A.S.A. Monographs, No. 2.

Southwold, M. 1960. *Bureaucracy and Chieftainship in Buganda*, East African Studies, No. 14, Kegan Paul, Trench, Trubner, London.

Stenning, D. J. *Chapter on Ankole*, in Richards, A. I. (ed.), 1959.

Tarantino, A. G. 1949. 'Lango Clans', *Uganda Journal*, Vol. 13, No. 1.

— 1949. 'Notes on the Lango', *Uganda Journal*, Vol. 13, No. 2.

Taylor, B. K. 1962. 'The Western Lacustrine Bantu', African Ethnographic Series, O.U.P. for I.A.I.

Uganda (Protectorate) *Statement of Policy on African Urban Housing, 1954.* Entebbe, Government Printer.

Uganda (Protectorate) *Annual Enumerations of Employees, 1956–62.* Entebbe, Government Printer.

Wagner, G. Vol. 1. 1949 and Vol. 2. 1956, *The Bantu of North Kavirondo*, O.U.P. for I.A.I.

Wilson, M., and Mafeje, A. 1963. *Langa*, O.U.P., Cape Town.

Wilson, P. N., and Watson, J. M. 1956. 'Two Surveys of Kasilang Erony. Teso, 1937 and 1953', *Uganda Journal*, Vol. 20, No. 2.

Worseley, P. 1952. *The Trumpet Shall Sound*, Macgibbon & Kee, London.

Wright, A. C. 1945. 'Notes of Iteso Social Organization', *Uganda Journal*, Vol. 9, No. 2.

INDEX

INDEX

friendships, 65–7; significance for women, 60–8; tenants' associations, 68, 70, 71; women's friendships, 65–7

Nilo-Hamitic group, 8–10, 200, 201

Nilotes (Nilotic group), 8–10, 32, 33, 68, 200–1: assimilation not desired, 143; dialects, 62; physique, 21

Non-tribal norms, 61–71

Nsambya, railway workers' housing estate, 14, 53

Ntinda house-ownership estate, 13, 17, 26, 52, 73, 77

Nubi tribe, 7, 8, 48, 117: business interests, 164; on housing estates, 20

Nuer tribe, 200

Nyamwongo, 163, 164

Nyoro tribe, 6, 7, 77, 198, 199: and marriage, 95; dialects, 199; occupations, 10; on housing estates, 20

Ogot, B. A., 186

Padhola (or Dama) tribe, 9, 77, 200: migration, 92

Political changes of independence, 87–9: retention of links, 90

Politics and the community, 44–51: attacks on Kenyan trade unionists, 44–5, 49; employment of Kenyans, 45–6, 49; labour market, 45–6; new franchise qualifications, 46–8; parliamentary elections (1963), 47

Population figures, 4–7: age groups, 6; increase in African population, 4; males and females, 6; tribal distribution, 7

Prostitution, 14–16, 94, 96

Religious figures for Naguru and Nakawa, 215–17

Rents and rent zones, 13–14, 17

Residential hierarchy, 52

Rivalries and 'tribalism', 78–87: case history, 78–83, 86–7

Ruanda tribe, 7, 9, 199–200: Hutu 'caste', 25, 199; migration, 25–6; occupations, 11, 25; Tutsi 'caste', 199

Samia tribe, 7, 9, 10, 39, 77, 164: on housing estates, 20; tribal rivalries, 79–84, 86

Sanctions among Migrants, 105–11, 116: deviants, 111; encouraging and discouraging change, 103–4; law and customs, 106; life histories, 107–11; marriage and bridewealth, 106

Sanitation, 18

Schwab, W. B., 187

Soga tribe, 6, 7, 9, 77, 198, 199: case histories, 128–31, 133–7; network, 133–5; on housing estates, 20; occupations, 10

Southall, A. W., 3–4, 20, 143, 188, 190, 192

Status divisions, 54–61: competition between localities, 55; debating societies, 55, 57; distinction between Upper and Lower Nakawa, 17, 52, 58–60; internal estate movement, 59–60; men and women, 60–1; sense of deprivation, 56–7

Subtribe associations, see Location associations

Sudanic group, 7–10

Swahili, xv, 19, 35, 62, 80–3, 85, 170: campaign for official recognition, 45; Kampala East dialect, xv, 19; status division between English and Swahili speakers, 80, 81

Tanganyika tribes, 7

Temne tribe in Freetown, 184–5

Tenants' associations, 41–3, 53–8, 68, 71: and city council, 88–9; and tribal rivalries, 79–89; arbitration in disputes, 70; attendance at meetings, 58; general meetings, 57–8, 83–7; leadership in, 72–4, 77; officers and committee members, 73–4, 79–81, 83–6

Teso tribe, 7, 10, 11, 201: migration, 92; occupations, 11, 25; on housing estates, 20

Toro, 92

Toro tribe, 7, 9, 77, 117, 198, 199: case history of two royal Toro, 137–41; dialects, 199; on housing estates, 20

'Townsman', notion of, ix, 187–8

Trade unions, 44–5, 147, 169, 171, 177, 180, 186: attacks on Kenyan trade unionists, 44–5, 49, 171; growth of Kenyan unions, 49

Tribal associations, 41–3, 50, 72, 150–69, 177–7, 181, 185, 186: and politics in Kenya, 169–78

227

For Product Safety Concerns and Information please contact our EU
representative GPSR@taylorandfrancis.com
Taylor & Francis Verlag GmbH, Kaufingerstraße 24, 80331 München, Germany

www.ingramcontent.com/pod-product-compliance
Lightning Source LLC
Chambersburg PA
CBHW070359270326
41926CB00014B/2619

9 7 8 1 1 3 8 8 6 1 9 1 6